Life of Petrarch

LIFE
of
PETRARCH

──────────── ❦ ────────────

BY ERNEST HATCH WILKINS

PHOENIX BOOKS

THE
UNIVERSITY
OF CHICAGO
PRESS

CHICAGO & LONDON

This book is also available in a clothbound edition from

THE UNIVERSITY OF CHICAGO PRESS

Library of Congress Catalog Card Number: 61-15939

The University of Chicago Press, Chicago & London
The University of Toronto Press, Toronto 5, Canada

© *1961 by The University of Chicago. Published 1961*
Second Impression 1963. First Phoenix Edition 1963
Composed and printed by The University of Chicago
Press, Chicago, Illinois, U.S.A.

Preface

PETRARCH was the most remarkable man of his time; and he is one of the most remarkable men of all time.

He was and is remarkable for his awareness of the entire continent on which the drama of European life was being enacted; for his awareness of the reality of times past and times to come; for the breadth and the variety of his own interests (he was, among many other things, a gardener, a fisherman, and a lutanist); for the high distinction of his writings; for his persistent belief in Rome as the rightful capital of a unified world, governed politically by an Emperor and religiously by a Pope; for his scholarly precocity and for the valiant industry of his old age; for the honors he received and for the hostilities he incurred; for his faithfulness to the study and writing that constituted his most important occupation; and most of all for the vast range, the deep loyalty, and the unfailing helpfulness of his friendships.

He is remarkable also—thanks mainly to his own hundreds of letters and to notes that he made on the margins of pages that have been devoutly cherished—for the fact that we know far more about his experiences in life than we know about the experiences of any human being who had lived before his time.

E. H.W.

Contents

I. *Childhood in Tuscany*

I F Y O U follow the Arno upstream from Florence, first to the east and then to the south, for about twenty miles, you will come to the little town of Incisa, where Petrarch's forebears had lived for three generations or more and where most of his own childhood was spent. But he was not born there.

Northern Italy, in the fourteenth century, was a patchwork of restless independent states, some of them, like Florence, governed more or less democratically; others, like Milan, ruled autocratically by powerful families. Incisa lay within the Florentine domain, not far from its southern border.

Petrarch's father, grandfather, and great-grandfather, Pietro, Parenzo, and Garzo, were all notaries. The family had no established surname. Pietro was known as Pietro di Parenzo, but he was more commonly called Petracco or Petraccolo. The title "Ser," appropriate for a notary, was often used before his name. Being able and ambitious, he went from Incisa to Florence, and became successful and prominent in his profession there. He was a man of some culture: he had a great respect for the writings of Cicero, and it was he who commissioned the famous manuscript of Virgil (now in the Ambrosian Library in Milan) that was to become one of the most precious possessions of his son.

The opening years of the fourteenth century were in Florence a time of political turmoil and of merciless injustice. In January, 1302, Dante, with whom Ser Petracco was acquainted, had been banished on the basis of a false charge of corruption in office; and in the following October Ser Petracco, who had incurred the enmity of a powerful politician, was sentenced, on the basis of a false charge and without a trial, to a heavy fine, the cutting off of a hand, banishment from Florentine territory, and confiscation of his property. (This confiscation did not apply to the family home at Incisa, which was owned by Ser Parenzo.) He was able to escape unharmed and take refuge, along with his wife, Eletta Canigiani, in Arezzo, the main city—not far south of Incisa—of a small independent state.

There, at dawn on July 20, 1304, in a house in the Vico dell'Orto, their son Francesco was born.

Early in the following year Eletta returned, with her little son, to the family home at Incisa. The journey from Arezzo, the first of Francesco's many journeys, came close to being his last: for as the servant who was carrying him was fording the Arno his horse slipped and fell, and in his struggle to save his precious burden the servant himself was nearly drowned.

At Incisa, Eletta and Francesco lived for about six years, and from time to time Ser Petracco managed to come there surreptitiously. In the course of these years the boy must have come to know several of his relatives—certainly his grandfather and presumably some uncles, aunts, and cousins. Two brothers were born: one died in infancy, and the other, Gherardo, born in 1307, was to be very dear to Francesco as long as his own life lasted. During these years he must have been told stories about his forebears: he once wrote at some length about his great-grandfather, Ser Garzo, a man of saintly life, keen mind, and sound judgment who lived to the age of one hundred and four, predicted the hour of his death, and when that hour came quoted the words of the Psalmist, "I will lay me down in peace and sleep," and thereupon fell peacefully into his final rest. In these same years the boy was presumably led to suppose that he would grow up to follow the profession of law. The teachings and the influences of this, the boy's first home, were deeply religious.

In 1311 Ser Petracco, taking his wife and sons with him, moved to Pisa—also the main city of a small independent state and a bitter rival of Florence—hoping, presumably (as Dante hoped), that the coming of the Emperor Henry VII, who had crossed the Alps late in 1310, would open the way for a return to Florence. Henry, however, made little progress; and in 1312 Ser Petracco decided to move to Avignon, where the French Pope, Clement V, had established the seat of the papacy. Clement's action, though not unreasonable under the circumstances then prevailing, came as a terrible shock to Italian conviction and Italian pride, but it also led many Italians to follow the papal court and seek their livelihood in the newly papal city.

It was probably in Pisa that Francesco saw, for the first and only time, his father's fellow exile, Dante. It may have been either in Pisa, or soon afterward in Carpentras, that Francesco was taught to read by Convenevole da Prato, an old man of simple heart and an excellent grammarian, who was in voluntary exile from his native city. From Pisa Ser Petracco and his family took ship for Marseilles, sailing first up the coast to Genoa, and stopping briefly there. The beauties of the Genoese riviera made an indelible impression upon Francesco, who recalls and celebrates them at some length in a letter written many years later to the Doge and Council of Genoa.

From Genoa the little family started westward by sea for Marseilles and a strange land.

II. *Boyhood in Provence*

THE arrival of Ser Petracco and his family in Provence was not auspicious: their ship was wrecked in a storm as they were nearing Marseilles, and Francesco's life was again endangered.

CARPENTRAS

Unable to establish his family in suddenly overpopulous Avignon, Ser Petracco found a home for his wife and their two sons in the town of Carpentras, about fifteen miles to the northeast. There the two boys and their mother lived for the next five years, visited often by Ser Petracco.

At about the time of their arrival in Provence members of the Sette family arrived also from Genoa, among them a boy, Guido, of about Francesco's age; and for Guido and his mother, likewise, a home was found in Carpentras. The two boys became fast friends. Their friendship was to endure unbroken as long as they both lived. In a late letter to Guido (then Archbishop of Genoa) Petrarch writes thus of their boyhood days at Carpentras:

> Do you remember those four years? What happiness we had, what security, what peace at home, what freedom in the town, what quietness and silence in the country!

Most of the children's talk that Francesco heard outdoors in Carpentras must have been in Provençal: it is accordingly very probable that he was soon able to understand and to speak that language.

It was in Carpentras that Francesco had his first regular schooling, studying (Latin) grammar and rhetoric with Convenevole da Prato, who had now come there to live. This first schooling must have been a wonderful experience for the boy: then, as always, he was intensely eager to learn. It was presumably at this time, also, that he discovered the infinitely fascinating world of books. It was at Carpentras, apparently, that he first developed his special enthusiasm for Cicero, though at first his pleasure came just from the sound of words that he could not yet understand.

Convenevole found it such a joy—and no wonder—to teach Francesco that his predilection for him became generally known. Cardinal Giovanni Colonna used to say to him, teasingly, "Tell me, Master, among your good scholars, whom I know you love, is there any place for our Francesco?" And Convenevole, if not too much moved to reply, would swear that he had never had such affection for any other pupil.

The irregular western fringe of the Basses-Alpes reaches points not far from Carpentras, both above and below that town. To the north the mass of Mont Ventoux rises to a height of more than 6,000 feet. A few miles to the south the river Sorgue gushes forth suddenly from the base of an immense cliff and then flows on through the lovely valley of Vaucluse. The spectacular interest of the Fountain of the Sorgue and the placid beauty of the valley drew many visitors, even then—among them King Robert of Naples (who was also Count of Provence).

In his reminiscent letter to Guido Sette, Petrarch recalls that once when his father and Guido's uncle had come to Carpentras, Guido's uncle decided to go to see the Fountain and Vaucluse, and the two boys, Francesco and Guido, begged to be allowed to go with him. Francesco's mother, fearing that something might happen to them, was reluctant to let them go, but she finally gave in, and they set out, amid her entreaties to be careful, each of the two boys mounted before a servant and within the protection of his arms. Francesco's imagination was so stirred by the strange beauty of Vaucluse that he said to himself, then and there, "this is the place for me; and if the chance ever comes to me I should rather live here than in any great city." It is also in this letter that the then aging Petrarch speaks of his mother as having been "the best mother I have ever known of, a mother to me in love as well as in blood."

MONTPELLIER

By 1316 Ser Petracco was satisfied that the time had come for Francesco to begin the study of civil law, and decided accordingly to send him in the autumn to the University of Montpellier, some fifty miles west of Avignon. Francesco seems to have accepted this decision unconcernedly. His real interests, however, already lay elsewhere. While in Montpellier he acquired copies of a few works of classic Latin literature, including some of the Latin poets and all the works of Cicero that he could get. Being quite sure that his father would not approve his spending on such books time that might have been devoted to the study of law, he hid them in a place in which he thought they would not be discovered. His father did discover them, however, and scornfully threw them into a fire. Suffering as if the fire were burning his own flesh, Francesco burst into grievous laments, which so affected his father that he rescued two books from the flames that had already singed them, a Virgil (not his father's great Virgil) and Cicero's *Rhetoric*, and holding them out to Francesco he said, smiling, "Here, keep this one for the sake of a little recreation now and then, and this other one to help you in the study of the law."

The years at Montpellier were by no means without happiness. Guido Sette was with him. In his reminiscent letter to Guido, Petrarch writes: "there too, what tranquillity, what peace, what rich merchandise, what a crowd of students, what a goodly number of masters!"

In 1318 or 1319 there came to him his first great sorrow, the death of his mother. His earliest surviving poem is a deeply affectionate elegy in Latin verse, written soon after her death. He speaks of her as "Electa" in truth as well as in name, and writes of her "honestas," her "pietas suprema," and her "maiestas animi." She will live in memory with him:

Vivemus pariter, pariter memorabimur ambo.

The little poem consists of 38 hexameters—as many as the years of her life.

It was very possibly in Montpellier that Francesco for the first time had need of a surname, and used his father's given name for that purpose: presumably his name appeared on the rolls of the University as "Franciscus Petracchi."

III. *Bologna*

AFTER his four years at Montpellier, Francesco was sent, to complete his study of civil law, to the University of Bologna, the greatest center of legal studies in Europe. With him went his brother Gherardo and Guido Sette, as well as a "preceptor," who was to act, apparently, *in loco parentis*, at least for Francesco and Gherardo.

Their studies in Bologna began in the autumn of 1320, but were soon interrupted. Early in 1321 a shameful riot for which a few students were responsible led to the civic trial and the execution of their leader; and in protest against that action virtually the entire faculty and student body left Bologna and went to Imola, the next city to the south. Francesco, Gherardo, Guido, and the preceptor certainly joined in this exodus. A political upheaval followed in Bologna; and the University seems not to have resumed full activity for more than a year.

Leaving Imola, the three boys and the preceptor, perhaps hoping that they might soon be able to return to Bologna, did some traveling in northeastern Italy, going first to Rimini and then up the coast to Venice. Return to Bologna continued to be impossible, however, and there seemed nothing for them to do except to go home to Avignon. They crossed northern Italy, amid many dangers, to Pisa or Genoa; and from one or the other of those ports they went on by sea to Provence.

It was not until the autumn of 1322 that they returned to Bologna, where they remained throughout the academic years 1322–23 and 1323–24, and through the first two or three months of the year 1324–25. Toward the end of 1324 they were called home—Francesco had to borrow a large sum of money in December—and there they stayed until the summer of 1325.

Francesco was already buying books: in February, 1325, he bought in Avignon a copy (now in the library of the University of Padua) of the *De civitate Dei* of St. Augustine, in which he made this notation:

> In the year 1325, in the month of February, in Avignon, I bought this book, *De civitate Dei*, from the executors of Don Cinzio, the chanter from Tours, for the price of 12 florins.

This is the earliest purchase by Francesco of which we have an exact record.

In the autumn of 1325 he was back in Bologna, and there he remained until the following April, when he was again recalled to Avignon.

During his years in Bologna Francesco applied himself seriously to the study of civil law. The study of legal theory held his contented interest: legal theory, noble in itself, was essentially derived from the laws of ancient Rome, and ancient Rome had already cast its spell over him. He thought well of his teachers, of whom, in his reminiscent letter to Guido, he writes: "You will remember . . . the orderliness, the vigilance, and the dignity of our professors, who looked like lawgivers of ancient times come to life again." He did so well in his work that it was said that if he had kept to the law he would have made a great success of it. But legal practice, with its petty details and opportunities for dishonesty, was unbearably repugnant to him.

Student life was by no means limited to study. In his reminiscent letter to Guido he writes:

> More venturesome than I had been before, I went off with other students, on holidays, going so far afield that we often got back late at night. The city gates were usually wide open; and if they were shut it was no matter, for the confident city was surrounded not by a wall but by an old and decaying stockade, and one could get in anywhere. . . . Things are very different there now: peace has given place to warfare, freedom to servitude, abundance to want, play to sorrow, singing to lamentation, and the dances of girls to bands of robbers.

He found new friends, of course, among his fellow students—Tommaso Caloiro, Mainardo Accursio, Luca Cristiani, and others, including some whom he was to meet again thirty years later in Basel. While in Bologna, also, he attracted the notice of Giacomo Colonna, of the great Roman family; but their friendship did not begin until later.

Francesco's years in Bologna were significant for him also in a respect not related to his studies. It was there, undoubtedly, that he first came into touch with men and boys who were writing poems not in the Latin of the schools but in their own living Italian speech. Many of his fellow students, doubtless, were writing sonnets and other lyrics in Italian, as Guido Guinizelli had done, in Bologna, in an earlier generation, and as Cino da Pistoia, who had once been a student in Bologna, was still doing. Dante had written his *Commedia* in Italian; and Giovanni del Virgilio, a professor in the University, had invited him to come to Bologna to receive the laurel crown. Presumably Francesco wrote some Italian verse while in Bologna, but no extant Italian poem of his appears to be of quite so early a date.

In April, 1326, probably on receipt of news of his father's death, he left Bologna to return to Avignon, knowing beyond the shadow of a doubt that the legal profession was not for him.

————————— ℰ —————————

IV. *Avignon*

AFTER their return to Avignon the two brothers lived for a time a life of fashionable gaiety. There seemed to be no need for them to earn their living: their father had always been successful in his profession.

In a letter written long afterward to his brother Gherardo Petrarch speaks in particular of the inordinate amount of time and effort they spent on their looks—their hair and their clothes. Inexpert with their curling irons, they were as likely as not to scorch their foreheads, and on the street they were in constant fear lest the wind should disturb the setting of their hair, or some animal should soil or disarrange their bright, pressed and perfumed gowns. Their shoes tortured them. But they succeeded in attracting much attention.

They busied themselves also with the writing of amatory verse in Italian, hoping thus to win praise and acclaim, as they did. Before long, however, love became for each of them a serious reality. Of Gherardo's lady we know only that Petrarch praised her gentleness and that she died young.

On the 6th of April, 1327, in the Church of St. Clare, Petrarch saw and fell in love with a young woman whose identity remains unknown. In an early sonnet, which is devoted to a play upon her name, he calls her Laureta; but elsewhere he refers to her as Laura. His love was not returned, but it endured, continuing as an affectionate memory even after her death. Giacomo Colonna once ventured to express a doubt of her reality; Petrarch's reply asserts convincingly that his love, only too real, held him in constant suffering and that, try as he might, he could not escape from it. It led him to the writing of a great many poems in Italian and a few in Latin.

By 1330, or perhaps a little earlier, the financial ease in which the two brothers had found themselves was fast diminishing, partly because of the faithlessness of Ser Petracco's executors, partly because of plundering by servants; and it became necessary for them to think of entering a profession. What Gherardo did at this time we do not know; he may have made some use of his legal training. Petrarch's disgust with legal practice, however, made it impossible for him to turn to the law; and for the practice of medicine he never had anything but scorn. Only the clerical profession remained, and to that profession, accordingly, he turned. His decision to do so was consonant with his early religious training and with his firm religious faith; but he never felt himself disposed or qualified to undertake the cure of souls, and never accepted the offer of any office that would have involved pastoral responsibilities. He must have taken the tonsure; he may or may not have taken the minor orders. His decision committed him to celibacy.

In the spring of 1330 Giacomo Colonna, who had recently been made Bishop of Lombez—which is in Gascony, among the northern foothills of the Pyrenees—invited Petrarch and at least two other young men to visit him through the summer. This proved to be one of the happiest seasons that Petrarch ever spent. In three later letters he writes: "No summer was ever happier for me"; "I saw Toulouse, the course of the Garonne, and the Pyrenees: the sky was often overcast, but the company was serene"; and "Near the Pyrenees I spent a well-nigh celestial summer, with a delightful host and delightful companions."

Two of these companions were to be intimate friends of Petrarch as long as they lived: Lello di Pietro Stefano dei Tosetti, a politically minded Roman, closely associated with the Colonna family, whom Petrarch called "Laelius"; and the Flemish Ludwig van Kempen, chanter in Cardinal Giovanni Colonna's chapel, whom Petrarch called "Socrates."

In the autumn of 1330 Cardinal Giovanni Colonna, on the recommendation of his brother Giacomo, took Petrarch into his service as a household chaplain, thus giving him his first ecclesiastical appointment. He remained an active member of the Cardinal's staff until 1337, and an occasionally active member for ten years after that. The Cardinal proved to be a friendly, generous, and understanding patron.

By early 1333 Petrarch, eager to see new places, had learned that Giacomo Colonna was planning to go to Rome at a somewhat later time, and had arranged to go with him. Meanwhile, in the spring and summer of 1333, he undertook a northern journey, with the consent of Cardinal Colonna. He spent some time in Paris, and then went on to Ghent, Liége, Aix-la-Chapelle, and Cologne. In Liége he found two of the orations of Cicero—one of them the *Pro Archia*—copied one himself, and had a friend copy the other. In Cologne, which he found very interesting indeed, he witnessed on St. John's Eve a curious traditional ceremony: a throng of women, some of them carrying flowers, gathered on the shore of the Rhine and washed their hands and arms in the river, murmuring words that to Petrarch were unintelligible. He found out, presently, that this procedure was supposed to wash away, for those who took part in it, any misfortune that might otherwise have befallen them in the next twelvemonth. From Cologne he turned homeward, traveling south through the forest of the Ardennes. This was a dangerous route for him to take—but Petrarch, himself a man of peace, scorned physical danger. On reaching Lyons he learned, from a servant of the Cardinal who met him there, that Bishop Giacomo had already left for Rome. There being therefore no hurry for him to return to Avignon, he rested in Lyons for a little while before going on, by boat, down the Rhone.

It was probably in or about 1333, and almost certainly in Avignon, that Petrarch came under the benign influence of the Augustinian monk Dionigi da Borgo San Sepolcro. Through Dionigi Petrarch came to recognize the dangers of the kind of life he had been leading and to realize even more fully than before that besides the literature of classic antiquity there existed a vast and equally important literature of Christian antiquity, in which the works of St. Augustine held first place. Dionigi gave him a tiny copy of the *Confessions* that Petrarch carried with him wherever he went until the very last year of his life.

In December, 1334, Pope John XXII having died early in the month, Benedict XII was elected in his stead. On the 25th of January, 1335, the new Pope, on the official recommendation of

Cardinal Colonna, appointed Petrarch to a canonry in the cathedral of Lombez. He was later to receive other canonries as well—plurality being common practice at the time. A man appointed to a canonry might or might not take resident possession of it: Petrarch never did take resident possession of his canonry at Lombez, but he did take resident possession of two canonries that he received in later years, and performed in some measure the normal canonical duties. Any appointment to a canonry carried with it the receipt of income.

The document notifying Petrarch of his appointment as canon is addressed "Francisco Petrachi de Florentia." In various other documents he is referred to as "de Florentia" or "florentinus": the fact that his father had been a Florentine citizen made Petrarch a Florentine citizen also; and he and others at times referred to Florence as his *patria*.

At some time in 1335, probably rather early in the year, Petrarch wrote a long letter in Latin verse to Pope Benedict, urging him to re-establish the papacy in Rome. The entire *epistola* is cast in the form of a plea by Rome, personified as a distressed and disheveled matron. This is Petrarch's first voicing of a conviction, already strong, that was to grow in intensity throughout his life: that Rome and only Rome was the proper seat of the papacy. Closely associated with this he cherished an equally intense conviction that Rome and only Rome was the proper seat of the empire.

On the first of June, 1335, Petrarch copied on a guard leaf in a manuscript containing the *De anima* of Cassiodorus and the *De vera religione* of St. Augustine a long and fervent prayer, certainly of his own composition. One of its sentences runs thus:

To Thy care, my God, I commit my thoughts and my actions, my silence and my speech, my goings and comings and my rest, my days and my nights, my sleep and my waking, my laughter and my tears, my hopes and my desires, the span of my life and the hour of my death.

Other prayers, written by Petrarch at various times, appear in this manuscript or in other manuscripts.

In the summer of 1335 Mastino della Scala, the lord of Verona, had seized Parma from the family of the Rossi. Both Mastino and the Rossi sought support from the Pope, who had some measure of feudal authority over Parma; and Mastino sent to Avignon, as envoys, his uncle Azzo da Correggio (one of the four sons of an earlier lord of Parma) and Guglielmo da Pastrengo, both of whom became friends of Petrarch. They persuaded Petrarch to undertake the presentation of their case to the Pope. Petrarch did so, and won papal support for Mastino. This seems to have been the only instance in which Petrarch acted in what was a legal capacity, though he was acting as a friend rather than as a lawyer.

In 1336, probably in the spring, Pope Benedict having made no move toward a return to Rome, Petrarch wrote him a second *epistola metrica*, again urging his return, and again building the poem around the figure of Rome as a distressed matron.

In the spring, apparently, the Sienese painter Simone Martini came to Avignon, called by the Pope to take part in the decoration of the papal palace that was then being built. Petrarch made his acquaintance and got him to paint a portrait—doubtless a miniature—of Laura; and soon thereafter he wrote two graceful sonnets in appreciation of Simone's work.

Much of Petrarch's early life had been spent in the near or distant presence of Mont Ventoux, and for many years he had thought of climbing that great mountain. In April, 1336, he carried out this long-cherished plan, taking his brother Gherardo with him. On the 24th they rode out from Avignon to Malaucène, a village on the northern side of the mountain, and there, staying at an inn, they spent the next day. On the 26th, starting before dawn, they undertook the long and difficult climb. At one point they passed an old shepherd who tried to dissuade them, telling them that he had climbed to the summit fifty years before, but had been worn out and had torn his flesh and his clothes: no one else, he said, had ever climbed it. But Petrarch was not to be dissuaded. The brothers pressed on, Gherardo looking for short cuts, and Francesco toiling after him more gradually. At last they gained the summit, and rested. When they began to look about, Petrarch was amazed and moved by what he beheld. Clouds lay beneath them. Turning toward Italy, he saw the snow-capped Alpine peaks in the distance. To the north he saw the mountains around Lyons; to the south Marseilles and the sea; and to the west Aiguesmortes (about 75 miles away). The Rhone flowed far below them. But it was growing late, and they could not linger. Having with him, as always, his tiny copy of the *Confessions* of St. Augustine, he opened it at random, so he tells us, and read this passage:

And men go about wondering at mountain heights and the mighty waves of the sea and broad flowing streams and the circuit of the sea and the wheeling of the stars: and to themselves they give no heed.

The brothers went down silently, reaching the inn late in the moonlit night.

ROMAN JOURNEY

In December, 1336, there came from Bishop Giacomo Colonna in Rome a letter from which Petrarch inferred that Giacomo would like to have him join him there. The Cardinal gave his consent, and Petrarch went by sea in stormy weather to Civitavecchia, where he landed.

Rome and its surrounding territory were at this time in a pitiable state. In theory Rome was an independent city; but it was customary that the city should confer the supreme governing authority on each new pope, who should appoint successive pairs of senators to serve, each pair for six months, as the actual governors of the city. The local government had also, at least occasionally, some democratic elements; but Rome was in practice controlled by the great noble families, of whom the most powerful were the Colonna and the Orsini, who were almost constantly engaged in virtual warfare with each other.

Petrarch was to be the guest of the Colonna family. Since the country around Rome was at this time infested by brigands and by roving bands of supporters of the Orsini, he went from Civitavecchia not directly to Rome, but to Capranica, about forty miles north of Rome, where Orso dell'Anguillara, who had married Agnese Colonna (a sister of Giacomo and of the Cardinal), had a castle. Even there danger was ever present: shepherds, ploughmen, hunters and fishermen went armed; and at night one heard the shouts of guards on the castle walls. Yet Petrarch wandered over the hills, meditating on some writing by which he might win favor with posterity: the desire for enduring fame was already strong in him.

Word having been sent to Rome of Petrarch's arrival in Capranica, on the 26th of January Giacomo and his oldest brother, Stefano, known as Stefano the Younger (whereas their father was known as Stefano the Elder), came out to Capranica with an armed escort; and after some days Petrarch returned with them to Rome. The Eternal City made a profound impression on him: he speaks in his letters of being overwhelmed with wonder and amazement.

While there he had a particularly memorable walk and talk with Stefano the Elder. They had been coming along the Via Lata (to which the modern Corso corresponds), and had stopped at a crossing from which another street led down to the Tiber. Petrarch, writing ten years later, recalls that as they talked they both leaned against a marble tomb that stood at the corner. Stefano had been at odds with one of his sons (probably Giacomo), who had ventured to remonstrate with him on his militancy; and Petrarch (who on more than one later occasion was to prove his ability as a reconciler) persuaded him, as they talked, to take his son back into his good graces. Stefano assured Petrarch that his militancy was due not to love of strife but to love of peace, which he valued above everything except freedom. As their talk came to an end, Stefano said that he greatly desired to leave a heritage to his (several) sons, but he prophesied sadly that they would all die before him (as, in the course of the next ten years, they did).

We do not know when Petrarch left Rome. He had certainly reached Avignon by July, but he did not stay there long.

During these early years Petrarch wrote a great many lyrics in Italian—many sonnets, a few *canzoni*, and a few lyrics in other forms. Many of the poems then written have been lost, but nearly a hundred survive in the *Canzoniere*, the selective collection of his poems that Petrarch made in later years. Most of these poems are love poems, varying widely in their special themes, but several are poems written to friends, and two rejoice eloquently in the hope, current in 1333, that the papacy might return to Rome, and that a new crusade might be undertaken. One poem was written in Lombez, three were written on Petrarch's northern journey, and several on his Roman journey. In the years 1336 and 1337 Petrarch himself copied a good many of the poems he had written onto a set of sheets, some of which are still preserved in the Vatican Library.

In a much later letter Petrarch says that in his youth he had thought of devoting himself entirely to composition in Italian, since the ancients had done so much in Latin verse and prose that little or nothing could be added to their achievements, whereas the situation in Italian was very different. He says also that he had planned, in his youth, to write a substantial work in Italian verse:

it seems probable that what he had in mind was an epic, with his favorite Scipio Africanus as its hero.

Yet it may well be that even before Petrarch's journey to Rome his idea of devoting himself entirely to composition in Italian had begun to fade. Whenever that fading did begin, it was due largely, as he writes in that same letter, to his distress at the way his Italian lyrics were being mispronounced and generally mistreated by the unqualified readers to whom they were available, and to his realization that such readers would inevitably prove to be incompetent judges of his work. He was beginning to think of writing primarily for a more select, less temporary audience. While at Capranica he had meditated on some writing by which he might win favor with posterity: he may have had in mind either the substantial work in Italian verse to which reference has just been made, or some other substantial work, as yet undefined, in the language of ancient Rome.

During these years in Avignon he did some writing in Latin, but not very much. In verse he wrote his two letters to Pope Benedict, one other letter—a notable poem on the plight of Italy—and a brief poem written at a time when he thought that Laura was dying. In verse or prose he wrote a lost "comedy" of some sort, entitled *Philologia*. For serious letters he necessarily made use of Latin prose, but in these early years the circle of his correspondents was not wide, and only a few letters written in this Avignonese period have survived.

Even his temporarily dominant concern with writing in Italian did not diminish his great interest in ancient Roman civilization and literature; and to this interest there was added, in and after 1333, an increased interest in early Christian life and literature. His journey to Rome must have served to intensify both these interests.

Nor was there any slackening in his eagerness to acquire books— which were necessarily in Latin. A list of his favorite books, "Libri mei peculiares," made probably in 1333 though perhaps somewhat later, contains some fifty entries, of which about a score are particular works of Cicero or Seneca. Since these were just his "favorite" books, the total number of the books that he then owned must have been considerably larger. He made every effort, in particular, to get copies of the works of Cicero. When men who had come from a distance to see Cardinal Colonna asked Petrarch what they could do for him, he always asked that they send him works of Cicero: he made such requests of men from Italy, France, Spain, Portugal, Britain, Germany, and Greece.

One Ciceronian incident involves a work, the *De gloria*, of which no copy is now known to be extant. After his return from Bologna Petrarch had not lost touch with his old teacher, Convenevole da Prato, who was now pitifully impoverished. Ser Petracco, as long as he lived, had helped him out generously, and thereafter Petrarch had done what little he could for him. Convenevole often asked to borrow books, among them one containing the *De gloria*. After a long time had passed, Petrarch asked him about it, and he confessed that he had pawned it. Petrarch offered him the money necessary to redeem it, but he protested that he would be able to redeem it himself, and would not accept Petrarch's offer. Eventually, however, he returned to his home in Tuscany without having recovered the book, which Petrarch tried in vain to trace.

One of the items in Petrarch's list of his favorite books is a "Virgilius." This cannot have been his father's Virgil, for that had been stolen in November, 1326. It was, however, to be recovered, as will presently appear.

In the course of his years in Avignon the still youthful Petrarch performed an extraordinary feat in the field of classical learning: he produced what may fairly be called the first scholarly edition of all the then known portions—the first, third, and fourth "Decades"—of Livy's *Ab urbe condita libri*. In the current manuscript tradition these three Decades had come down separately; the Fourth Decade was virtually unknown; and the text was corrupt. Petrarch brought the three Decades together, using an old manuscript of the Third Decade and having new copies made of the First and Fourth. Most of the transcription was done by copyists employed by Petrarch; but he did some of it himself. Since several passages were lacking in the old manuscript of the Third Decade, Petrarch located these passages in other manuscripts, copied some of them himself, and had others copied, and had them placed at convenient points in the old manuscript. He made many emendations in the text, moreover, some of them variants found in other manuscripts and some of them conjectural; and he annotated the First and Third Decades extensively and the Fourth scantily. He had all his three Decades sewn together in a single volume (which is now in the British Museum). Copies of Petrarch's text served not only as bases for early Italian and French translations, but also indirectly for the texts of Livy contained in Italian humanistic manuscripts and the earliest printed editions.

By the end of this period Petrarch was in his early thirties and a marked man in Avignon. He was indeed a man of impressive personality, handsome and strong. He was an easy talker, had traveled widely, and was highly intelligent, well informed, even learned. He was uniquely gifted as a writer of Italian verse. He was much concerned about public affairs, especially about the continued absence of both Pope and Emperor from Rome. He stood well in papal circles. Above all, he was a friendly man, possessed already of cherished friends, and quite ready to admit new friends into their company.

———————————— ❧ ————————————

V. *First Residence in Vaucluse*

SOON after returning to Avignon, Petrarch acquired a modest house in Vaucluse, on the south bank of the Sorgue, not far from the cavern from which the river gushes forth, and went there to live. His friends in the city were amazed; but he had two compelling reasons for his move: Vaucluse *was not* Avignon, and Vaucluse *was* Vaucluse. Avignon, to Petrarch, meant crowds, clamor, confusion, elegance, demands upon his time, knowledge of unworthy doings in the papal court, and nearness to Laura, which brought him an active consciousness of love and pain. Vaucluse, he thought, would mean to him the realization of a boyhood dream, solitude, peace, simplicity, the fascination of the river, woods to wander in, and beauty everywhere. Most of all it would mean freedom: freedom to think, to study, and to write. All this and more Vaucluse was indeed to mean to him; and it soon became for him the dearest spot on earth. By his move to Vaucluse he had taken charge of his own life.

His settlement in Vaucluse brought him a new friend, who was to be one of the dearest of all his friends, Philippe de Cabassoles, the Bishop of Cavaillon. His diocese included Vaucluse, of which, as Bishop, he was the feudal lord: he had a castle there on the mountainside. The two men were of about the same age, and their interests and likings were the same, for Philippe, also, loved books and country life. He came often to Vaucluse, to be with Petrarch there.

Aside from Philippe, Petrarch had few visitors. One of them, probably, was Dionigi da Borgo San Sepolcro, to whom Petrarch had sent an invitation in the form of an *epistola metrica*, setting forth most persuasively the many attractions of Vaucluse. Other friends seemed to fear the austerity of the life that Petrarch was now leading. Parties of visitors came now and then to see the Fountain of the Sorgue: Laura came once as a member of such a party.

It was presumably in the course of the summer of 1337 that Petrarch learned that a son had been born to him, in Avignon, of a mother whose identity is unknown. Such parentage, in four-teenth-century Avignon, cannot have been uncommon, and it seems not to have led Petrarch's friends and associates to have thought ill of him. What was uncommon, as the coming years were to prove, was Petrarch's sustained effort to be a good father to the boy, whom he took into his own care after he was ready for schooling.

He had servants in Vaucluse. It is probable that Raymond Monet served as his overseer from the start, though the happy familiarity of their relationship was doubtless a matter of gradual growth. He must always have kept horses, and he usually had a dog. Later, if not at once, he began the development of gardens on his property.

Though living now in Vaucluse, Petrarch was still on the staff of Cardinal Colonna and subject to call by him. In the autumn of 1337 the Cardinal asked Petrarch to accompany a personage of some importance on a visit to the Cavern of the Sainte-Beaume, not far from Marseilles, in which, it was believed, St. Mary Magdalene had lived as a penitent for thirty years. Petrarch and his charge spent three days and nights at the Cavern, and while there Petrarch wrote a Latin poem on St. Mary Magda-lene's life there as a penitent.

Bent on the attainment of fame, converted now to the use of Latin for his major writings, and ready to undertake serious scholarly production, Petrarch began work, before the end of 1337, on his *De viris illustribus*, with which he was to be concerned, from time to time, to the very end of his life. As first conceived, it was to consist of a series of biographies of ancient heroes, chiefly Roman, beginning with Romulus and extending, presumably, to the early emperors. How many of these biographies he wrote during his first years in Vaucluse we do not know: by 1343 he had written twenty-three, the last being that of Cato the Censor. Most of the early ones are very brief, but some are considerably longer, and one, that of Scipio Africanus, Petrarch's favorite hero, presumably ran, even in its first form, to ten thousand words or more.

As Petrarch was wandering among the hills of Vaucluse on a Good Friday—either in 1338 or in 1339—the idea came to him, with compelling force, that he should write a Latin epic, with Scipio Africanus as its hero, and he began it forthwith, calling it the *Africa*.

This involved discontinuing work on the *De viris*, but Petrarch never felt constrained to finish one work before beginning another one. There was indeed in his nature a certain restlessness— frequently shown in his changes of residence and his thoughts of still other changes—that manifested itself, in his literary activity, in a turning from one to another of the works that he had on hand at a given time, or in the undertaking of an entirely new work. As a result of this readiness to shift his attention from one task to another, he ultimately left several works unfinished, among them both the *De viris* and the *Africa*. For both of these works Livy was his main source of information.

One of Petrarch's friends, Pierre Bersuire, who was on the staff of a French cardinal, was allowed, in or before 1341, to see a passage in the *Africa* that interested him, and apparently to copy it. The passage was one briefly describing several pagan divinities: Bersuire was writing a work in one portion of which he wanted to describe such divinities as a basis for allegorization. Petrarch's permitting him to see this passage and apparently to make a copy of it constituted his first release, and his only willing release, of any part of the *Africa*; and Bersuire's borrowings from this passage in a portion of his *Reductorium morale*—a portion that came to be known separately as the *Ovidius moralizatus*—constituted the earliest instance in which the influence of any work of Petrarch appears in the work of any other author.

In addition to the portions of the *De viris* and the *Africa* that he wrote in these years, and to the Latin poem on St. Mary Magdalene and the *epistola metrica* to Dionigi that have already been mentioned, Petrarch, in these same years, wrote several other *epistolae metricae*, some of which are comparable in beauty and power to the best of his Italian lyrics. His thought moves freely in its epistolary setting, dealing now with the charms of Vaucluse, now with his life there, now with a terrific thunderstorm, now with the love that pursues him even in his Vale Enclosed.

One of these *epistolae metricae*, addressed to Giacomo Colonna, is a very remarkable poem indeed. It was written in answer to a request from Giacomo that he give an account of himself. He is content, he says, with his little field, his little house, and his books, and wants no greater possessions. He has sought to rid himself, by travel, of the love that torments him; but that effort has failed, and even in Vaucluse the image of Laura pursues him:

> When I think
> To be alone in pathless forest shades,
> I see the face I fear, upon the bushes
> Or on an oaken trunk; or from the stream
> She rises; flashes on me from a cloud
> Or from clear sky; or issues from a rock,
> Compelling me, dismayed, to hold my step.

Turning to the manner of his life at Vaucluse, he says:

> Light is my evening meal, seasoned with hunger
> And with the toil and fasting of the day.
> Companions have I none, save only three:
> My faithful dog, my servants, and myself . . .
> The Muses, from their exile now released,
> Share my retreat, but visitors are few
> Save those who come to see the famous Fount.

Letters from absent friends come constantly; and secret friends—his books—are always with him:

> They come to me from every century
> And every land . . .
> Sometimes they sing for me;
> Some tell me of the mysteries of nature;
> Some give me counsel for my life and death;
> Some tell of high emprise, bringing to mind
> Ages long past; some with their jesting words
> Dispel my sadness, and I smile again;

> Some teach me to endure, to have no longing,
> To know myself. Masters are they of peace,
> Of war, of tillage, and of eloquence,
> And travel o'er the sea.

The concept of books as persons was an abiding concept with Petrarch. A book, to him, was not a mere object: it was the emanation of a personality; and he consistently sought acquaintance—at times even friendship—with the personalities thus revealed.

One of the shorter *epistolae*, addressed to Mastino della Scala, reports the first moves in the long Anglo-French conflict that was to be known as the Hundred Years' War. Another *epistola*, written either in this period or in Petrarch's next period of residence in Provence, was sent to Guido Gonzaga, son of the lord of Mantua, with a copy of the *Roman de la Rose*. Guido had apparently asked that Petrarch send him a copy: Petrarch's accompanying comments are disparaging.

Despite his conversion to Latinity, the poetic impulse that was so strong in Petrarch compelled him still to write many Italian lyrics. Some forty such poems written in this period are included in the *Canzoniere*. As a whole, they show an advance in maturity of thought, of feeling, and of artistry. Most of them are love poems, but several are poems of friendship, one is political, one is a poem to Gherardo on the death of his lady, and now for the first time a few poems of religion appear. Finest of all are two *canzoni*, one inspired by Laura's visit to Vaucluse, the other a most eloquent voicing of the plight of Rome, summoning a newly elected Senator to restore Rome to its ancient glory, and its early Christian churches to their pristine sanctity.

Very characteristic in its expression of a need for solitude and in its pervading reflectiveness is the sonnet beginning *Solo e pensoso:*

> Alone and deep in thought I measure with slow and lingering steps the loneliest fields, ready to flee if my eyes discern a human footprint on the ground.
>
> No other defense have I that will save me from others' clear perception of my plight. For in my looks, bereft of joy, one may read outwardly how I flame within,
>
> so that I think that mountains, now, and hillsides and streams and forests know the temper of my life, that from all men is hidden.

Yet ways so rough or wild I cannot find that Love comes not with me ever, holding converse with me, and I with him.

Although Petrarch regarded his love for Laura as being in itself a worthy love, he was aware that it involved him in a conflict with a strictly religious attitude toward life. That awareness finds its first, though not its greatest, expression in the sonnet beginning *Padre del ciel*, written in 1338 on the anniversary of the crucifixion:

> Father in Heaven, after my wasted days, after my nights spent in vain dreaming, because of the fell desire kindled in my heart by the beholding of one who, to my sorrow, was so lovely,
>
> may it please Thee now that by Thy light I may turn to a better life, and to fairer tasks, so that my cruel adversary shall have spread his nets in vain.
>
> 'Tis now, my Lord, the eleventh year since I took upon me the pitiless yoke that presses most fiercely on those who are most submissive.
>
> Have pity on my sinful suffering! Recall my straying thoughts to a better theme: remind them that Thou wast on the Cross today.

In the days of ancient Rome a general returning after a great victory might be given the honor of a triumph—an elaborate procession, including captives, that ended in a ceremony on the Capitoline. Having in mind these ancient celebrations, Petrarch conceived the idea of a poetic "triumph"—the triumphant figure being Cupid, and the captives being lovers; and he began, either in this period or a little later, the writing of a fairly long poem embodying this idea and relating ostensibly what he had beheld in a dream. Though the poem is in Italian, he gave it the Latin title *Triumphus Cupidinis*. It is divided into *capitoli* ("chapters," or "cantos"). The first three of these *capitoli* may have been written in this period; the fourth was probably written a little later. For his metrical form Petrarch chose the *terza rima* devised by Dante for the *Divine Comedy*—a series of tercets in each of which the first and third lines rhyme with each other, enclosing a line that rhymes not with them but with the first and third lines of the following tercet. Petrarch was the first of a great many poets to make use of Dante's great metrical invention.

The poem consists mainly of a review of the captives, most of whom receive only an identifying line or two. Successful poetic handling of a processional plan would have called for more dramatic power than Petrarch possessed. The poem as a whole is a piece of erudite virtuosity; such poetic values as it has are to be found chiefly in certain memorable epigrammatic characterizations and in certain non-processional passages.

At the head of the procession the triumphant Cupid is borne in a chariot drawn by four white horses. All of the thirty-odd captives listed in the first *capitolo* are figures of classic history, legend, or mythology, among them Caesar, Aeneas, Paris, Helen, Venus, and Jupiter. The long classic series is continued through the second *capitolo*, in which a passage of exceptional length is devoted to Masinissa and Sophonisba, and into the third *capitolo*, where it is followed by a Biblical series, which includes David and Samson, and a brief medieval series: Lancelot, Tristan, Isolde, Guinevere, and Paolo and Francesca. The *capitolo* ends, however, with a passage of a very different kind. Petrarch has been a mere spectator hitherto; but Laura (not in the procession) now appears to him, and he himself joins the throng of captives. The closing lines of the *capitolo*, in which he sets forth his experience in love, are like his lyric poems in their personal and poetic character.

In April, 1338, Petrarch's father's Virgil, which had been stolen several years before, came again into his possession: this manuscript contained the *Bucolics*, the *Georgics*, and the *Aeneid*, all with the commentary of Servius. Soon thereafter he got Simone Martini to paint a frontispiece for it (on the verso of the second guard leaf). It must have been Petrarch himself, however, who planned the picture: he evidently specified that it should contain figures of Virgil, as a poet with pen and book, seated under a laurel tree, of Servius, as an interpreter drawing a curtain, of Aeneas, of a pruner, representing the *Georgics*, and of a shepherd, representing the *Bucolics*. He specified also that two blank scrolls, on which he himself was to write, should appear, one related to the figure of Virgil, the other to the other figures. Simone did his work faithfully and delightfully. On each of the two scrolls Petrarch wrote an appropriate rhymed Latin distich, and below the painting he wrote a third similar distich:

> Mantua Virgilium qui talia carmina finxit
> Sena tulit Symonem digito qui talia pinxit.

This manuscript is now in the Ambrosian Library in Milan. It bears hundreds of marginal and interlinear notations in Petrarch's hand.

Petrarch's property ended, at the east, in a small and stony field close to the Fountain of the Sorgue; and in the summer of 1340, apparently, he decided to turn part or all of that field into a meadow fit for his guests, the Muses. With his own hands he cleared a space; turf was brought in; and he had his desired smiling meadow. The Nymphs of the Fountain—to use his own figure—objected to this appropriation of land they regarded as their own; and with a great flood they undid all that he had done. He would not admit defeat, however, and reconstructed his meadow.

It lasted until the following summer, when, as he puts it in an *epistola metrica*, he beheld a host of Nymphs assaulting and destroying all his work. Just as he was about to renew it, however, he received a summons to Rome—as will presently appear—so he gave up the struggle for the time being, and left the Nymphs in possession.

It was perhaps within this period that Petrarch began to use as surname the form *Petrarca*, rather than the form *Petracchi* that he had presumably used thitherto—the new form being more Latin, more euphonious, and more distinctive.

‿

VI. *Coronation*

IN THE days of imperial Rome there had been held on the Capitoline, once in every five years, a multiple contest that included a contest in poetry, the winner receiving a crown of oak leaves. According to the inaccurate tradition that Petrarch accepted, the crown was of laurel, and the last poet to have received it was Statius. Petrarch also thought, mistakenly, that the ancient ceremony had something in common with the proclamation of a "master" in the medieval universities.

In 1315 Albertino Mussato, who was both a poet and a historian, had received the laurel crown in Padua, his own city. Dante, who desired coronation, had been invited to receive the laurel crown in Bologna, but had declined: Florence, for him, would have been the only desirable scene of coronation. It is probable that at Dante's funeral in Ravenna a laurel crown was placed on his head. Petrarch himself states that his old teacher Convenevole, who had returned to Prato, had received posthumous coronation.

Petrarch's knowledge of the coronation tradition and of one or more recent local coronations, together with his great desire for lasting fame, kindled in him, inevitably, the desire for coronation. He confided this desire to Dionigi da Borgo San Sepolcro and to Giacomo Colonna, and it was made known also to someone connected with the University of Paris. In a letter written in Vaucluse, in 1339 or 1340, to Dionigi, who had now been called to Naples by King Robert, Petrarch implied that he would very much like to have King Robert's sponsorship for a coronation.

On the morning of the first day of September, 1340, he received a coronation invitation from the Chancellor of the University of Paris; and on the afternoon of the same day he received another such invitation from the Roman Senate. His preference must have been for Rome, but he thought it best to ask the advice of his Cardinal, to whom, therefore, he wrote on the evening of the same day. The Cardinal replied on the next day, advising acceptance of the Roman invitation; and Petrarch of course accepted that advice.

Petrarch's sense of need for an authoritative sponsor was due, at least in part, to fear that without such a sponsor the coronation might bring him more adverse criticism than acclaim, and in part, perhaps, to a mistaken idea that in ancient times an examination had preceded the award. He felt strongly that King Robert, an enlightened and highly respected monarch, would be, for him, the ideal sponsor. Preliminary arrangements were made accordingly in the autumn of 1340, presumably through Dionigi, for Petrarch to go to Naples, prior to his going to Rome, and be examined by King Robert as to his fitness to receive the laurel crown.

It must have been in the last months of 1340, also, or in the first few weeks of 1341, that Petrarch drafted, and perhaps put into final form, the oration that he was to deliver on the great occasion. The structure of this oration is that of a medieval sermon; but the opening text is taken not from the Bible but from Virgil, and the whole oration is richly studded with quotations taken not from Biblical but from classic sources. The first of its three main parts discusses the difficulty and the ardor of poetic achievement; the second, the allegorical character of poetry; and the third, the rewards of the poet's task.

By 1340, Azzo da Correggio and his brothers had determined to wrest control of Parma from Mastino della Scala, who was ruling through a tyrannous governor. They needed assurance of support from the Pope and from King Robert, as well as from some other persons. Azzo, therefore, came again to Avignon, and evidently won there the support that he desired. Since both he and Petrarch were about to go to Naples, it was arranged that they should go together. They left Avignon on the 16th of February, 1341, and took ship at Marseilles.

Petrarch reached Naples about the end of February and remained there for about a month. King Robert made him welcome and was greatly pleased that Petrarch had chosen to ask him to serve as his sponsor for the coronation. The examination was not held at once; and on the days preceding it (and perhaps on some days following it) Petrarch was often with the King. Some of their conversations have been reported by Petrarch: one of them, concerning the French king's lack of interest in literary matters, partly in direct discourse. Another concerned the Grotto of Posilipo, King Robert asking Petrarch whether he believed that Virgil had made it by means of magic incantations; and when Petrarch replied that he had never read of Virgil's being a magician, the King assented, saying that the grotto had been made by excavation. The King, according to Petrarch, was thoroughly familiar with the Scriptures and remarkably well versed in philosophy, and had an extraordinary knowledge of mechanical matters: he said repeatedly to Petrarch that he had had little interest in poetry, and that now, in his old age, he regretted that this was so. Petrarch showed him the *Africa*—it may well be that he read him some lines of it—and Robert asked that the poem be dedicated to him. He asked also that Petrarch write something in verse in his honor.

There are extant two or three bits of Latin verse that are credibly supposed to have been improvised by Petrarch at the King's request. On one occasion Petrarch discussed with him the allegorical meaning of the *Aeneid;* and on another occasion the King asked Petrarch to make every possible effort to find Livy's lost Second Decade. Despite his age, the King engaged every day in a sport of a military type—apparently shooting with a cross-bow

—and excelled in it. Petrarch rode with him on several occasions, once, in all probability, to the summit of the hill of San Martino, which affords a magnificent view over the city and its marvelous Bay.

During Petrarch's stay in Naples he found at court two men, Barbato da Sulmona and Giovanni Barrili, whom he was to count as friends from that time on. With one or both of them, apparently, he made some brief excursions. While in Naples he undoubtedly saw Giotto's frescoes in the Royal Chapel, painted about 1330 (nothing of these frescoes now remains).

The appointed day having come, King Robert began his formal examination at noon and continued it until the vesper hour. Sessions were held also on each of the two following days. Of the content of the examination we know only that in one of the sessions Petrarch spoke of the poetic art, of the various purposes of poetry, and of the properties of the laurel; and that thereafter the King declared that if he in his youth had heard Petrarch give such an exposition he would have devoted much of his time to the study of poetry. At the close of the examination the King pronounced Petrarch worthy to receive the laurel crown. He offered to perform the coronation himself, in Naples; but Petrarch held the Roman invitation to be compelling.

Before Petrarch left for Rome the King appointed him to a chaplaincy, which must have been merely honorary. Had it not been for his age, the King would have come to Rome with Petrarch, but since he could not come himself he commissioned Giovanni Barrili to serve as his representative and to place the crown on Petrarch's head. The King gave Petrarch one of his own robes to wear at the coronation ceremony, in conformity with the Oriental practice of the giving by rulers of robes that they had worn, robes so given being called "robes of honor." He gave Petrarch also a letter to the Roman Senate. His last words to Petrarch were a request that he should soon return to Naples.

Petrarch reached Rome safely, probably on the 6th of April, but Giovanni Barrili was waylaid at Anagni and missed the ceremony, at which, however, someone to whom Petrarch refers as a messenger of the King was present.

The coronation ceremony, the most spectacular event in Petrarch's life, took place on the 8th of April, in the audience hall of the Senatorial Palace on the Capitoline (that palace is still standing, but has often been restored and altered). The hall was filled with an excited crowd of Roman citizens. Petrarch wore King Robert's "robe of honor." Trumpets sounded, and ceased, and the crowd was quiet. Petrarch then delivered his oration: at the end of his introductory paragraph he recited an *Ave;* and at the very end he made a formal request for coronation.

Orso dell'Anguillara, one of the two Senators then in office, read a long statement listing the eight awards that were to be given to Petrarch. These were (1) the declaration that he was "magnum poetam et historicum"; (2) his designation as a "magister"; (3) the conferring of the laurel crown; (4) accreditation as a professor of the poetic art and of history; (5) the right to confer poetic coronation on others; (6) approval of his writings, present and future; (7) all the rights and privileges enjoyed by professors of the liberal and honorable arts; and (8) Roman citizenship. When he came to the end of the list, Orso asked the Roman citizens present whether they approved the granting of those awards: the approval—one imagines a shouted *sic*—was unanimous. Orso then placed the laurel crown on Petrarch's head amid the applause of the audience; and either then or thereafter he gave Petrarch a diploma, known as the *Privilegium lauree domini Francisci petrarche*, which was in all probability virtually identical, in content and in wording, with the statement that Orso had just read. (It is clear that Petrarch had had something to do with the preparation of Orso's statement, but it is not possible to determine just what he did or when he did it.)

The ceremony ended with a laudation of Petrarch by Stefano Colonna the Elder. Petrarch then, with an attendant company, went through the city to St. Peter's, and there he laid his crown upon the altar.

He stayed on in Rome for several days, and in the course of those days he went all through Rome with another Giovanni Colonna (a Dominican monk, who belonged to a minor branch of the family), visiting sites that had ancient Roman or early Christian associations: in a letter written a little later to this Giovanni he mentions about eighty such sites. At times, tired of walking, they went to the top of the vaulting of the ruined Baths of Diocletian, and sat there enjoying the clear air, the view over all Rome, and the solitude, and talking of ancient Roman and early Christian history, of moral philosophy, and of the arts. One day Giovanni asked Petrarch to talk to him about the origin of the liberal and the mechanical arts; and Petrarch did so.

It was perhaps on one of their walks that a laborer came up to Petrarch with a Roman coin that he had found as he was digging, and asked him whether he wanted to buy it. He did; and thus he began the making of his collection of Roman coins, a collection in which he took great pleasure. Other laborers, perhaps on this same visit, perhaps on one or another of his other visits to Rome, brought him Roman coins or bits of Roman jewelry, sometimes wanting to sell them, sometimes just wanting to find out whom the head on a coin represented.

Petrarch had now become a famous man—the most famous private citizen then living. But the coronation, in Petrarch's intention and in fact, was more than a personal triumph: he was endeavoring, and endeavoring successfully, to re-establish great cultural values in the position of high honor that they had held in ancient Rome, and were to hold again, thanks largely to his efforts, in the age that was to come.

VII. *First Residence in Parma*

As THEY were starting north from Rome, Petrarch, Azzo da Correggio, and their companions fell into the hands of a band of brigands; on being released they returned to Rome; and on the next day they set out again, with an adequate armed escort.

Azzo went on to Parma, accompanied or followed by Petrarch. In Parma a popular revolt, instigated and led by Azzo's brothers, began on the 21st of May and succeeded on the 22nd, when Azzo arrived with troops sent by Mantua, and perhaps some other troops. Petrarch arrived on the 22nd or the 23rd. The victorious Correggi invited him to spend the summer with them, promising him "wonderful quietness"; and he accepted, planning to return to Provence at the coming of winter. He wrote accordingly to Cardinal Colonna expressing both his confident hope that the Cardinal would agree to his plan and his willingness to return earlier if the Cardinal should so desire. In point of fact he remained with the Correggi through January, 1342.

Soon after his arrival in Parma he wrote an appropriate *canzone* celebrating the restoration of liberty by the Correggi: it contains some fine lines; but he did not include it in the *Canzoniere*.

Parma is not far from the Apennines. About a dozen miles to the south of the city two spurs of the great range enclose a pleasant valley through which the Enza flows downward to the plain. High on the northern spur is a wooded plateau called Selvapiana, which affords a remarkable view, extending even to the Alps. At the entrance of the valley, on the north side of the river, stood the castle of Guardasone (apparently a stronghold of moderate size, not needed, at this time, for military purposes). In accordance with their promise of "wonderful quietness," the Correggi invited him to spend the summer there, and he did so, visited occasionally, no doubt, by Azzo. From time to time he climbed up to Selvapiana; and there, on one memorable day—as he writes in a later *epistola metrica*—the beauty of the place itself and the glorious view brought him a renewal of poetic inspiration: he resumed work on the *Africa* and continued to work on it daily.

At the end of the summer he returned to Parma, where he occupied a quiet house, remote from the centre of the city, with two gardens for trees and plants, one nearer the house and one farther from it, and a little stream running between them. The house was close to the church of San Stefano. Petrarch liked the church, and made friends with its rector, a Don Luca whose surname is not known.

In Parma he finished a draft—but only a draft—of the *Africa*. At least one considerable portion of the poem as it had been planned was never written, and the poem as a whole never received final revision. There are several references to it in Petrarch's later correspondence as being incomplete.

At about the time of his return to the city he heard that Giacomo Colonna, then perhaps the dearest of his friends, was seriously ill; and one night in September he had a most distressing dream, which he described thus in a later letter:

> He appeared to me, alone, in my garden, just crossing the little stream. I hastened to meet him, and asked him whence he came, whither he was going, why he was hurrying, and why he was alone. He replied, smiling: "Do you remember how much you minded the Pyrenean storms when you were in Lombez? I am tired of them; and I am leaving,

never to return, and going to Rome." I asked him to take me with him; but he held up his hand in refusal, and changing his manner and his voice he said: "Cease your asking; I do not want you to come with me." I looked at him intently, and saw from his pallor that he was dead.

After Petrarch woke, he made a note of the date, and in about a month he learned that it was on that date that Giacomo had died.

Late in the year Petrarch received a visit from an old and blind schoolteacher of Pontremoli, who had been so much impressed by Petrarch's fame that he had resolved to "see" him. Guided by his son, he had gone first to Naples, then to Rome; finally, hearing that Petrarch was in Parma, he came there. Petrarch tells the last part of his story, in substance, thus:

For three days he was with me constantly, and one day he said: "I don't want to be a bother to you, but I am enjoying my visit so much, after coming all this way to see you." His use of the word "see" made the bystanders laugh; but he exclaimed: "I call you to witness that I, blind as I am, see you better and more clearly than do any of these people who have their eyesight."

Early in January Petrarch wrote to his Cardinal a long and impressive *consolatoria* (that is, a letter of condolence) on the death of Giacomo. Petrarch wrote many such letters, sometimes long after the death of the man concerned. At about the same time he wrote a brief letter of sympathy to Laelius, to whom Giacomo had been very dear.

Within this period Petrarch wrote the fine *canzone* beginning *Di pensier in pensier* ("From thought to thought"), a poem of love in absence, written in anticipation of a return to Provence.

Either in this period or early in the next, Petrarch added a fourth *capitolo* to the *Triumphus Cupidinis*. The captives listed here are poets, first a classic series, then Dante, Cino da Pistoia, and other Italians, and then Arnaut Daniel and several other troubadours. Thereafter he sees his own friend Tommaso Caloiro (word of whose untimely death had reached him in Parma); and this leads him to speak of two of his living friends, Socrates and Laelius, and to an incidental mention of his coronation. Then the *capitolo* turns to its conclusion: the procession moves to the island of Cyprus, and there Cupid celebrates his triumph, inflicting all the sufferings of love upon his pitiable captives. Before Petrarch finished this *capitolo* he had decided to write a second *Triumph*, which should celebrate resistance to love, the two *Triumphs* constituting together a single twofold poem.

In February or March Petrarch started back to Provence.

VIII. *Vaucluse and Avignon: 1342 - 1343*

ON HIS arrival in Provence early in the spring of 1342 Petrarch learned that Pope Benedict was dying. He wrote forthwith to Philippe de Cabassoles a confidential letter containing an extremely severe characterization of Benedict and a distressed portrayal of the plight of the papacy. Benedict died on the 25th of April; and on the 7th of May Clement VI was elected to succeed him. Petrarch was to have much to do with Clement, of whom, in the course of time, he was to speak as bitterly as he had spoken of Benedict. His scathing criticism of these two popes was due primarily not to personal hostility but to the high reverence in which he held the papal office, and to his consequent conviction that they were not filling it worthily.

On the 22nd of May Clement, acting on a recommendation by Cardinal Colonna, appointed Petrarch to a canonry—of which he never took resident possession—in the cathedral of Pisa.

Before the end of the spring Petrarch must have heard of the death of Dionigi da Borgo San Sepolcro, who had done so much for him and whose influence upon him had been so great and so good. Dionigi in his last years had been closely associated with King Robert; and Petrarch now wrote to the King a deeply felt *consolatoria* in Latin verse, which ends with an eight-line epitaph that is compact of praises of Dionigi—for his fidelity, his benignity, his serenity, his piety, his modesty, his high intelligence, his poetic gift, and his knowledge of the stars.

At some time before the 30th of May Petrarch received from the monk Giovanni Colonna, who had been his companion on his walks through Rome, a mournful letter complaining of his sufferings from his old age, his poverty, his gout, and the absence of Petrarch. On the 30th Petrarch replied in a comforting letter notable chiefly for its account of Petrarch's great-grandfather

Garzo and for its long conclusion, in which Petrarch tells Giovanni exactly how to come from Tivoli to Vaucluse by water, so that he will not have to walk at all: from Tivoli to the Tiber, from the Tiber to the Tyrrhenian sea, thence to the mouth of the Rhone, thence to the point where the Sorgue empties into the Rhone, and thence up the Sorgue to Vaucluse. Each turn is to the right; and when Giovanni reaches Vaucluse he will find Petrarch on the right bank of the river. Of his life at Vaucluse he writes thus:

> You will see him whom you wish to see, in good health, wanting nothing, and expecting nothing from the hands of Fortune. You will see him, from morning to night, wandering alone over hill and dale, through woods and fields, avoiding human footprints, seeking pathless ways, loving the shadow, enjoying dank caves and green meadows, thinking with hatred of the cares of the papal court, far from the tumult of the city, crossing no wealthy thresholds, laughing at the concerns of the commonalty, midway between joyousness and sadness, free for whole days and nights, glorying in the companionship of the Muses, the songs of birds and the murmuring of the river, attended by few servants but by many books, now at home, now walking, now standing still, now laying down his weary head and his tired body on the bank of the rippling stream or on the soft grass . . . now communing with himself, and ever holding earthly affairs in low esteem.

Much as he loved Vaucluse, however, and much as he hated Avignon, the city held him most of the time from the summer of 1342 until the following spring. In the opening sentence of a letter written in mid-August he says that his ears are wearied with the noise of the populace; and in an *epistola metrica* written in the same summer he speaks of

> The uproar that resounds within the walls
> Of the straitened city, where the very ground
> Cannot contain the crowds, nor the very sky
> Contain the clamor.

During the summer the Basilian monk Barlaam, an able Calabrian who had spent some years in Constantinople but had recently transferred his religious allegiance to the Western Church, was teaching Greek in the papal Curia (that is, the immense complex of administrative, legal, and other departments necessary for the functioning of the papal government). Beginning perhaps in August, Petrarch studied Greek privately with Barlaam, in daily sessions, giving him in return some help with his imperfect Latin. Petrarch himself, however, was responsible, at least in part, for the early termination of this study, for he recommended the appointment of Barlaam to a bishopric in Calabria, and the appointment was made early in October. Petrarch's knowledge of Greek remained elementary, but he liked to remember that he had once studied it with Barlaam—and he treasured the two or three Greek manuscripts that came into his possession.

In August, moved by the desire to gather into an artistic whole those of his Italian lyrics that he himself approved, Petrarch began the making of a selective collection of them—a collection that constituted the first form of his *Canzoniere*. The making of this form, and of the later forms as well, involved several processes: the selection of the poems to be included, the determination of the order in which they should stand, a careful revision of each poem, and the transcription of each poem onto one of the sheets that were together to make up the master-manuscript of the *Canzoniere*. In many cases a preliminary transcription, allowing for further revision, intervened between the first revision and the final transcription. It is probable that this first form of the *Canzoniere* began with the sonnet *Apollo, s'ancor vive il bel desio* ("Apollo, if the fair desire still lives"), and that it contained about a hundred poems in all.

On the 6th of October Pope Clement appointed Petrarch to the priorate of S. Nicola di Migliarino, near Pisa. This appointment, however, brought Petrarch nothing but trouble: the right to the priorate was claimed by another man; and although Petrarch endeavored to have that man's claim annulled in the papal courts, it was finally sustained—the case having dragged on for about two years.

At some time before the end of 1342 the city of Rome sent to Avignon a deputation, headed by Stefano Colonna the Younger, to make three requests of the new Pope: that he accept the position of Senator for life (this request continued the custom of offering the supreme governing authority to each new pope); that he come to Rome; and that he designate the year 1350 as a Year of Jubilee.

Apparently Stefano asked Petrarch, by his coronation a Roman citizen, to do whatever he could in support of these requests. In any case, Petrarch now wrote to Pope Clement an *epistola metrica* in which, though without referring to the deputation, he does in fact support the second and third requests—the second at great length, the third briefly. Advocacy of the return of the papacy to Rome was nothing new for Petrarch, and this cause, in view of his recent Roman experiences, was now dearer than ever to his mind and his heart. His *epistola* to Clement, like his earlier *epistolae* to Benedict, presents Rome as a distressed matron, but this new poem is much more successful than the earlier ones, both in its argumentation and in its poetic quality.

Pope Clement, after some delay, granted the first and third requests—the Bull designating 1350 as a Year of Jubilee was issued on January 27, 1343. With regard to the second request his answer was that he could not leave France until the conflict between France and England had been brought to a peaceful settlement.

Meanwhile there had been a popular uprising in Rome; the government that had sent the deputation had been overthrown; and control was placed in a Council composed of the heads of the several guilds of merchants. This change led to the political emergence of the most spectacular figure of the fourteenth century, Cola di Rienzo. Of plebeian birth, Cola was a brilliant, eloquent, highly imaginative, and inordinately ambitious young notary, a studious enthusiast for ancient Rome and for Early Christian Rome, obsessed with visions of a new Rome possessed of its pristine power and glory. He proposed to the new Council that it send a representative to the Pope, to give him a true picture of the pitiable state of the people of Rome and to seek his approval for their new and democratic form of government. Naturally enough, the Council agreed and appointed Cola as its representative. He arrived in Avignon early in 1343.

Cola took immediate advantage of the opportunity to send good news back to Rome by reporting, in a magniloquent and fantastic letter, the Pope's designation of 1350 as a Year of Jubilee. But he never had any good news to report as to his own mission. Clement granted him several hearings, and seemed well disposed toward him, but his request for approval of a democratic form of government met with decisive opposition from the cardinals, and Clement, reverting to the form of the government that had been overthrown, appointed two nobles as the new Senators.

Cola stayed on in Avignon for several months, and in the course of those months he and Petrarch became friends. Cola was as yet young and undistinguished; but the two men had in common great enthusiasm for ancient and Early Christian Rome, great distress over the present plight of the city, and great hope for a restoration of Roman power and glory.

In February Petrarch must have heard, with deep sorrow, of the death of King Robert. As a result of his pre-coronation experience in Naples his early admiration for the King had become a firm personal devotion, which finds expression in many of his letters and in some of his other writings, especially in the *Rerum memorandarum libri*, which is presently to be mentioned. He was much concerned, also, and with ample cause, as to what might happen to the young queen, Robert's granddaughter Joan, and her even younger consort, Andrew of Hungary. The King's death put an end to the possibility that Petrarch might take up residence in Naples, but he was to see Naples again sooner than he thought.

Since King Robert's son Charles had died and Charles' daughter Joan was still a minor, the King had provided in his Will for the establishment of a regency council consisting of the Queen Dowager, Philippe de Cabassoles, as Vice-Chancellor of the Kingdom (there was no Chancellor just then), and three nobles. Philippe had been in Naples for some time, and it had been at the King's request that he had agreed to remain.

In April Petrarch's brother Gherardo, who had been his companion through so much of his youth, became a Carthusian monk. The possibility that he might take this step had been considered by the brothers for some time; but Gherardo's final decision seems to have been sudden. To Petrarch it brought not only the knowledge that their dear companionship was at an end, but also a personal challenge and a sense of need for thorough self-examination. Despite the unquestionable sincerity of his religious faith and his constancy in his religious observances, his religion was by no means in complete control of his life: he felt that it ought to be, and that his brother had chosen the better part, but the active life held so much for him that he could not achieve renunciation. Gherardo was sent to the monastery of Montrieux, in the hills north of Toulon. There Petrarch was to visit him, twice, in later years; and there Gherardo lived to the end of his long life, a life of simple fidelity starred once by extraordinary heroism.

At some time in 1343 Petrarch's daughter Francesca was born, of an unknown mother. This also brought a challenge to him, and it led to a more resolute self-mastery. We have no information as to Francesca's upbringing; but she must have been with Petrarch soon after she had grown into young womanhood. Petrarch's relations with his son were to be extremely unhappy, in spite of his efforts to be a good father; but his relations with his daughter, with her husband, and with their children were to be a blessing to him in his last years.

The stresses and strains of these two years led Petrarch to the writing of one of his two or three most distinctive and most notable works: the *Secretum*, which is his equivalent to the *Confessions* of St. Augustine. It is a searching self-analysis in dialogue form, the interlocutors being "Augustinus," a relentless examiner who represents the strictly religious ideal, and "Franciscus," who represents Petrarch the man, ready to admit faults, but ready also to defend values which, though not religious, seem to him to be in themselves true and worthy. The first of the three Books contains a general introductory discussion of Petrarch's inability to gain spiritual peace. In the second Book Augustine examines Petrarch with regard to each of the Seven Deadly Sins: Petrarch comes through this ordeal fairly well, except in the cases of incontinence and accidie. He uses this latter term to designate not sloth, but certain recurring fits of extreme depression. The intensely personal third Book deals with "sins"—if indeed they are sins—that concern Petrarch alone. The charge that Augustine now brings against him is this:

> You are bound, right and left, by two adamantine chains
> . . . you resemble a miser held in prison by chains of gold:
> he would like to be free, but he cannot bear to part with his
> golden chains.

Petrarch's two "chains" are his love of Laura and his desire for glory. An extraordinary debate about these two chains rages throughout the third Book, Augustine attacking with an impressive display of logic and authority, Petrarch defending valiantly, maintaining the essential purity of his love for Laura and the essential nobility of his desire for glory. No agreement is reached; there is no yielding on the part of Augustine; and Petrarch, though greatly troubled, does not renounce his chains.

The same stresses and strains led him to the writing, in a single day, of his seven Latin *Penitential Psalms*. These, like the Biblical psalms, are short prose poems, written in "verses" that consist typically of short and balanced clauses. The first three of these psalms and the last three are moving outcries of spiritual distress: the plea for forgiveness sounds throughout—"Miserere, Domine, miserere." The fourth psalm—a poem of great beauty, written, Petrarch says, in order that his sense of shame for his sinfulness may be made still stronger—sets forth the blessings that God has showered upon him and upon all men:

Thou hast created for me the heavens and the stars. . . .
The sun and the moon, days and nights, light and darkness.
The air is the work of Thy fingers; Thou didst make the clear sky and the clouds, and the winds and the rains.
Thou hast enfolded the earth in waters; Thou hast made mountains and seas, valleys and plains, fountains and lakes and rivers.

He goes on to give thanks for growing things and for living things, for rest, and shade, and (intellectual) freedom, and for God's endowment of man:

Thou hast given him a visage commanding and serene, and a spirit that may know Thee and may contemplate that which is celestial.
Thou hast added innumerable arts whereby life may be adorned; Thou hast given also the hope of eternal life.

The same stresses and strains are reflected also in some of the letters and some of the Italian poems that were written in this period, notably in a sonnet that begins thus:

My ship is passing through a rough sea, at midnight, in winter, between Scylla and Charybdis; at the helm sits my lord—nay, rather mine enemy—and at every oar a quick and restless thought that seems to scorn tempest and fate alike; my sails are rent by a dank and ceaseless wind of sighs, of hopes, and of desire.

Before leaving Provence Petrarch began the writing of a treatise on the cardinal virtues, entitled *Rerum memorandarum libri*—a work which, if it had ever been completed, would have been of great extent. In Provence he wrote only an introductory Book, on solitude and study as conducive to virtue, and a bit of a second Book, which initiates his treatment of Prudence. The most interesting feature of this work is that the sections devoted to general statements are followed by groups of examples—the first group being ancient Roman, the second group ancient non-Roman (chiefly Greek), and a third group (not always present) modern. Essentially, indeed, the work is a rich thesaurus of classified examples, drawn mainly from Petrarch's already vast knowledge of ancient history and literature and from the already wide range of his own experience.

In September, a mission in Naples having been entrusted to him by his Cardinal and by the Pope, he set out for Italy.

IX. *Mission to Naples*

IN 1 3 3 8 and the next three years the powerful family of the Pipini, who held great possessions in the eastern part of the Kingdom of Naples, had engaged first in warfare against a rival family and then in open rebellion against the King; and on the suppression of that rebellion in 1341 the three brothers who were then the heads of the family were imprisoned in the Castel Capuano in Naples, and their properties were confiscated and given or sold to others. Some signs of clemency had been shown after the death of King Robert, but the three brothers were still imprisoned. An influential relative had secured for them the interest of the Colonna family, and Cardinal Colonna had secured the interest of the Pope; and in August or early September, 1343, it had been decided that Petrarch should be sent to Naples with a letter from the Pope urging the release of the three prisoners.

Petrarch accordingly left Provence about mid-September, taking with him two unfinished works, the *Africa* and the *Rerum memorandarum libri*. He went first by land to Nice, where he took ship, expecting to make the rest of his journey by sea. That same evening the ship put into the harbor of Monaco for the night. The next day the weather was so bad that the ship did not venture to leave the harbor. On the following day, although the weather was still bad, they sailed on as far as Porto Maurizio, where they put in for the night, which Petrarch spent in a rough sailors' tavern. Disgusted by the sea, he decided to send his servants and his baggage on by ship and to go himself by land, with a single companion. They bought horses in Porto Maurizio; and all went well with their journey by land until they approached the southern border of Lombardy: Milan and Pisa were at war, and both armies were encamped near the border. There was nothing for it but to take to the sea again, though only for a short stretch from Lerici to a point north of Pisa. Thence they were able to ride to Rome without hindrance, going through Pisa, Siena, Perugia, Todi, and Narni.

They reached Rome on the evening of the 4th of October; and although it was late Petrarch went at once to pay his respects to Stefano Colonna the Elder, whom he found as impressive and vigorous as ever. The next day was spent with Stefano, who shared the Cardinal's hope that the Pipini might be released. On the 7th Petrarch left Rome, Stefano accompanying him beyond the walls of the city, and went as far as Palestrina, the ancestral home and stronghold of the Colonna. Here he was made welcome by still another Giovanni Colonna—a son of Stefano the Younger. At Palestrina he had a chance to talk once more with the much older Giovanni Colonna, the monk who had been his companion in 1341 on walks through Rome.

While in Naples Petrarch lived in the Franciscan monastery of San Lorenzo.

He was greatly shocked by the state of affairs in Naples, where he found "no piety, no truth, no faith," and "clear signs of impending disaster." He was shocked, most of all, by the apparent dominance of a certain Roberto da Mileto, a monk of the dissident party of the Franciscan Order known as the "Spirituals" or as the "Brethren of the Life of Poverty"—a party at odds not only with other Franciscans but with the papacy. Petrarch, a realist when he chose to be, describes him thus:

> I have seen here a three-legged creature, barefoot, bareheaded, proud of his poverty, foul with indulgences, bald, red-faced, with fat haunches, half-covered by his scanty gown . . . bent not so much by age as by hypocrisy. Impressive not by eloquence but by a frowning silence, he

traverses the halls of the queens, overthrowing the humble and trampling on justice.

The one and only champion of justice, according to Petrarch, was Philippe de Cabassoles, who could do little among the wolves that surrounded him.

In point of fact conditions in Naples were very bad indeed, though the dominance of Fra Roberto was probably not as extensive as Petrarch thought it was. Grave inner tensions had arisen from the ambitions of the families of two younger brothers of King Robert; there were tensions with the Pope, who claimed the overlordship of the Kingdom and was known to be planning to send a Legate to take control of the government; and there were tensions with Hungary, whose royal family had also some claims upon Naples and was insistent that Prince Andrew should be crowned as king.

Soon after his arrival Petrarch went to see the two Queens and attended a meeting of the Council. Decision on the Pope's request for the liberation of the Pipini was deferred. Petrarch visited the Pipini in their prison three or four times, and came away disheartened, especially by the realization that many influential men were now enjoying possession of the confiscated Pipini properties.

During his weeks of waiting for an answer—which he was sure would be a refusal—Petrarch had certain memorable experiences that were not related to his mission. The happiest of these was an excursion with Barbato da Sulmona and Giovanni Barrili along the northern shore of the Bay, an excursion full of delight for Petrarch because of the classical associations of scenes visited. Among the places they saw were Pozzuoli, the Solfatara, with its sulphureous fumes, Lake Avernus, the Lucrine Lake, the Cave of the Sybil, and Baia. At Pozzuoli he saw a then famous amazon, Maria, and witnessed a display of her extraordinary strength. He would have liked very much to visit the site of Scipio's villa of Linternum, but he could not find anyone who could guide him there.

A local bishop who dabbled in astrology had predicted that on the 25th of November an earthquake would leave Naples in ruins; and in consequence of this prediction most of the people of Naples were abandoning their occupations and devoting themselves to acts of penitence: on the evening of the 24th crowds were filling the streets and pressing into the churches. Petrarch did not believe in astrology, but he was enough concerned to stay up until nearly midnight, watching, from his window, the setting of the moon. He then went to bed; but he was soon wakened by a terrific noise, and by the shaking of the building. The monks—Petrarch with them—gathered in their church, where they prostrated themselves in momentary expectation of death. The wind was raging, rain was falling in a deluge, thunder was rolling and lightning flashing, the earth was quaking, the Bay was roaring, men were wailing. As the morning brought some lessening of terror, Petrarch and some others rode down to the shore. The Bay was a mass of white fury: all but one of the ships that had been in the harbor had been dashed to pieces, and death tossed on the huge waves. Buildings along the shore had been undermined and had collapsed. In the course of the morning Queen Joan, barefoot and dishevelled, with a great company of women, hastened to a church dedicated to the Virgin. The storm raged throughout the day—Petrarch himself was in danger at one time—but ceased suddenly at nightfall (it had wrought havoc not only at Naples but to the north and the south as well: most of Amalfi slid into the sea). Petrarch resolved never again to venture on the sea—and he never did.

On the following day, as it chanced, Queen Joan, following the example of her grandfather, appointed Petrarch to an honorary chaplaincy.

At some time during Petrarch's stay in Naples Barbato da Sulmona begged him for a copy of one short passage of the *Africa*, a passage on the death of Mago (the younger brother of Hannibal). Petrarch at first refused, being unwilling to release anything that was not yet in final form. Barbato persisted, however, and Petrarch finally let him have a copy of the passage on the condition that he keep it for himself alone. Barbato promised to do so, but he soon broke his promise, and copies of the passage, often very incorrect, were to circulate widely, much to Petrarch's distress. His friendship for Barbato was too strong, however, to be seriously injured even by this episode.

Late in November, apparently, Petrarch went with some companions to a gladiatorial show. Queen Joan and her consort, many nobles, and a host of commoners were there. Petrarch had not been told that in this show men would fight to the death. While he was looking for something worth while to happen, a sudden burst of applause drew his attention to a handsome youth who had just fallen dead at his feet, killed by a dagger thrust. Astounded and horrified by such a display of cruelty and folly, he left his companions immediately, and spurred away.

On the afternoon of the last day of November he attended a meeting of the Council at which he had reason to think that a decision as to the Pope's request would be reached; but nightfall came without a decision; violence ruled the streets after dark; and without further waiting he rode back to his monastery. On the next day, unable to endure Naples any longer, he decided to leave for Parma soon, even if no decision as to the Pope's request should have been reached.

Before he left Naples Barbato da Sulmona and Giovanni Barrili urged him to settle there permanently. He of course declined; but he suggested that they send a similar invitation, through him, to his friend Rinaldo Cavalchini, a Veronese teacher. They agreed; and Petrarch sent the invitation in the form of a long *epistola metrica*.

Before he left Naples, also, Niccolò d'Alife, a prominent official, requested him to write an epitaph for King Robert, and he promised to do so.

During his weeks in Naples Petrarch had plenty of time on his hands, and he naturally spent much of it in writing. To Cardinal Colonna he wrote four letters from which much of our information about his stay in Naples is derived, and one other letter that is not extant: this was a confidential letter, and its contents were to be made known to the Pope.

He wrote also three *epistolae metricae*. one to Niccolò d'Alife, devoted to praise of King Robert; one to Barbato, proposing just such an excursion along the north shore of the Bay as they were presently to take; and the one to Rinaldo Cavalchini that has just been mentioned.

His main literary activity at this time, however, was his continuation of the *Rerum memorandarum libri*. Before leaving Provence he had completed only the first Book and a small part of the second: while in Naples he finished the second Book (though this did not bring him to the end of his treatment of Prudence). This Book contains treatments of Memory and of Ingenuity, the lengthy treatment of Ingenuity being divided into four parts:

ingenuity and eloquence, jests and witty sayings, biting jests, and the ingenuity of poverty. Among the moderns quoted are Azzo da Correggio, Clement VI, and Dante.

At about the time of Petrarch's departure from Naples a letter sent to the Pope, apparently in the name of the Queen Dowager, reported that his request for the liberation of the Pipini had been refused.

X. *Parma and Verona: 1344 - 1345*

A<small>T SOME</small> point of pause in his northward journey, perhaps in Rome, Petrarch wrote an effectionate farewell message to Barbato da Sulmona in the form of an *epistola metrica*, which, however, is concerned less with Naples than with Parma. Petrarch had been happy there, two years before, in his relations with Azzo da Correggio, in the renewal of inspiration that had come to him at Selvapiana for work on the *Africa*, and in the tranquillity that he had found in a house in Parma itself. His *epistola* to Barbato makes it clear that he was now hoping to find in Parma and at Selvapiana a similar happiness and a similar renewal of inspiration.

He reached Parma toward the end of December, 1344. The Correggi were still in control of Parma, and Petrarch evidently had no reason to suspect that their control was not to be lasting. Early in 1344 he bought the house in which he had lived during the latter part of his previous stay. He did more than buy it: he had it extensively repaired, and improved its appearance by some decoration in marble. Apparently he was planning to make Parma his permanent home.

Perhaps in the spring, perhaps somewhat later, he received from his Veronese friend Guglielmo da Pastrengo a letter asking what he was doing and how he was faring. He replied in an *epistola metrica*, of which the main elements—partly in translation and partly in summary—are these:

> What am I doing? Like all men, I toil.
> What am I thinking of? My final rest.
> What hope have I? No hope for peace on earth . . .
> Where am I now? In Parma. How do I spend

My days? Now in my orchard, now at church,
And now in woods far from the city walls . . .
What am I working on? the *Africa*.
And why? For empty glory . . .
And I am working on my house, to which
I am adding marbles rare . . .
There are cracks in the walls: the workmen scoff,
   and say
That the house will last my time and more; and yet
I cannot leave it so, for the repairs
I have begun must now be carried through . . .
Desires do vary, but as I weigh them all
I laugh at myself and all the world besides.

Presumably the church referred to was San Stefano, and the woods were those of Selvapiana.

Azzo da Correggio was at this time employing Moggio dei Moggi, a citizen of Parma, as a teacher for his young sons. Petrarch thought that Moggio would be a good teacher for his Giovanni, who was now about seven years old; and he therefore had someone bring him to Parma. It was a wise move: writing to Moggio many years later, he says of his son: "In his childhood he learned to admire you, and to be fonder of you than of anyone else."

In the spring Petrarch suffered severely, for a time, from an attack of scabies; and in consequence, presumably, of this illness a rumor that he had died gained wide circulation. Similar rumors of his death were to circulate repeatedly in later years. One of the results, in this first instance, was the composition of a lament in *canzone* form by Antonio da Ferrara (a minor poet, well known at the time), to which Petrarch replied in a sonnet, assuring Antonio that while he had indeed been seriously ill he had not died.

His growing fame, due largely to his coronation, caused both adulation and hostility: both of these attitudes found written expressions that reached Petrarch in 1344. An *epistola metrica* that is full of high praise and asks that the writer be admitted to friendship with Petrarch came from Gabrio Zamorei, a Parmesan jurist and writer, and was answered by an *epistola metrica* that is typical in its combination of protest that the praise is undeserved and obvious pleasure in the receipt of it.

Perhaps about the same time there came to Petrarch a hostile and insolent letter, written ostensibly by Lancellotto Anguissola, a Lombard noble who was associated with the Visconti. The letter attacked not only Petrarch as an individual but also the art of poetry in general. Petrarch's coronation was said to be undeserved and premature, and his poetry was said to be generally unknown; and poets were called mendacious and mad, and their writings puerile.

To this attack Petrarch replied in a long *epistola metrica*, originally addressed to Lancellotto. While this reply is severe and sarcastic, it is devoted mainly to an able self-defense and an able defense of poetry. Poets are moved by a certain divine energy; their "madness" is the excitement of inspiration; and what they write has not only an obvious charm, but the deeper value of hidden meanings.

Perhaps before he had the *epistola* ready to send, perhaps after he had sent it and Lancellotto had received it, a letter arrived from Lancellotto saying that he had not written the hostile letter to which his name had been attached; and either through Lancellotto's letter or in some other way Petrarch learned that the actual writer of that hostile letter was Brizio Visconti, a powerful, cruel, and unscrupulous son of Luchino Visconti, who was at this time one of the two co-rulers of Milan (the other being his brother, the Archbishop Giovanni): Brizio had simply chosen to attach Lancellotto's name to the letter that he himself had written.

Petrarch then wrote a brief and grateful *epistola metrica* to Lancellotto, and a violently sarcastic *epistola metrica* to Brizio, who has nothing in common, Petrarch says, with him or with poets. To Brizio Saturn had given wealth, avarice, and stupidity; to Petrarch Mercury had given modest means, the love of poetry, and a restless mind. Let Brizio revel in all the selfish indulgences that his wealth makes possible; but let him restrain his words. In later years, when Petrarch was making a collection of his *epistolae metricae*, he included all three of these letters, giving to the first the heading: "To a certain unnamed envious man who had indulged in manifold insults, shielding himself under a name that was not his."

In the autumn, apparently, Petrarch received from Socrates a letter urging him to return to Provence. To this urging he replied in two *epistolae metricae* that are notable chiefly for Petrarch's statement that he does not intend ever to leave Italy again.

The first nine months of 1344 were a period of remarkable productivity for Petrarch, in spite of his illness in the spring and the signs of trouble for Parma, from within and from without, that were becoming more and more apparent. During these months he worked on the *Africa* and on the *Rerum memorandarum libri*, and wrote the *epistolae metricae* that have been mentioned and a considerable number of poems in Italian.

One of the greatest of his *canzoni* was written, probably, at this time: the unique *I' vo pensando* ("I live and move in thought"), which he chose eventually for the position of honor as the opening poem of the second of the two parts into which the *Canzoniere* was divided. This *canzone* is the poetic equivalent of the third Book of the *Secretum:* it voices an intense conflict between the thought of salvation, on the one hand, and the thoughts of glory and of love on the other hand—thoughts that are in reality desires infused with thought. After an introductory stanza the thought of salvation, speaking in direct discourse, attacks the thoughts of glory and of love; Petrarch then defends them as best he can; and the concluding stanzas depict the plight from which he cannot free himself. The stanza devoted to the defense of the thought of glory reads in part:

> A thought that is sweet and sharp abides in my soul, a wearying and a delightful burden. It fills my heart with desire and feeds it with hope, for when I think of glorious and generous fame I know not whether I freeze or burn, or whether I be pale and gaunt; and if I slay it, it springs up again stronger than ever. This thought has been growing in me ever since I slept in swaddling clothes, and I fear that it will go down with me into the tomb.

In a later stanza, having in mind both of the thoughts that endanger his salvation, he cries out thus:

> My Lord, why takest thou not this shame from my face? For I am as a man who dreams, and it seems that Death is before me, and I seek to defend myself, but have no weapon.

Probably within this period, though perhaps a little later, Petrarch wrote a second *Triumph* as a pendant to the *Triumphus Cupidinis*. The earlier poem had celebrated the triumph of Cupid over a host of lovers. This new poem, entitled *Triumphus Pudici-*

tie, opens with a battle between Cupid and Laura, who is supported by a group of her many Virtues. Laura is victorious; Cupid is bound; and the poem now becomes processional. Among its persons are Lucretia, Virginia and her father, Judith, and Piccarda Donati. The procession, led by Laura, with Cupid as its single captive, starts on the northern shore of the Bay of Naples—the places mentioned being places that Petrarch had visited recently—moves to Linternum, where Scipio Africanus joins in, and then proceeds to Rome, where Cupid is left in the temple of Pudicitia Patricia, under a guard that includes Hippolytus and Joseph.

The Correggio brothers had at first been successful as rulers of Parma, but later on they had incurred serious difficulties, and by the autumn of 1344 their position had become so bad that Azzo, at least, was convinced that they could no longer maintain themselves. In October, therefore, he sold the lordship to Obizzo d'Este, the Marquis of Ferrara, who was welcomed in November by the people of Parma. Azzo's action, however, aroused the jealousy of the Marquis of Mantua and the hostility of the Visconti. In 1341 Azzo had made a secret agreement with the Visconti according to which they had promised him substantial support (the extent of which is not a matter of record) and he had promised to turn the lordship of Parma over to them in four years. He may well have had reason to believe that they were not keeping their promises and that his agreement with them was therefore null and void; but the fact of their hostility remained. The Marquis of Mantua, certain allies of his, and the Visconti sent troops to Parma, and a loosely organized siege of the city began in December. Among the troops employed were foreign mercenaries—there was already disastrous Italian precedent for such employment. The besiegers bided their time, refraining from assault and repelling sallies by the defenders; but the situation was very dangerous.

Under these circumstances Petrarch's freedom and tranquillity vanished. During the last months of 1344 and the first weeks of 1345 he probably kept on, nevertheless, with his work on the *Rerum memorandarum libri*. By the middle of February he had completed Book III of the *Rerum* and most, but not all, of Book IV. These Books are still devoted to Prudence: Book III completes the discussion of the understanding of things present, and Book IV discusses foresight for the future. The completed portion of this Book deals with such matters as oracles, prophecies, and dreams. Among the moderns quoted in these two Books are Pope Hadrian V, Henry VII, and King Robert.

It seems probable that it was in the course of these months that the tragic situation of Parma, which reflected the tragic situation of Italy as a whole, forced from Petrarch's anguished mind and heart—but under the control of an unsurpassed artistry—what is perhaps the greatest of all his *canzoni*, his *Italia mia*. It is an exceedingly powerful appeal to the rulers of the many parts of Italy to cease their jealous warfare, and in particular to cease their employment of foreign mercenaries. It opens with a cry of distress: the poet must speak, even though his speaking may be vain. He implores divine help:

> Ruler of heaven, I entreat Thee that the same pity that brought Thee to this earth turn Thine eyes now to this beloved and favored land of Thine ... do Thou, oh Father, soften and open the hearts that War has hardened and has shut.

The rulers of Italy are then addressed directly:

> You in whose hands fortune has placed the rule of these fair regions, for which you seem to feel no pity, why should so many foreign swords be here?

The folly and shame of the employment of foreign mercenaries are then protested most convincingly. Very different thoughts should pervade ruling minds:

> "Is not this the ground that first I touched? Is not this the nest wherein I had my nurture? Is not this my fatherland, in which I trust, a mother benign and holy, wherein my own father and my own mother are at rest?" In God's name let such thoughts as these stir in your minds, and look with pity on the tears of the grieving people, who look only to you, after God, for surcease of their distress. And if you will only show them some sign of sympathy, virtue will take arms against fury, and the combat will be short, for ancient valor is not yet dead in Italian hearts.

The *envoi* reads:

> My song, I charge thee to give thy message courteously, for thou must go amidst proud folk whose minds, through

old and evil habit, are hostile to the truth. Thou wilt find welcome with the few noble souls who follow after that which is good. Say to them: "Who will give me aid? I go crying out 'Peace, peace, peace.'"

As the winter wore on and conditions in Parma became worse and worse, Petrarch began to think of the possibility of returning to Provence after all. By the middle of February the situation had become unendurable, and Petrarch may well have felt that his close association with Azzo might lead to personal disaster. In any case, he then determined to attempt to escape from Parma and to return to Provence. He made his escape on the evening of the 23rd of February. In a letter written two days later to Barbato da Sulmona he tells of his experiences:

At sunset on the 23rd I started out with a few companions; and we made our way between enemy positions. About midnight, when we were near Reggio, which was hostile to us, a band of marauders broke out of an ambush, shouting noisily, and threatening to kill us. There was nothing for it but to flee. But after we were safe from them my horse stumbled, in the darkness, and fell, carrying me down with him, injuring me and knocking the breath out of me. Nevertheless, gathering all my strength, I got to my feet; and although today I can hardly lift my hand to my mouth, I managed to get onto my horse again. . . . Our guides had lost their way; and we were standing still, off the road, exhausted and dismayed, and within the sound of the voices of enemy guards on walls that we could not place. Meanwhile a thunderstorm was raging, and rain, mixed with hail, was coming down in a deluge. . . . We spent that hellish night lying on the bare ground; and the arm that had been hurt in my fall was swelling and paining me severely. . . . In the first dim light of dawn we followed a path through the brush that took us to the friendly town of Scandiano, where we learned that a force of enemy troops had been looking for us in the night, but had abandoned their search because of the storm. . . . That day, after a makeshift bandage had been put on my arm, we went by a mountain road to Modena; and on the next day we came here to Bologna.

At some time in the spring, after he had recovered somewhat from the experiences of his escape, he journeyed northward to Verona, where he had at least two good friends, Guglielmo da Pastrengo and Rinaldo Cavalchini, to whom he had written from Naples. He probably knew, also, that Azzo da Correggio had either taken refuge already in Verona, or was planning to do so. There seemed, indeed, to be no other North Italian city to which Petrarch might better go: he had as yet no connections with any one of the three great cities—Milan, Padua, and Venice—in which he was to spend most of the latter part of his life.

While in Verona, probably soon after he got there, he made an attempt to resume work on the *Rerum memorandarum libri*. Not having with him what he had already done, he did not try to go on from the point he had reached in Parma, but began a section on Modesty, which would presumably have formed part of a treatment of Temperance. He wrote only two or three pages, however, and thereafter he never resumed work on the *Rerum*.

In Verona, and well before the middle of June, he made his greatest find. He discovered in the library of the cathedral a volume containing the sixteen Books of Cicero's collection of his letters to Atticus, as well as the minor collections of Cicero's letters to his brother Quintus and to Brutus. This volume, if known at all, had been known only to men who had not realized its importance

Greatly excited, Petrarch started at once to make a copy of these collections, for no local copyist had the competence necessary for this particular piece of work. This task, undertaken at a time when his arm was still troubling him, must have kept him busy for several weeks, even if he worked at it quite steadily. The finished volume was so huge and unwieldy that he could not keep it in a book-chest, but had to stand it on the floor.

This discovery was to have extraordinary results. It was to enrich the classical heritage of all later generations; it was to lead Petrarch to write to Cicero and to other classical authors; and it was to give him the idea of making a collection or collections of his own letters. It was also to be responsible for a serious injury to his left leg.

His first letter to Cicero, composed in the irresistible flush of a vast amount of new knowledge of Cicero the man, as revealed in his correspondence, is concerned not with Cicero's literary achievements but with his political and personal inconsistencies, for which Petrarch takes him severely to task, though he maintains that he is one who dearly loves Cicero's name. He subscribes his letter thus:

> In the upper world, on the right bank of the Adige, in the city of Verona in that part of Italy that lies beyond the Po, on the sixteenth day before the Kalends of July, in the year that is the 1345th since the birth of the God of whom thou hadst no knowledge.

The idea of writing such a letter, while directly suggested by his recent discovery, was a natural outgrowth of his lifelong feeling that books, far from being mere objects, were emanations of personality. Within a few months, Petrarch was to write again to Cicero; and in later years he was to write to Seneca, Varro, Quintilian, Livy, Asinius Pollio, Horace, Virgil, Homer, and also, bridging time in the opposite direction, to Posterity.

While in Verona Petrarch enjoyed acquaintance, perhaps friendship, with Dante's son Pietro. On one occasion they exchanged written messages, Petrarch's being a brief *epistola metrica*.

It seems probable that Petrarch had taken his son with him when he escaped from Parma; that on reaching Verona he had employed Rinaldo Cavalchini as a teacher for the boy; and that when he left Verona he left Giovanni in Rinaldo's care.

At some time in the autumn Petrarch set out from Verona to return to Provence. He was going on his own initiative: the rush of untoward events at Parma had determined him to give up the idea of continued residence there. He had, however, a mission of a sort to Pope Clement: someone—we do not know who it was—had requested him to plead with the Pope to come to Italy.

Wishing evidently to avoid Lombardy, he decided to take a long and difficult route through the Alps. Guglielmo da Pastrengo accompanied him to Peschiera (at the southern end of Lake Garda). There they talked far into the night. Early the next morning they went on westward to the boundary between the territories of Verona and Brescia, where they parted, affectionately and tearfully, Petrarch saying that he was going to live thenceforth in a foreign land, that they might never see each other again, and that their separation did not mean any lessening of their friendship. He then turned north, keeping to the west of Lake Garda, but returning then to the valley of the Adige. He saw and marvelled at the vast mass of huge rocks, fallen in a landslide (or glacially deposited), known as the Slavini di Marco, and went on, certainly through Trent and Merano, to the source of the Adige at the Pass of Resia (which leads into the Tyrol). There he was greatly impressed by the adamantine majesty of the Alps. What route he followed from the Pass of Resia to Provence we do not know.

XI. *Vaucluse: 1345 - 1347*

D URING this two-year period Petrarch found it possible to stay in Vaucluse nearly all the time: once in a while he had to go into Avignon, but never for a stay of any considerable length. For the greater part of the period he had as house guest a younger Florentine relative, Franceschino degli Albizzi, whom he counted as a very dear friend. Franceschino was evidently a man of fine spirit and a writer of Italian verse.

LATE 1345

Petrarch's Neapolitan forebodings had been all too well founded; for probably soon after he reached Provence he learned that Queen Joan's consort, Andrew of Hungary, had been murdered in September.

Soon after reaching Provence he complied at last with Niccolò d'Alife's request that he write an epitaph for King Robert. The twenty-five hexameters of which the epitaph consists are filled with praises of the king. It was sent to Niccolò with a covering *epistola metrica,* in which he bids Niccolò to make use of as much or as little of it as he may think wise.

Petrarch's second letter to Cicero, written in Avignon on the 19th of December, would have pleased its supposed recipient more than the first letter, since this second letter is devoted largely to praise of Cicero's intellectual attainments and of his eloquence, and to the assurance that he had won great and widespread fame. Of the present state of Rome, Petrarch says, he will forbear to speak.

It was doubtless not long after his arrival in Provence that Petrarch, on behalf of those in Italy who had commissioned him to do so, presented to the Pope the plea that he come to Italy. In the course of their conversation Petrarch said that Italians wished greatly that Clement might know Italy as well as he knew France and England. The Pope replied that he wished so too. But he was not to be moved from Provence.

1346

In January Philippe de Cabassoles arrived in Provence: he and another man had been sent by Queen Joan on a mission to the Pope. It had been expected that Philippe would return to Naples; but he remained in Provence.

The almost simultaneous returns of Petrarch and Philippe after long absences must have brought a joyous sense of reunion to both of them. It was in all probability soon after Philippe's arrival that Petrarch wrote and sent to him a charming *epistola metrica,* beginning *Exul ab Italia* (excluded from the collection of the *Epistolae metricae,* presumably because it is written in rhymed hexametric couplets), inviting Philippe to live with him in Vaucluse. Here Philippe will find a Naples free from treachery, as Petrarch is finding a Parma free from the clamor of war. Here all is quietness and simplicity; here are care-dispelling books; here are the woods and the river. Some of Petrarch's old trees have decayed: let Philippe's servants find and bring young fruit trees to replace them; and under the shade of these new trees, planted by the riverside, Philippe and Petrarch may sit and fish. Here Petrarch expects, barring unforeseen circumstances, to spend the rest of his life.

Philippe soon spent a fortnight with Petrarch in Vaucluse; and their contented companionship in the beloved valley led Petrarch, in Lent (Easter, in 1346, fell on the 16th of April), to write his unique treatise *De vita solitaria,* "On the Life of Solitude," which is dedicated to Philippe. By "the life of solitude" Petrarch meant not hermitage alone, but quiet country life, fruitful in its leisure, with or without a companion or two, as contrasted with the noisy, crowded, and bustling life of cities. The first of the two Books of the treatise discusses the life of solitude and city life. The second Book is devoted chiefly to examples of men and women who had loved and sought solitude. These examples embrace a great variety of persons, times, and places: Biblical figures, saints early and recent (St. Benedict and St. Francis), the Brahmans and other non-Christians, and ancient philosophers, poets, orators, emperors and men of war (among whom Scipio Africanus is dominant). There is a long digression on the failure of contemporary popes and princes to recover the Holy Land; and there is an ample and appropriate conclusion.

It is quite possible that the treatise was begun during Philippe's visit: certainly he must have heard much of it while it was being written or soon afterward. But Petrarch, knowing that he would want to undertake extensive revision, would not let Philippe have a copy of the first draft. In point of fact it was not until twenty years later that he sent a copy to Philippe—and even after that he made one considerable insertion.

Petrarch was not by any means insensitive to the difficulties and the hardships of the villagers and the peasants of his valley. In an *epistola metrica* of uncertain date, filled with a remarkable description of what must have been a terrible storm and flood, he writes thus:

> The plowman,
> Bewildered, can no longer find the ground
> His feet were wont to tread, but with his arms
> Struggles in fear to keep above the waters:
> His cattle and his plow, his humble cottage
> And all his hopes drift past him on the flood. . . .
> Mothers are weeping, pressing to their breasts
> Their little ones. A sound of mourning rises
> From villages where poor and suffering folk
> Lament their ruin: in his painted vestments
> The priest intones his vows, as if he ruled
> The clouds, and with a knotted rope he wakes
> The clangor of his bells.

A letter that was probably written in 1346 contains this passage:

> Here before my eyes are fishermen worn out with cold and hunger . . . hungry and half-naked, they spend whole days and whole sleepless nights casting their lines or their nets over and over again, catching nothing, in extreme discomfort . . . yet . . . they cannot tear themselves away from the fatal stream.

Villagers and peasants came to him from time to time to ask his advice as to their legal rights, as to household problems, and even as to possible marriages.

In April, 1346, a desperate call for help came to him from the village of Thor, a few miles down the Sorgue, that was the feudal property of an evil lord. This lord, Geraud Amic, had sought to seduce a girl of the village, who had resisted him but had yielded to her betrothed lover what she had refused to his master. Under the law that was then and there in force, Geraud had the right to condemn the young man to death; and he was holding him in jail, apparently intending to exercise that right. The young man's friends appealed to Petrarch, who was certainly the greatest man in the valley. Petrarch, realizing that the only hope lay in intervention by someone in a position of great influence, decided to turn to his Cardinal. He therefore wrote a letter to Laelius, who was then with the Cardinal in Avignon, stating the case and asking Laelius to try to secure the Cardinal's intervention; and he sent the letter into Avignon by a peasant who could give Laelius more information if he wanted it. Three days later, no answer having been received, and the danger that the young man would be put to death being imminent, he sent a second letter to Laelius by the same messenger —who on his own initiative, hoping to win favor with Laelius, took him a bottle of pure olive oil that he himself had pressed. How the matter turned out we do not know.

In April the young Charles of Bohemia was in Avignon, seeking the support of Pope Clement in his candidacy for election as Emperor. Clement agreed to support him, but only if he made certain promises, among which were these two: that he would never enter any state subject to the Church without formal permission from the Pope; and that on going to Rome to be crowned he would enter the city only on the day set for the coronation and would leave it before night. If Petrarch learned of these promises, as he probably did, they must have left him with little hope that Charles could ever be the means of restoring Rome to its ancient imperial greatness.

In the spring or summer Petrarch learned that a canonry in the cathedral of Parma and the archdeaconate of the cathedral had become vacant through the death of the man who had held them; and he applied, doubtless through Cardinal Colonna, for appointment to the double position.

In the autumn of 1341 Petrarch had given up what he calls his "warfare with the Nymphs," and had left them in possession of the disputed ground near the Fountain of the Sorgue. In

1343 he seems to have left things as they were; but now, in the spring or summer of 1346, he renewed the struggle. Employing peasants, shepherds, and fishermen, he had large rocks sunk at the edge of the river, forming a breakwater; a stone walk was made along the bank; and on the ground now reclaimed he had a shrine built for the Muses. All this and more he tells in an *epistola metrica* to Cardinal Colonna, inviting him to come and see it all for himself, and to enjoy a visit in the quietness and beauty of the country.

In the course of the summer Petrarch began the writing of his Latin Eclogues, which he was to gather eventually in a collection called *Bucolicum carmen*. These poems, twelve in all, are pastoral in their nomenclature and terminology, but they deal with actual persons, circumstances, and events, all presented in pastoral disguise. The first four Eclogues, written certainly or probably in 1346, deal respectively with the contrast between Petrarch's life and that of his brother Gherardo, with the death of King Robert, with Petrarch's love for Laura and his coronation, and with the nature of the poetic task. The first part of the Twelfth Eclogue, dealing with the early phases of the Hundred Years' War, may also have been written in 1346, but the last part is much later.

The three persons of the Second Eclogue, Idaeus, Pythias, and Silvius, represent Giovanni Barrili, Barbato da Sulmona, and Petrarch himself.

On the 29th of October Pope Clement appointed Petrarch to the vacant Parmesan canonry but not to the archdeaconate, there being a prior commitment for that post. It was presumably also in October that Petrarch learned that the fighting around Parma had come to an end, and that the conflict had been settled, in September, by Luchino Visconti's purchase of the lordship from Obizzo d'Este.

At some time in 1346, in all probability, Petrarch wrote to an older Florentine kinsman, Giovanni dell'Incisa, a letter in which he tells of his constant eagerness to build up his library, and asks Giovanni's help:

> I am possessed by one insatiable passion, which I cannot restrain—nor would I if I could. . . . I cannot get enough books. It may well be that I already have more than I need; but it is with books as it is with other things: the more you have, the more you want. Books have indeed a special

fascination. Gold, silver, gems, fine raiment, a marble palace, well-cultivated fields, paintings, a splendidly caparisoned horse—such things as these give one nothing more than a mute and superficial pleasure. Books delight us through and through, they converse with us, they give us good advice; they become living and lively companions to us. . . .

So then do please arrange to have competent and trustworthy men go through Tuscany for me, examining the book-chests of the religious and of other studious men, looking for things that might either alleviate or intensify my thirst. And although you know in general what I want, I am enclosing a list of the things that I am especially eager to get. And to stimulate your helpfulness let me tell you that I am sending similar requests to friends of mine in Britain, France, and Spain.

1 3 4 7

On the 18th of January, Laelius being about to leave for Naples on an errand that was probably for Cardinal Colonna or for the Pope, Petrarch wrote a letter of recommendation for him, addressing it to Barbato da Sulmona, and enclosed with it a graceful supplementary recommendation in Latin verse. He enclosed a copy of his Second Eclogue, on the death of King Robert; and in the letter itself he identifies the three persons of the eclogue, and says that it is to be regarded as a small gift for Barbato, Giovanni Barrili, and Niccolò d'Alife. The letter is dated "in inferno viventium," which of course means Avignon.

Early in 1347 Petrarch journeyed to Montrieux to visit his brother, whom he had not seen since Gherardo had become a monk. He spent one day and one night in the monastery: no day and no night had ever seemed shorter to him. He was greatly impressed by all that he saw and heard; and though he had come to see Gherardo, and did have opportunity for good talks with him, he found a brotherly welcome from all the other monks, with some of whom he had brief and pleasant individual talks. He was particularly impressed by the devout silence that prevailed at the appropriate times, and by the midnight singing of matins. Gherardo gave him three pieces of advice: that he make confession frequently; that he be instant in prayer and praise, not only by day but at night; and that he abstain from carnality. When he left the monastery several of the monks kept him company as far as their Rule allowed.

Petrarch's experience at Montrieux led him to write, in Lent (Easter, in 1347, fell on the first of April), a treatise *De otio religioso*, "On Monastic Freedom," which is in reality a long sermonic exhortation, with a text, "vacate et videte quoniam ego sum Deus," taken from the 46th Psalm. The *otio* of the title and the *vacate* of the text carry the same idea of freedom from all concerns that might interfere with religious insight or religious conduct. The perilous concerns from which liberation is to be sought are those of the devil, the world, and the flesh: those of the first group are treated in the first of the two Books of the treatise, those of the second and third groups in the second Book. There are hundreds of quotations from the Bible, from St. Augustine and other Fathers of the Church, and from Virgil, Cicero, and other classic authors. There are many *exempla* also, some ancient and some modern. The treatise is addressed, in a grateful preface, to the monks of Montrieux; but Petrarch states that he is writing it not for their benefit but for his own.

At some time in the spring or summer Petrarch submitted to the Pope a petition containing five requests. The nature of the first two requests is not clear, but they seem to have indicated the existence of a plan (never carried out) for Petrarch and Socrates to settle together in the neighborhood of Montrieux. The third request was for the legitimation of Azzo da Correggio's son Barriano; the fourth was for the legitimation of Petrarch's son Giovanni; and the fifth was for the granting of a benefice to a man who was apparently a Veronese friend or acquaintance of Petrarch.

In June Petrarch learned, with great excitement, that Cola di Rienzo had become the ruler of Rome. The story of his relations with Cola during the year 1347 will be told in the following chapter.

In the preceding summer Petrarch had renewed his warfare with the nymphs of the Sorgue, and had thought that the defenses then constructed would withstand any onslaught; but the winter storms had ruined them. He now surrendered—retaining for himself and the Muses, in the disputed territory, just one rocky nook, which he fortified so strongly that he was sure that nothing less than a tremendous earthquake could destroy it. This he reports to Cardinal Colonna in another *epistola metrica*.

On a day, probably in the spring, when Petrarch, having been in Avignon, was just leaving for Vaucluse, Cardinal Colonna, knowing that Petrarch liked dogs, gave him a big white dog of Spanish breed. Petrarch took him to Vaucluse, where he was to become a constant companion.

Soon, probably, Petrarch wrote another *epistola metrica* to the Cardinal, this one giving an account of the dog that the Cardinal had given him—of his contentment in the country, of the care he takes of his master, and of his exploits and his antics:

> If I sleep too long
> He whimpers, telling me the sun has risen,
> And scratches at my door. When I go forth
> He greets me joyously, and runs ahead
> Toward places often visited, and turns
> Around from time to time to see if I
> Am following. . . .
>
> Continually
> He gives amusement: with great bounds he goes
> Through woods and waters; with his shrilly bark
> He imitates the children when they sing;
> His sudden twists and turns are laughable.
> He is forever chasing the wild geese:
> Over the shore and over the rocks he leaps;
> They find no safety even in the stream;
> He plunges in, catches them in his mouth,
> And brings them out, offering them as a prize.

There could hardly be a finer poetic appreciation of caninity.

Before the end of the summer Petrarch had decided to return to Italy, thus abandoning whatever plan he may have had for settlement near Montrieux. His reasons for making this decision are indicated in an eclogue that is to be mentioned presently.

At some time in August or September he must have heard that Queen Joan had taken as her second husband Louis of Taranto, a nephew of the late King Robert. This news may or may not have been of any great interest to Petrarch at the time, but this marriage was to affect him indirectly in later years, since it involved the advancement of the able and ambitious

Florentine, Niccolò Acciaiuoli, who had long been Louis' chief adviser, to a position of great influence in Neapolitan affairs.

On the 9th of September Pope Clement approved the fivefold petition that Petrarch had submitted earlier in the year—the approval of its first two items having been rendered needless, however, by Petrarch's decision to return to Italy. In a letter written two days later Petrarch invites Barbato da Sulmona to come and live with him in Parma, if driven out of Sulmona by warfare in the Kingdom of Naples.

Three more eclogues and part of a fourth were written in the summer or the early autumn of 1347. The Fifth Eclogue, which concerns Cola, will be mentioned in the next chapter. The Sixth and the Seventh (of which only the first part was written at this time) are violent denunciations of the corruption of the papal court.

The Eighth Eclogue tells of Petrarch's decision to leave the service of Cardinal Colonna and to return to Italy. The interlocutors are Ganimedes, an old shepherd who represents the Cardinal, and another shepherd, Amiclas, younger but conscious of the approach of old age, who represents Petrarch. Amiclas, who has served Ganimedes for many years, has told him of his decision to leave his service and return to his own country. The main reasons for his decision are these: Ganimedes, once cheery, has become intractable and gruff; Amiclas' sheep are thin and dirty, their fleece is torn by thorns, their water is foul, and their forage is unhealthy (these conditions represent the corruption of the papal court); Amiclas desires now to cease servitude and to be free; he wants to return to his fatherland; and Gillias (Azzo da Correggio) is calling him. Ganimedes accuses him of ingratitude; but Amiclas denies the accusation, protesting that he is mindful and grateful, that he has always loved Ganimedes, and that as long as life shall last he will continue to love him.

The most notable of the several poems in Italian that were written in 1346 and 1347 are the three sonnets known as the "Babylonian" sonnets: they, like the Sixth and Seventh Eclogues, are violent denunciations of the corruption of the papal court. The first of the three begins thus:

> May fire from heaven rain down upon thy head, thou
> evil one, who ... through thy plundering of others art
> become rich and great.

The second begins thus:

This greedy Babylon has filled its sack with the wrath of God and with evil and wicked vices.

The third begins thus:

Fountain of dolor, abode of wrath, school of falsity, temple of heresy . . .

It was in all probability within these two years, also, that Petrarch began the making of the second form of the *Canzoniere*, and that he wrote as its initial poem the introductory sonnet that opens also all later forms of the collection. This second form, like all later forms, was divided into two parts, the second part begining with the great *canzone I' vo pensando*. This form probably contained about 130 poems.

Before Petrarch left Provence the Pope, apparently knowing that he was planning to go to Verona, entrusted him with a special message to Mastino della Scala, urging him to oppose the entrance into Italy of the King of Hungary, who was intending to invade the Kingdom of Naples. On the 13th of November the Pope addressed to Mastino a letter establishing Petrarch's status as a papal envoy, and on the 20th Petrarch started for Italy.

1346–1347

At some time or times during the two-year period now ending, Pope Clement offered Petrarch a bishopric and a papal secretaryship. Both positions would have been honorable and lucrative; but Petrarch refused them, as he was to refuse similar offers made thereafter: they would have interfered far too much with his cherished freedom to study and to write.

He had a standing request from Giovanni Coci, the librarian of the papal library, to prepare a correct list of the works of Cicero. Before he left Provence Clement himself had seconded that request, and Petrarch had agreed to do what he could while in Italy; he was evidently contemplating a task that would have entailed a considerable amount of work in Italian libraries.

XII. *Petrarch and Cola di Rienzo*

EVER since his return from Avignon Cola had been busily and ingeniously preparing himself and the people of Rome for a revolutionary change in the government of the city, a change designed to rescue Rome from its still worsening plight and in particular from the lawless violence of the great noble families, and to lead to the restoration of Roman dominance in Italy and in the world.

The revolution, carefully planned and perfectly timed, took place on May 19 and 20, 1347. On the 19th the people of Rome were summoned to meet on the next day as a parliament to decide on a new constitution. Cola spent the night in the church of Sant'Angelo in Pescheria praying and hearing Mass after Mass in honor of the Holy Spirit: he believed firmly that he was acting as an instrument of that Spirit.

On the morning of the 20th Cola went in a procession from Sant'Angelo to the Capitoline. There he addressed a vast assembly—in effect, the Roman People—blasting the great noble families as responsible for the plight of the city. An aide then read the new constitution, which placed the government of the city and its territory in the hands of the Roman People and provided for a whole series of salutary laws. The people were then asked whether they approved the constitution, which they did. Then they were asked to whom, on the basis of the new constitution, they would entrust the governing authority: Cola was named by acclamation. Nothing in all this was anti-papal: indeed the Pope's vicar, Raimondo di Orvieto, was at Cola's side on the Capitoline, and Cola had Raimondo named as his colleague, the two men being called "rectors of the city"—a title later confirmed by the Pope. At a second parliament, held a day or two later, Cola assumed the title of Tribune and was accorded dictatorial powers.

It became his custom to begin each day, at dawn, by making confession and receiving communion.

By early June Petrarch had heard the extraordinary news of Cola's successful revolution: he must have heard it with the utmost excitement and the utmost enthusiasm. Of all men then living Cola and Petrarch were doubtless the two who most passionately and intelligently desired the rescue of Rome from its shameful plight and the restoration of Rome to its pristine power and glory. Petrarch, to be sure, had supposed hitherto that such rescue and restoration could come only through an emperor; but now that a Roman citizen was actually undertaking the great task and had made so triumphant a beginning, Petrarch was quite ready to transfer his hope to Cola: that Rome restored should be republican rather than imperial was in itself a matter of little consequence. Despite his close associations with members of the Colonna family, Petrarch was bound by his ideals for Rome and by what he himself had seen in Roman territory to support Cola's attitude toward the great noble families that had been wrecking the city. All Cola's striving, highly aimed and widely beneficial though it was, contained a large element of histrionic self-glorification. Petrarch was content to give his whole-hearted assistance with no thought of personal aggrandizement: his part was simply to strengthen as best he could Cola's determination and that of the Roman People.

His first effort toward this end was the writing, at some time in June, of a long letter of exhortation addressed both to Cola and to the Roman People. Most of it reads less like a letter than like an oration—an oration that would indeed have stirred Roman souls if it could have been delivered on the Capitoline. The opening theme is liberty: the Roman People have won a joy-bringing liberation from their enslaving tyrants. Liberty is supremely precious, more precious than life itself: let the Roman People defend it, then, at any cost. The past slavery has been the more shameful in that the enslavers were not Romans, but interlopers of foreign origin (it was generally believed that the Colonna were of Germanic stock, and that the Orsini had come originally from Spoleto). Cola is compared to the two famous liberators of ancient Rome—the Brutus who drove out Tarquin and the Brutus who struck Caesar down. The evils wrought by the now ousted tyrants are rehearsed; and warning is given that these same tyrants will strive to regain the ruthless power they have lost. Unity, now providentially achieved, must be maintained: there must be no toleration of traitors, to whom no mercy should be shown. The rescue of Rome, now accomplished, will be an inspiration to all Italy.

Turning then to Cola himself, Petrarch exhorts him to advance steadfastly on the difficult road on which he has entered—a road that will lead to undying fame and to the gratitude of posterity. Cola's custom of daily confession and communion is praised, and Petrarch then makes one special request of him: that he constantly feed his mind by reading the annals of ancient Rome or by having them read to him. Finally, the Roman People are bidden to give Cola absolute support. Ancient instances of Roman devotion to Rome are cited effectively. No other task is comparable in importance to the maintenance of the welfare of the state. The letter has been written in an effort to fulfil what Petrarch has felt to be his duty as a Roman citizen. At some later time, perhaps, if Cola and the Roman People persevere in their great effort, Petrarch will celebrate it, more worthily, in poetry. The letter, splendidly eloquent throughout, ends with farewell wishes to Cola, the Roman People, and the glorious City of the Seven Hills.

Even before this letter reached Rome, Cola had rushed far ahead in his revolutionary course. He had summoned the nobles to appear before him and take an oath that they would not attack him or his new constitution: almost all of them did so, and military operations brought about the submission of the rest. He had taken steps to secure the support of all the cities that lay within the Roman territory; and early in June he had sent letters to all the great cities of Italy, bidding them send delegates to a gathering to be held in Rome to provide for the safety and the peace of "universa sacra Italia." In the superscription of these letters Cola had referred to himself as "Nicholas the Severe and Clement, Tribune of Liberty, of Peace, and of Justice, Liberator of the Holy Roman Republic." After the first of July he dated his letters "in the first year of the liberated Roman Republic."

He wrote frequently to persons in Avignon: his letters were eagerly received and widely circulated in the papal court. The general impression seems to have been favorable. The suppression of the tyrannical nobles was not incompatible with papal policy—Cardinal Colonna being apparently the only member of the Sacred College whose family interests were adversely affected.

On the 22nd of July Cola proposed to an assembly of the Roman People the adoption of a legal principle of far-reaching significance: that the Roman People should reclaim all their ancient rights of sovereignty, annulling all concessions, donations, and conferrals of dignity made in the course of the centuries that were in conflict with those ancient rights. Adoption followed immediately.

He continued to affect personal display. On the Feast of St. John he rode at the head of a procession to the Lateran, dressed in a white costume trimmed with gold, and mounted on a white horse, although processional use of a white horse was normally reserved for popes and emperors. A few days later he rode through the city to St. Peter's in a still more pompous procession. He planned also two even more audacious ceremonies: he was to be knighted on the first of August, and crowned as Tribune on the 15th. Invitations to these two ceremonies were sent out far and wide.

Petrarch's second extant letter to Cola was written before the end of July, and before he had received Cola's answer to his long letter of exhortation. He opens this second letter with the statement that he has been writing to Cola every day, but no letter written by him to Cola between these two is still extant. This second letter shows no special knowledge of Cola's current moves: it tells instead of the eagerness with which Cola's letters are being received in Avignon; praises their caution and their combination of respect for the dignity of the Roman People with respect for the Pope; commends Cola's custom of keeping copies of all his letters, and his use of the dating formula "in the first year of the liberated Roman Republic"; urges him to persevere as he has begun, and in particular to continue the caution with which he has been writing hitherto; and promises that he (Petrarch) will serve Cola with his pen as best he can—even if that means postponing work on the *Africa*.

On the 28th of July Cola wrote to Petrarch a letter beginning "Dulcissima literarum vestrarum series" that answers both Petrarch's original letter of exhortation and other letters that he had received from Petrarch. Cola's letter is brief but appreciative of Petrarch's support. It assumes the permanence of the revolution —"liberty is now the soul of the Roman People"—and expresses the wish that Petrarch might be in Rome.

On the last day of July Cola, with the papal vicar riding by his side, went in procession to St. John Lateran, gave a banquet there, addressed the crowd from the loggia on the façade, and then, in the Baptistery, heard Mass, and bathed in the great font in which, according to the general belief, the Emperor Constantine had been cured of leprosy and baptized a thousand years before. He spend the night in a bed that had been set up by the font. On the next morning the papal vicar celebrated Mass in the church, and Cola, standing, dressed in scarlet, on the balcony, was duly knighted by Roman officials. He immediately caused to be read, from the loggia, a decree whereby the Roman People reclaimed their ancient rights. This decree asserts that Rome is "caput orbis," that all cities and peoples of Italy are free and have Roman citizenship, and that the right of election of a Roman Emperor belongs to the Roman People. All emperors, electors, kings, dukes, princes, counts, marquises, peoples, universities and other persons (Charles of Bohemia is among those mentioned by name) who might desire to protest this electoral claim are summoned to appear and state their cases in Rome at the Feast of Pentecost in the next year. Cola is referred to as "White-mantled Knight of the Holy Spirit, Nicholas the Severe and Clement, liberator of the City, zealot for Italy, lover of the world, and august Tribune."

On this same day, as soon as the papal vicar heard this decree, or heard about it, he protested vigorously, on the ground that it was contrary to the freedom of action of the Church, and urged that it be withdrawn. His protest was of no avail, but he reported it in a letter to the Pope. Nevertheless, he did not resign his co-rectorship, and Cola did not oust him at this time.

Probably early in August, before he had heard of the knighting of Cola, Petrarch wrote his Fifth Eclogue, which is a poetically unsuccessful but still not uninteresting attempt to present Cola's revolution in pastoral terms; and shortly thereafter he sent a copy of it to Cola, with an expository covering letter.

The first two weeks of August were filled with ceremonies, festivals, and tournaments arranged for the entertainment of the delegates—two hundred or more—who had been sent to Rome by other cities in response to Cola's invitations.

At the ceremony of coronation, held on the Capitoline on the 15th, each of five prelates, one after another, crowned Cola with a wreath, each wreath being immediately removed by an attendant. The existing records indicate that the first prelate said:

Receive this crown of oak leaves, for that thou hast liberated citizens from death.

The second:

Receive this crown of ivy, for that thou hast loved religion.

The third:

Receive this crown of myrtle, for that thou hast remained faithful to thy duties.

The fourth:

Receive this crown of laurel, for that thou hast loved knowledge and hast abhorred avarice.

The fifth:

Thou humble man, receive this crown of olive leaves, for that thou hast overcome pride by humility.

A sixth prelate then gave him a silver crown and a scepter, saying:

Eminent Tribune, receive the gifts of the Holy Spirit, together with this crown and this scepter and a spiritual crown.

Finally, the mayor of Rome gave him a terrestrial globe, saying:

Eminent Tribune, receive this globe, exercise justice, and give us liberty and peace.

It was Cola who in May had named the papal vicar as his co-rector: on the day after the coronation he dismissed him.

After news of the knighting of Cola, of his bathing in the font of Constantine, and of the decree reclaiming sovereignty reached Avignon, the attitude of the papal court toward Cola underwent a decided change. He was assuming titles that had not been authorized by the Pope; his use of the font was regarded as sacrilegious; and the assumptions of the reclaiming decree appeared to jeopardize papal authority.

Petrarch also, when he heard of these matters, was perturbed, but he did not lose faith in Cola. On the contrary, he did his best to defend him, even though his efforts cost him friendships that he had long enjoyed. Toward the end of August, and probably before he had heard of the coronation, he wrote to Cola a letter in which he tells of the hostility to Cola that has developed, and of his efforts to defend him. He feels, he says, as if he were himself present and militant in Rome: his days are filled with anxieties and his nights with troubled dreams. One such dream, or waking fantasy, which he reports at length, may be summarized thus, with some bits of quotation:

I saw thee enthroned at the summit of a mountain loftier than any that I had ever seen. The clouds were far below thy feet, the sun not far above thy head. I beheld a vast throng of people, twenty times more numerous, it seemed to me, than the entire population of the earth. Of one who stood near me I asked the meaning of this marvel, and he answered:

"There are gathered here not only those who are living in this present age, but also all those who will live in the ages still to come. . . . They are waiting to see what will befall this man, because of whom both earth and sky are filled with conflict."

"What," I asked, "will be the end of it all?" And he replied:

"God only knows; but as far as human conjecture may foresee, the glory of this man will endure forever, provided only that he fear not the winds. One thing I dread: that the faith of some of those who are with him at the summit may waver, and that they may think that if he be destroyed they may gain his throne."

"Alas," I said, "can there be anyone of such fierce inhumanity as to plot the ruin of the very man under whose leadership he has attained so glorious a height?" At this point he was about to leave me, though I was eager to hear more. I grasped his hand, saying "Whither art thou hasting?" "The night is fleeing," he said, "and I must away." "At least tell me this," I said, "what toil is it, or what study, or what fortune, that has raised this man so high?" And he replied, "He is one of those few whom—as Virgil says—'Jove has justly loved, or ardent virtue has raised to the heavens.'" Thus saying—the dawn now being red—he disappeared.

The letter, written clearly as a loyal message of warning, ends with the words: "Farewell, thou unique champion of liberty."

Early in September a young courier who was bringing letters from Cola was set upon as he was approaching Avignon and was badly beaten; the silvered wand that marked him as an envoy was broken over his head; his letter box was taken from him and destroyed; the letters it had contained were torn to pieces; he was forbidden to enter Avignon; and he was told that any other messenger from Cola would be similarly received.

When Petrarch heard of this outrage he wrote to Cola an exclamatory letter that is extremely violent in its denunciation of Avignon. For upstart Avignon to commit such an outrage against sacred Rome was an act of both wickedness and folly. Cola's envoy would have been safer among hostile barbarians than among these men of Latin blood: the assault upon him violated both the law of nations and the natural law of humanity. There is an avenging God in heaven; and vengeance for this outrage will come when Rome is itself avenged. Cola has nothing to fear: he has begun gloriously, and Petrarch bids him to go forward boldly and constantly upon the course that lies still before him.

At about the same time the cardinals in consistory engaged in a discussion of the question whether it would be expedient for the Church if Rome and Italy should be unified. The conclusion reached was negative. The news of this discussion and its outcome again roused Petrarch's ire. He proceeded to argue the matter, taking the opposite stand, among his friends; and he wrote another letter to Cola, reporting the discussion and his own efforts, begging Cola and the Roman people to prove by their deeds the rightness of what he had been maintaining in words, and ending with the wish that Cola might live long and prosperously, and rule happily the state that he had so happily set free.

Early in September Cola had become doubtful of the loyalty of the nobles who had taken oath to support him—there was at least suspicion that they were conspiring against him. He decided therefore to get them into his power and try to discover their real attitude toward him. On the 14th, accordingly, he invited the leading nobles to a banquet. Those who came—several did not come—included Stefano Colonna the Elder, his grandson

Giovanni, and some of the Orsini. In the course of the banquet Stefano ventured to make an unfavorable comment on the expensiveness of Cola's costume: Cola took that comment as an evidence of hostility, and had all the nobles who were there arrested forthwith, and taken to the Capitoline prison.

On the next morning Cola, in the hope of eliciting information as to the suspected conspiracy, sent to the prisoners friars who told them that they were about to be condemned to death, and gave them communion. No information was disclosed, however, and Cola seems to have been satisfied that the report of the conspiracy was false. Meanwhile the Capitoline bell had been ringing, and a large crowd—which Cola chose to consider as representing the Roman People—had gathered. Cola, addressing the crowd, took as his text the words "Forgive us our debts as we forgive our debtors"; praised the nobles for their loyalty, and asked the People to pardon them. Pardon was accorded: and in sign of reconciliation Cola gave to each of his recent guests an honorific title, a gold ring, and other gifts. But the Colonna and the Orsini left the city, and put their castles in readiness for defense.

Pope Clement and his advisers had become more and more concerned about Cola's activities and pronouncements. In September the Pope had directed his legate, Cardinal Bertrand de Déaulx (who was then in Naples) to go to Rome and establish relations with the papal rectors of various places near Rome, and to direct those rectors to put their strongholds in readiness.

Early in October Cola, with a considerable body of troops, laid siege to the castle of the Orsini at Marino, on a spur of the Alban Mountains. About the middle of the month Cardinal de Déaulx came to Rome, with plenipotentiary authority from the Pope. Cola was to retain his rectorship only on these three conditions: he must swear not to engage in any activity contrary to the rights of the Church and to act only within the limits of the rectorship that had been conferred upon him; he must revoke the illegal laws that he had promulgated; and he must swear fealty to Pope Clement and to his successors. If Cola should not accept these conditions, the legate might even order his excommunication, and the Roman People might be ordered to cease to support him, under pain of interdict if they should disobey. The legate demanded also that the siege of the Orsini castle be raised.

Cola at first complied with the demand that the siege be raised, but he refused defiantly to accept Clement's three conditions, and he presently renewed the siege.

Just before Petrarch left Provence on the 20th of November he received from Laelius a letter that he answered, two days later, in a letter that ends thus:

> I have received and read the letter concerning the Tribune that you sent me: there is nothing that I can say in reply. I foresee my country's fate, and everywhere I look I find causes and grounds for grief. For if Rome is lacerated, what will become of Italy? And if Italy is despoiled, what will become of me? In this hour of public and private distress some may offer their wealth, some their bodily strength, some their power, others their counsel: I do not see what I can offer except my tears.

We do not know the contents of the letter from Laelius, or of one by or concerning Cola of which Laelius had enclosed a copy. Whatever their contents, the two letters shattered Petrarch's confidence in Cola and distressed him extremely. In his reply to Laelius he says that he has not slept for three nights. A week later, being then in Genoa, he had recovered his poise sufficiently to write to Cola a letter that is an outcry of bitter reproach and impassioned entreaty. In summary it is as follows:

> Cola's ascent has been glorious: "facilis descensus Averni." He is in danger of a terrible fall from the height he has attained. He must take a firm stand if he is not to be laughed at by his enemies and wept for by his friends. He is now relying not on the Roman People as a whole but on their worst elements. Petrarch had desired to join him in Rome; but he is unwilling to behold a Cola so different from the Cola he had known; and he bids a long farewell to Rome—if the tidings that have come to him are true he would rather go to India or to the land of the Garamantes. Yet perhaps, after all, the tidings are not true. To send untrue tidings would indeed be wrongful; but to betray one's country would be beyond any possible forgiveness. If Cola has no thought for his own reputation let him at least think of Petrarch's: Cola must know what a storm

hangs over Petrarch, what a crowd of reproachers will assail him if Cola falls.

The letter ends thus:

Remember what you are, what you have been, whence you came, whither you have come, how far you may go without offending liberty, what part you are playing, what hopes you have raised, what promises you have made; and you will see that you are not the master of the Republic, but its servant.

In November Cola began to suffer from what seems to have been a severe form of nervous exhaustion, one of his troubles being the recurrence of a fearful nightmare.

The Colonna and other nobles, encouraged by the arrival and the support of the papal legate, joined forces with a view to the overthrow of the Tribune. On the 20th of November—the day on which Petrarch left Provence—a plan of the nobles to gain entrance into Rome failed disastrously in a battle in which Stefano Colonna the Younger and his son Giovanni were killed.

Although Cola made this affair the occasion for a triumphal celebration he was clearly losing ground with many of those who had been supporting him, and his self-confidence was deserting him. Before the end of November he had renewed contact with the papal legate; and negotiations thus begun led early in December to Cola's complete submission to the papal demands: he renounced the titles he had assumed and cancelled the decree that he had proclaimed at the time of his knighting. On the 15th he abdicated, riding in procession from the Capitoline to the Castel Sant'Angelo (where he was assured of personal safety) with banners flying and trumpets sounding—but weeping, amid weeping crowds. He remained in Sant'Angelo through the following month; but soon thereafter his wanderings began.

Petrarch never forgave Cola for his failure. The letter from Genoa was the last letter, as far as we know, that he ever wrote to him—though he once wrote a letter to the Roman People on Cola's behalf, as will appear in a later chapter.

XIII. *The Year of the Black Death*

THE fearful plague known as the Black Death appeared
in Sicily before the end of 1347 and soon reached Naples.
In January it appeared in Genoa and in Venice, whence it spread
to Padua and Verona. It had arrived in Florence by March:
the introduction to the *Decameron* records its raging there. It
seems not to have affected Parma until June, but by that time
it was general in northern Italy, where the worst was over,
in most places, by the end of the year. Before the end of 1347
it had appeared in Marseilles, whence it spread through Provence.
The plague reached Avignon in January: it is said that 150,000
persons died there within the next seven months.

Petrarch had been commissioned by the Pope to carry to
Mastino della Scala, the lord of Verona, a message urging
him to oppose the Italian expedition of King Louis of Hungary.
His natural route to Verona from Genoa (where he had been
on November 29) led through Parma, and he presumably
followed that route. King Louis, moving with extraordinary
speed, reached Verona on the 5th of December, and won
Mastino's approval and support. If Petrarch reached Parma before
the news of the King's arrival in Verona did, he presumably
went on to Verona almost immediately; but if he heard that
news on or after reaching Parma, he presumably made no attempt
to deliver the Pope's message. In any case, however, he went
on soon from Parma to Verona, where, as he knew, he would
find his son, his son's teacher Rinaldo Cavalchini, Azzo da
Correggio, Moggio dei Moggi—and Cicero.

He was certainly in Verona on January 25. Toward the end
of the day, as he was sitting alone among his books, he suddenly
felt the floor tremble beneath his feet, and his books came tum-
bling down around him. He rushed out of the house and found
the townsfolk milling about in the streets, pale with fright, and
thinking that the end of the world had come. This earthquake,
the first that Petrarch had experienced, was extremely severe:
it shook all Italy, the Alps, and much of Central Europe.

While Petrarch was in Verona three Byzantine officials passed
through that city on their way to Avignon, where they were

to confer with the Pope on the possibility of the unification of the Greek and Roman churches. Petrarch met at least one of them, Nicholas Sygeros, told him of his interest in Greek, and indicated that he would be glad to add a manuscript of Homer to his library.

By early March Petrarch had left Verona for Parma. It is probable that he took his son Giovanni with him, and that in Parma he had him study with Giberto Baiardi, whom he regarded as an able teacher. After his return to Parma he undertook his duties as a canon of the cathedral—if indeed he had not done so before going to Verona.

Parma was now in the possession of Luchino Visconti, who had sent there, as governor, his counsellor Paganino da Bizzozzero, a very intelligent and able man, who either was already or soon became a friend of Petrarch.

Before the 13th Petrarch received from Luchino a letter in which Luchino made two requests: that Petrarch send him some scions from his fruit trees, and that he send him some verses. Petrarch complied with both requests. In his answer to Luchino he says that while his gardener is busy with herbs and trees he will busy himself with words and verses, sitting among his trees, and listening to the murmuring of the little stream that flows among them. He takes occasion, in his letter, to set forth as exemplary the honor in which certain ancient rulers held the Muses. In his brief poem, addressed *Ad arbores suas*, he bids them to grow tall and fruitful, to renew their foliage in the spring, and to furnish shade in the summer for the great lord for whom they are to flourish.

There had been expectation in Florence that Petrarch on his return from Provence would come there. This expectation not having been fulfilled, several of his Florentine admirers wrote to him early in 1348, protesting his stay in northern Italy. Among them were his older kinsman Giovanni dell'Incisa, and two younger men whom he did not know personally, Bruno Casini and Zanobi da Strada: Bruno and Zanobi sent *epistolae metricae* with their prose letters. Bruno's prose letter evidently indicated that his admiration for Petrarch had been derived from the older poet, Sennuccio del Bene (who was then living in Florence). All these Florentine letters reached Petrarch at Parma on March 24.

By the 6th of April Petrarch had returned to Verona, where, on the 7th, he wrote his reply to Giovanni dell'Incisa. His failure to come to Florence, he says, was due to the failure of hopes that he had cherished (apparently his hopes for Cola and for Rome): if those hopes had been fulfilled he would have come. There are references to the universal raging of the plague, and to a lawsuit, which perhaps concerned family property.

On the 8th, in the dead of night (a time at which Petrarch wrote many of his letters), he replied to Bruno Casini, sending him both a brief prose letter and a brief *epistola metrica*, a mournful poem that contains an expression of Petrarch's grief for the deaths, in recent years, of five members of the Colonna family. At about the same time, doubtless, he replied to Zanobi: the *epistola metrica* that he sent to him is a pleasant little poem on poetry.

By early May Petrarch had returned to Parma; and there he remained for the rest of the year, busy, as always, with his study and writing and his correspondence, and busy now, from time to time, with his garden, and with duties connected with his canonry.

It was probably at some time in the spring that Petrarch wrote to Cardinal Colonna a long *consolatoria* on the deaths of his brother Stefano and of Stefano's son Giovanni, who had been killed in the fighting at Rome on the preceding November 20.

This year was a year of death; and knowledge of two deaths that brought him great distress came to Petrarch in the course of the month of May.

His kinsman, Franceschino degli Albizzi, who had been Petrarch's house guest at Vaucluse during much of the two previous years, had left him at some time in 1347 to go to Paris, and finding, on his return to Provence, that Petrarch had gone to Italy, he had set out to follow him; but he died on the way. News of his death reached Petrarch early in May: and on the 11th he wrote to Giovanni dell'Incisa, who was also akin to Franceschino, the most heartbroken of all the many letters that he wrote after hearing of the death of a friend.

The 19th of May brought him a letter from Socrates telling him of the death of Laura. Perhaps immediately, perhaps somewhat later, he made this entry on the verso of the first guard leaf of his precious Virgil—facing the frontispiece that Simone Martini had painted for him:

> Laura, illustrious through her own virtues, and long famed through my verses, first appeared to my eyes in my youth, in the year of our Lord 1327, on the sixth day of April, in the church of St. Clare in Avignon, at matins; and in the same city, also on the sixth day of April, at the same first hour, but in the year 1348, the light of her life was withdrawn from the light of day, while I, as it chanced, was in Verona, unaware of my fate. The sad tidings reached me in Parma, in the same year, on the morning of the 19th day of May, in a letter from my Ludovicus. Her chaste and lovely form was laid to rest at vesper time, on the same day on which she died, in the burial place of the Brothers Minor. I am persuaded that her soul returned to the heaven from which it came, as Seneca says of Africanus. I have thought to write this, in bitter memory, yet with a certain bitter sweetness, here in this place that is often before my eyes, so that I may be admonished, by the sight of these words and by the consideration of the swift flight of time, that there is nothing in this life in which I should find pleasure, and that it is time, now that the strongest tie is broken, to flee from Babylon; and this, by the prevenient grace of God, should be easy for me, if I meditate deeply and manfully on the futile cares, the empty hopes, and the unforseen events of my past years.

The deep and lasting grief that the death of Laura brought to Petrarch necessarily sought and found poetic expression. It may well be that the sonnet beginning *Oimè il bel viso* ("Alas, her lovely face"), which stands in the *Canzoniere* as the first of the poems written after her death, was indeed the first that he then wrote. It is a poignantly simple one, through which the lamenting *Oimè* echoes. Before long he began work on a *canzone* on which he was to spend a vast amount of loving care. First, on a work sheet that is still preserved, he wrote eight lines, but being dissatisfied, he cancelled them, making above them the notation *Non videtur satis triste principium* ("This beginning does not seem sufficiently sad"). His new lines, of which the first is *Che debb'io far? che mi consigli, Amore?* ("What shall I do? What counsel dost thou give me, Love?") came closer to satisfying him; but before he entered the poem in the *Canzoniere* he had made more than a hundred changes in it, as his work sheet still attests. One of the later stanzas introduces a motif—the return of Laura in vision or in dream—of which he was to make use repeatedly:

> More beautiful and lovelier than ever she comes to me,
> as knowing where she is most welcome.

Still another sorrow came to Petrarch, probably toward the end of July, when he learned that Cardinal Colonna had died early in that month.

In 1345 Petrarch had addressed two letters to Cicero, the first critical of his life, the second praising his intellectual attainments and his eloquence. On or about the first of August, 1348, he addressed to Seneca a letter in which criticism of his life and praise of his writings are combined. When he wrote this letter he assumed that the tragedy *Octavia* was by Seneca, and blamed him in particular for having written of Nero with such bitter condemnation after having been Nero's tolerant tutor (at a later time Petrarch rightly questioned Seneca's authorship of this tragedy). He mistakenly accepts as genuine the letters supposed to have been exchanged by Seneca and St. Paul.

In 1346 Petrarch had petitioned Pope Clement not only for appointment to a Parmesan canonry, which he had received, but also for appointment to the archdeaconate of the cathedral, which he had not received, there being a prior commitment in that case. When in the spring or early summer of 1348 it became probable that the archdeaconate would soon fall vacant again, Petrarch again petitioned for it and was assured that he would receive it when it became vacant. In the course of the summer it did become vacant; and on August 23 Clement appointed him to the archdeaconate. This position carried with it the right to the occupancy of a certain large house; but Petrarch continued to live in the house that he had bought.

On an 8th of September that was probably that of 1348 (though possibly that of 1349) Petrarch wrote to Stefano Colonna the Elder, now a very old man, a long letter that was occasioned by the death of the Cardinal, Stefano's first-born son, but is a *consolatoria* not just for this one death, but for the whole series of deaths that had taken from Stefano his five brothers, his wife, seven of his sons, and his grandson Giovanni. It is also a tribute to Stefano's nobility, his great gifts of mind and body, and his achievements. It contains a detailed account of the conversation that Stefano had had with Petrarch when they were walking through Rome together in 1337—a conversation in the course of which Stefano had prophesied that he would be so unfortunate as to outlive all his sons.

When the messenger who had taken this letter to Stefano returned to Parma, he reported to Petrarch that Stefano—usually a man of iron—had been so deeply moved as he read it that he wept as if his weeping would never end, gaining relief thereby from long pent-up grief; and that when he had finished reading it he dried his eyes and said that he had wept his full and would never weep again.

On the 26th of November Petrarch, always an eager horticulturist, had some vine-stocks cut from his vines and planted. The planting was done, as he well knew, under poor conditions and not in accordance with local custom or with Virgilian precept: the season, the wind, and the phase of the moon were all unfavorable. Soon afterward he wrote a detailed note about this planting on a blank page near the end of a manuscript containing the *De agricultura* of Palladius. This note, which records his doubt as to the outcome of the planting, ends with the words "Sed placet experiri" ("But I like to experiment"). This was the first of a considerable series of such notes made in this same manuscript at various times up to 1369. To each such note Petrarch eventually added a brief indication as to the success or failure of the planting.

On the 8th of December, still experimenting, he planted some hyssop and rosemary and noted the planting in his Palladius.

Late in the year, in the midst of the raging of the Black Death, Petrarch wrote in Latin a somber, even despairing, poem expressive of the plight of his own soul. He treated it as if it were a letter addressed to himself, and eventually included it, under the title *Ad se ipsum*, in the collection of his *epistolae metricae*. It begins thus:

> Alas, what lies before me? Whither now
> Am I to be whirled away by the force of fate?
> Time rushes onward for the perishing world,

And round about I see the hosts of the dying,
The young and the old; nor is there anywhere
In all the world a refuge, or a harbor
Where there is hope of safety. Funerals,
Where'er I turn my frightened eyes, appall;
The temples groan with coffins, and the proud
And humble lie alike in lack of honor.
The end of life presses upon my mind,
And I recall the dear ones I have lost,
Their cherished words, their faces, vanished now.
The consecrated ground is all too small
To hold the instant multitude of graves

Throughout the poem Petrarch wrestles with the problem whether he should not now abandon all earthly interests; but even under the present terrifying circumstances he cannot bring himself to do so.

Three Eclogues suggested by the Black Death in general or by the death of Laura in particular were written (certainly the Ninth and probably the Tenth and Eleventh) before the end of the year. In the Ninth a shepherd laments the ravages of a pestilence among both shepherds and their sheep. In the Tenth the plague is figured as a windstorm that uproots many trees, among them a laurel that represents both literary glory and Laura: most of the poem consists of references to more than a hundred famed writers of classic antiquity. The Eleventh is devoted entirely to the death of Galathea (Laura), "than whom Nature never fashioned aught more beautiful." To Niobe, who bitterly laments her death, the sad but earth-bound Fusca counsels resignation: what is past is past, and death puts an end to cares and bonds. The heaven-dwelling Fulgida then joins them and bids them cease their sorrow, assuring them that Galathea has attained immortality.

In earlier years Petrarch had written two *Triumphs*—the *Triumphus Cupidinis* and the *Triumphus Castitatis*. The Black Death and the death of Laura suggested to him the writing of a third *Triumph*, that of Death. Two *capitoli* written for it are preserved: the first may well have been written before the end of 1348.

This first *capitolo* is like the earlier *Triumphs* in that it is ceremonial, but is unlike them in that it is not processional and mentions no individual person other than Laura. The scene is a great valley, wherein are gathered to witness her death a vast throng of the dead from many ages and lands, and a group of living ladies, who speak of her with sorrow and with praise. Her passing is serene:

> Not like a flame that by some force is quenched,
> But one that of itself consumes itself,
> Her soul, contented, went its way in peace.
> Her dearness lasted to the end of life,
> Like to a light that is both sweet and clear
> But burns more faintly till its oil has failed.
> Not pale, but whiter than the snow that falls
> On a fair hillside where there is no wind,
> She seemed to rest, as one who had been weary.
> And when her soul was parted from her frame,
> What is called death by those who are but fools
> Was a sweet closing of her lovely eyes;
> And even death seemed fair in her fair face.

XIV. *Parma, Padua, and Mantua: 1349 - 1350*

THE Black Death, though now on the wane in most regions, continued to take a heavy toll in Parma in the first six months of 1349.

It may well have been quite early in 1349 that a rift developed between Petrarch and the Bishop of Parma, Ugolino dei Rossi, that was to become more and more serious as time went on. What its cause was we do not know.

Probably in 1349, though possibly before the end of 1348, Petrarch added to his letters to ancient Roman writers one addressed to Varro.

In February Petrarch had an apple tree and two peach trees transplanted, and he himself planted more rosemary; and in the first week in March he planted, or had his servants plant, vines that were to form an arbor running from tree to tree in one of his gardens.

Before the end of February, doubtless, he heard of the death of Luchino Visconti, which left his brother, the Archbishop Giovanni, as the sole lord of Milan.

For some years Jacopo da Carrara, the lord of Padua, had been trying to get Petrarch to come to Padua, and early in March he finally went there. He was received most cordially and most honorably; and Jacopo, in order to ensure that his visits should be repeated, arranged for him to receive a canonry in the cathedral. Petrarch took possession of this canonry on the 18th of April, in a largely attended ceremony in which he was formally installed by Cardinal Gui de Boulogne, who had stopped in Padua on his way to Hungary as a papal legate. The Bishop of Padua, Ildebrandino Conti, who was to accompany the legate in his mission, took part in the ceremony, speaking of Petrarch in terms of high praise. The Bishop was much older than Petrarch, but they were to become fast friends.

Either while Cardinal Gui de Boulogne was in Padua at this time or while he was there early in the following year Petrarch and the Benedictine Abbot Pierre d'Auvergne, a member of the Cardinal's suite, became friends.

The holding of his Paduan canonry gave Petrarch the right to occupy a house in the cathedral close. This canonry and this house were to mean much to him, but for the present he maintained his residence in Parma, though spending much time in Padua.

Before returning to Parma after his installation as canon Petrarch visited Venice and Treviso, and spent at least a day or two in Verona. It was probably while he was in Venice at this time that he bought, for a hundred pounds, a great breviary that became one of his most cherished books.

When he reached Parma, early in May, he was distressed to find that during his absence he had missed a visit from two friends who had recently come from Avignon to Italy: the Florentine Mainardo Accursio (whom he called Simplicianus) and Luca Cristiani (whom he called Olimpius). Both had been fellow students of his at the University of Bologna, and both had served Cardinal Colonna in Avignon. Luca had been made Provost of Sant'Antonino in Piacenza. Just when they had come to Parma and when they had gone we do not know. They had left a letter in which, apparently, they had said that they would return, and had suggested that they, Petrarch, and Socrates (who was still in Avignon) should live together from this time on, perhaps in Parma.

On the 19th of May Petrarch wrote to Luca a letter that was

intended also to be seen by Mainardo and Socrates. He agrees heartily, especially in view of the deaths of so many of their other friends, with the suggestion that the four of them should live together, discusses at length the question of the place in which they might best make their common home, and concludes in favor of Parma. His own house there would be too small; but the Archdeacon's house, which he has the right to occupy, would provide plenty of room for all four. They would be within easy reach of Bologna, where they had been together in the days of their youth; Luca himself might serve as their host if they should wish to go to Piacenza. They might even visit Milan and Genoa. If they should tire of Parma, they could find an equally tranquil and suitable home in Padua, whence they could readily visit Venice and Treviso. The essential thing, however, is that they should be together; and if Mainardo and Luca should think some other place better than Parma he will accept their judgment and join them there. The letter contains a long reminiscent account of Petrarch's life in Vaucluse, and implies, incidentally, that he is still revising the *Africa*.

In the midst of his anxiety about Mainardo and Luca, the plague dealt him a shocking blow. On the evening of the 22d of May Paganino da Bizzozzero, who had become one of his closest friends, came to see him, and they had a long talk together. On the evening of the 23rd a messenger brought word to Petrarch that in the morning Paganino had died of the plague. Within the next three days all of the several members of Paganino's family died also. Soon afterward Petrarch wrote this note in his Virgil, on the page preceding that on which he had written his note about Laura:

> After sunset on Saturday the 23rd of May, in the year
> of our Lord 1349, my ears were wounded by the distressing
> news of the death of my special and most excellent friend,
> Paganino of Milan.

This was the first of a series of obituary notes that were to be entered on this page at various times up to 1372. The second note was to be entered only a few days after the first one.

Petrarch had thought that his letter to Luca Cristiani would serve to recall Mainardo and Luca speedily to Parma. When, after several days had passed, they had neither reappeared nor sent any word to him, he sent one of his servants to Florence with a letter for Mainardo. A week later this servant returned, at night, drenched with rain, weeping, and bringing tragic news. Mainardo and Luca, when crossing the Apennines, had fallen into the hands of a band of robbers; Mainardo had been killed; and Luca, fighting valiantly, though one against ten, had been wounded, but had escaped: what had happened to him Petrarch's servant did not know. Peasants brought to the scene by the noise of the fighting would have seized the robbers, but they had been rescued by certain unworthy nobles who had given them shelter in their castle.

Unspeakably distressed and extremely anxious to find out what had become of Luca, Petrarch sent messengers to make inquiries in Piacenza, Florence, and Rome. To Florence he sent also, on the 2nd of June, an impassioned letter addressed to the rulers and people of the city, lamenting bitterly the death of Mainardo, holding the Florentines responsible for their shameful failure to guard their own roads, urging them to maintain justice, to put an end to the sheltering of wicked bands, to see to it that all roads leading to Florence should be kept safe—especially in view of the throngs that would traverse them in the coming Year of Jubilee—and asking that diligent inquiries be made as to the fate of Luca.

In June, since Petrarch wanted to turn part of his inner garden into a hayfield, he had some salvia plants transferred to another part of the garden, arranging for irrigation for them in their new location, and put in some new salvia plants also. At the same time he moved a horehound plant, and planted something that he calls "like hyssop." Later in the month he had seed sown in his new field and planted some rue given to him by Don Luca.

Early in September a series of terrific earthquakes shook Italy and the Alps and Germany. The damage to churches and other buildings in Rome was very great. Petrarch, in a later letter, refers to these earthquakes, which he must have felt.

On the 25th of September Petrarch was in Carpi (about 25 miles east of Parma). There, on that day, he wrote to his brother Gherardo a very affectionate letter, commending him for his choice of the monastic life, and contrasting that life with his own restless and troubled secularity. In reminiscent portions of this letter Petrarch tells of the sacrifices to fashion that Gherardo and he had made in the days of their youth. The letter also contains a long, though incidental, diatribe against the depravity of servants in general, a subject to which Petrarch often returns (there were cases, however, in which he had good things to say of certain servants). He did not send the letter at once. The circumstances of his going to Carpi remain unknown: it is probable that he went there as the guest of the ruling Pio family.

At some time within the years 1349–1351, and more probably in the autumn of 1349 than at any earlier or later time, he visited Ferrara. In this case also the circumstances of his visit remain unknown: it is probable that he went there as the guest of the ruling Este family. While in Ferrara he was attracted by an unknown Ferrarese woman: love tempted him again, he says, but the thought of Laura sufficed to prevent him from yielding to this temptation. Either while he was still in Ferrara or soon afterward he wrote a few Italian lyrics that are related to this episode.

While Bishop Ildebrandino Conti was still in Hungary with the papal legate, Petrarch sent him an *epistola metrica* in which, after referring to the Bishop's acquaintance with all Europe and to his own travels, he asserts the superiority of Italy to other lands. France, he says, is lacking in olives, fruit, cultivated shrubs, metals, springs, and flocks; and he goes on to tell of lacks suffered in snowy Germany and in other northern regions: all that Italy lacks is peace.

In November, apparently, Petrarch went to Padua, where he seems to have stayed—living presumably in the house to which his canonry entitled him—until about the first of March. It seems probable that he had his son with him during at least part of this stay, and that he arranged for some continuation of Giovanni's schooling.

Before the end of November, having heard of the death of the poet Sennuccio del Bene, he wrote a sonnet addressed to him in which he sends a faithful message to Laura and bids Sennuccio give his remembrances to four other poets, Guittone d'Arezzo, Cino da Pistoia, Dante, and Franceschino degli Albizzi. In November, also, he wrote a sonnet on the dawn, which in its beauty always brought to him the realization that Laura was now in Heaven. On the 28th of November he made a fresh copy of the *canzone Che debb'io far*, on the death of Laura; and later on the same day he made some revisions, and wrote above it, on his work sheet, a note that means "I am ready now to finish work on this poem, because of the sonnets on the death of Sennuccio and on the Dawn that I have just written—and they have stirred me deeply"—"et erexerunt animum."

On the second of December he wrote to Gherardo a letter that was designed to serve as a covering letter to be sent with his First Eclogue, in which he had contrasted his own secular life with his brother's monastic life. In this important letter he achieves a certain harmony between their interests: theology is a poem on the nature of God, and poetry originated as a form of public prayer.

On the 26th of December he wrote in memory of Laura a gentle *ballata* beginning *Amor che 'n cielo e 'n gentil core alberghi* ("Love that dwellest in heaven and in the gentle heart"); on the 30th he rewrote it: and on the first of January he made a fair copy of it as he had written it. This little poem, however, did not receive admission into the *Canzoniere*.

Before the end of 1348, in all probability, Petrarch had written a *Triumphus mortis* consisting of a single *capitolo*. That *capitolo*, ceremonial in nature, appeared to constitute a complete *Triumph* in itself; but at a somewhat later time, probably in 1349, he was moved to write a second *capitolo*, which is very different from any other *capitolo* in the series of the *Triumphs*—so different, indeed, as to be virtually an independent poem. It is devoted entirely to an account of an imagined appearance of Laura to him in a vision on the night following her death, and consists largely of a report of their conversation, much of which is given in direct discourse. The unique feature of this conversation is that in answer to Petrarch's question as to whether Laura ever, within the bounds of honor, returned his affection, she replies that she did indeed care for him, but that for his sake she tempered her dealings with him, checking him when he was too ardent, comforting him when he was too deeply sad. "Can this indeed be so?" he asks; she chides him for doubting her; and in the course of her reply she asks, in turn:

> But was not every veil between us rent
> When in thy presence I received thy verse,
> And I in answer sang to you the song
> *Dir più non osa il nostro amor?*

(The Italian words mean "Our love dares not say more.")

It may well have been fairly soon after writing this *capitolo* that there came to Petrarch the idea of a fourth *Triumph*. Death triumphs over life; but there is that which triumphs over Death— namely, Fame. So he began work on a *Triumph of Fame*, writing a *capitolo* that begins with the words *Nel cor* ("In my heart"), the first lines of which refer to his vision of Laura. But the new *capitolo* presently becomes processional, with a personified Fame leading the procession. In her train are more than a hundred identified figures of Roman or Greek history or legend, and a few others: Hannibal, Masinissa, David, Judas Maccabaeus, and Joshua, with King Arthur and Charlemagne bringing up the rear. Before many years had passed, however, Petrarch was to discard this *capitolo*, replacing it by two new *capitoli*.

Petrarch's discovery in 1345 of three of Cicero's letter collections had given him the idea of making a collection of his own letters; but he had not as yet made any substantial progress in this enter- prise. Although he had kept copies of many of his letters, the making of such a collection as he had in mind would involve much more than recopying them and letting them stand in a merely casual order: it would involve decisions as to the inclusion or exclusion of particular letters, revision of the letters that were to be included, and decisions as to arrangement and various other matters.

By January, 1350, he was ready to begin work on the actual making of the collection; and on the 13th, in Padua, he wrote a long letter to his Socrates, dedicating the collection to him. This letter was designed to serve as an introduction to the entire (though as yet non-existent) collection, and in point of fact it serves its intended purpose excellently well. It tells, among other things, of his writing of letters to Cicero and Seneca, which are to find place at the end of the collection; of his intention to make not only a collection of his prose letters, but also a collection of his *epistolae metricae*, which he is going to dedicate to Barbato da Sulmona; and of his burning of a great many of his letters and poems. It contains also a brief incidental account of his earliest years, and a sentence in which he says that he is working on a sort of self-portrait, which he may send to Socrates at a later time.

He thought of his collection not as a series of documents but as a work of art in itself, every element of which was to be made as perfect as he could make it: this idea governed his decisions as to inclusion, revision, and arrangement, and all other relevant decisions. The general principle of arrangement that he adopted was roughly chronological; but he made no attempt at chronological exactness, and even his general principle was subject to infraction for one or another of several possible reasons. He wanted, naturally, to include the letters he had written to Cicero and to Seneca, and any other letters to classical authors that he might write at later times. These were, of course, fictional letters; and he felt free to write, for insertion in the collection, other fictional letters addressed to contemporaries of his own, or having no addressees. At times, also, he was to break a long letter into the semblance of two or more separate letters, and in a few instances, to combine two originally separate letters into the semblance of a single letter.

After Cardinal Gui de Boulogne had returned from his mission he stayed on in Padua for a time in order to preside over the ceremonial translation of the body of St. Anthony of Padua from its first burial place to a newly finished sepulchral chapel in the great church of Sant'Antonio (which had itself been built not long before). The translation took place on the 13th of February, and was witnessed by an immense throng of the devout, Petrarch among them.

The Cardinal showed to Petrarch a letter in French that he had received from one of Petrarch's French friends, Philippe de Vitry, in which Philippe commiserated the Cardinal on his absence from France—an absence which he termed an exile. This letter roused Petrarch's indignation, and he proceeded to write to Philippe, reproving him severely for his excessive attachment to France and his scorn for all the rest of the world. The Cardinal's mission was a holy and a glorious one, entrusted to him by the Pope. "You think it a pitiable exile to be in Italy: were it not that to the strong man all the world is fatherland, to be anywhere but in Italy would rather seem to be an exile." Much of the letter is devoted to the praise of travel in general, the wide travels of various ancients—philosophers and others— being cited. The Cardinal's journey has already given him the opportunity to visit many noteworthy places; and after he leaves Padua he is going on to Rome—this being a Year of Jubilee—where he will behold many sacred treasures and many scenes rich in sacred memories. On his way to Rome and on his return he will visit also many other famous Italian cities; and when he returns to France he will himself bear witness to his admiration of Italy.

When the Cardinal left Padua he started westward, accompanied both by his own suite and by many Italian gentlemen. Petrarch was a member of the party; and in a letter written many years later he gives this account of an incident that was to him a very memorable one:

> When we had come to noble Lake Garda he [the Cardinal] stopped on a grassy hill and looked all around. To his right he could see the Alps, covered with snow although it was midsummer, and the deep and undulating waters of the lake; before him and behind him were low hills; and to his left was a fertile and smiling plain. Finally, being of an agile mind and ready of speech and jovial, he called me, and said to me in a loud voice, so that everyone heard him, "It is clear, I confess, that your fatherland is much more beautiful and productive than ours"; and seeing that I was well pleased with this outspoken confession, and was confirming it by nodding my head and clapping my hands and by what I said, he added "But we have a more tranquil state and a more stable government"; and having said that he started on, as if he were a victor. Unwilling to admit defeat, I—or rather not I but truth—called to him and said, "There is nothing to prevent our having a state and a government like yours, if only we would: but Nature prevents you from having a land like ours." He smiled and held his peace, realizing that what I had said was true, but not wanting either to agree with it or to oppose it; and so he rode on.

On the 22nd of February Petrarch, being still in Padua and having in mind the fact that Padua was the birthplace of Livy, addressed to him the fifth letter in his series of letters to ancient writers. His letter opens with the wish that either he might himself have lived when Livy did, in which case he would have been one of the many pilgrims who sought Livy out, or that Livy might be living in Petrarch's own age, which would have benefited greatly by his presence. The letter then goes into some detail as to the portions of Livy's work that had been lost, and continues with an expression of gratitude to Livy for introducing him (Petrarch) to some twenty-five individually named men who, thanks to Livy, have become welcome companions of his thought. Greetings are sent to Pliny (the Elder) and to other less famous Romans; and the letter was originally subscribed thus:

> In the land of the living, in that part of Italy in which I am now dwelling and thou wast born and buried, in the portico of [the monastery of] the Virgin Justina and before the very stone of thy tomb, in the year MCCCL since the birth of Him whom thou mightest have beheld if thou hadst lived a little longer.

There had recently been found in the monastery a tombstone which was long thought (mistakenly) to be that of Livy. When Petrarch revised this letter for inclusion in the collection of the *Familiares*, he changed the MCCCL to MCCCLI, for the sake of a smoother chronological sequence in the series of letters.

Shortly before he left Padua, apparently, Petrarch made arrangements for his son to be taken to Parma, to be again a pupil of Giberto Baiardi.

On the 12th of March, being then in Verona, Petrarch wrote again to Socrates, lamenting the loss of many friends, and urging Socrates to come and live with him, either in Parma or in Padua, or elsewhere if Socrates should so prefer. In the course of this letter he indicates that he had still had no definite word as to whether Luca Cristiani was or was not still alive.

In May Petrarch spent some time in Mantua, doubtless as the guest of the ruling Gonzaga family. He had had some correspondence with Guido Gonzaga, and in Avignon he had met the chancellor of the Gonzaga, Giovanni Aghinolfi, whom he counted as a friend. Mantua held a special appeal for Petrarch: Virgil had been born in Mantuan territory, in the village of Andes (now Pietole), which is near the city. What more natural, then, than that while there he should write a letter to Virgil? He did so on the 19th. This letter, since it was addressed to a poet, was to be an *epistola metrica*. In Petrarch's first intention it was to find a place not in the series of letters that he was writing in prose to certain other ancients, but at the end of the collection of his *epistolae metricae* that he was planning as a companion to the collection of his prose letters. Eventually, however, he changed his mind, and placed this letter, though in verse, with his prose letters to ancient writers, in his major collection.

It opens with many questions: "Where dwellest thou? Is it in some circle of Avernus? Dost thou charm the Elysian groves with thy sweet song? Or art thou now among those redeemed by Him who conquered Tartarus? Who now companion thee, and what manner of life do ye lead? How close to the truth were thy dreams?" Three cities, Naples, Mantua, and Rome, had been dear to Virgil: Petrarch sends him sad news from Naples and good news from Mantua—and refrains from telling him what has been happening in Rome. As he writes of Mantua he has this to say:

> Here have I written what thou readest now,
> In the dear peace of this thy countryside,
> Wondering whither thou wast wont to roam,
> What was thy path in darkling forest depths,
> Through meadows fair, or by the banks of the stream
> Or the bays of the curving lake; under what trees
> Or in what glades remote thou didst find shade;
> Upon what gentle hillside thou wast wont
> To sit and gaze, or where in weariness
> On the soft turf or by some lovely spring
> Thou didst recline. And sights and scenes like these
> Bring thee in very presence to mine eyes.

Toward the end of the letter Petrarch tells Virgil of the fame of his three great works—the *Bucolics*, the *Georgics*, and the *Aeneid*. At the very end he sends his greetings to Homer and to Hesiod.

By the 24th of May Petrarch was back in Parma. On that day he had grass seed sown in the field near his house: the notation that he made thereafter in his Palladius indicates that he had recently enlarged that field by the purchase of adjacent property.

From time to time, when in Parma, Petrarch did some work on his Italian poems—drafting, revising, or copying. A notation made on one of his work sheets, above the first line of a *canzone*, reads in translation: "1350, Wednesday the 9th of June. After vespers I wanted to begin this, but I was called off to supper. The next morning I started work."

Late in June Petrarch was again in Mantua. There, on the 28th, he wrote to Socrates, desiring him to make the acquaintance, in Avignon, of Pierre d'Auvergne: Pierre and Socrates, he believes, will become good friends.

Late in the afternoon of that same day Petrarch started with companions to return to Parma, planning to spend the night at Luzzara, a small town in Mantuan territory near the Po. The sirocco had been blowing, the snow on the mountains had been melting, and the Po was in flood: the horses had hard going through the mud. The Gonzaga had sent word in advance that preparations should be made to receive Petrarch and his party, and a delicious meal was served to them; but the house was full of flies and mosquitoes, and an army of frogs came out of holes and swarmed over the floor of the dining room. Petrarch escaped to his bedroom, but although he was tired and sleepy and not much of the night was left, he wrote to Laelius a letter of introduction for an unknown bearer and took occasion to tell Laelius of the circumstances under which the letter had been written.

On the 6th of July he was back in Mantua, where, on that day, he bought his copy (now in the Bibliothèque Nationale) of the *Natural History* of Pliny the Elder, on the last leaf of which he made the entry "Emptus Mantue. 1350. Iul. 6°." At the point in Book XVIII at which Pliny mentions the Sorgue, Petrarch made, in the lower margin of the page, a simple pen-and-ink drawing intended to suggest Vaucluse. It shows a rocky height from the base of which a river flows forth. Atop the height is a chapel (which no longer exists). Plant life is suggested by a few trees and bushes on the height and by a group of reeds at the edge of the river; and in the lower left corner of the drawing a relatively large figure of a heron is depicted with a fish in its beak. To the right of that figure is the inscription, in Petrarch's hand, "Transalpina Solitudo mea iocundissima." The chances are that this drawing was made fairly soon after the manuscript came into Petrarch's possession.

In January Petrarch, ready to begin work on a collection of his prose letters, had written a letter to Socrates, dedicating the collection to him. In that letter he had said that he was planning to make also a collection of his *epistolae metricae*, and to dedicate that collection to Barbato da Sulmona. By late spring, apparently, he was ready to begin the making of this other collection; and it was probably in the late spring or early summer, during one of his stays in Mantua, that he wrote a dedicatory *epistola metrica* to Barbato. He did not complete this poem, however, until after he had returned to Provence, and not until several years later, and after he had revised it to his own satisfaction, did he send it to Barbato.

At some time in the summer Petrarch received from a Florentine with whom he was not acquainted, Giovanni Boccaccio, an *epistola metrica* in which, declaring himself an avid collector of the writings of Petrarch, Boccaccio bemoaned the fact that he had never been able to get copies of some of Petrarch's writings that had been obtained by men who had no real literary interests. Petrarch wrote an appropriate *epistola metrica* in reply, but he promptly mislaid it. This incident was, however, the beginning of the warm friendship of the two great Italian writers of the mid-century—a friendship in which Boccaccio, who was about ten years younger than Petrarch, was definitely a disciple as well as a friend.

Late in the summer, apparently, Petrarch, having determined to make his Year of Jubilee pilgrimage to Rome in the autumn, wrote to Guglielmo da Pastrengo an *epistola metrica* inviting him urgently to accompany him. Guglielmo, however, did not accept the invitation.

XV. *Roman Pilgrimage*

PAPAL pronouncements regarding the Year of Jubilee had promised plenary indulgence to all who in that year should make pilgrimage to the Holy City and visit there, with contrite hearts, the churches of St. Peter, St. Paul, and St. John. Hordes of pilgrims, mindful of the recent horrors of the Black Death, most of them presumably regarding those horrors as a manifestation of divine wrath and hoping to escape a still more fearful and more enduring wrath, made their way to Rome in the course of the year. It was a Year of Jubilee, but not of jubilation. Journeying was fraught with peril; conditions in Rome itself were extremely bad; and the pitiably impoverished inhabitants were making the most of their opportunities to overcharge the pilgrims for food and lodging.

Petrarch, who had supported the Roman plea for the designation of 1350 as a Year of Jubilee, set out for Rome about the first of October. He took his large breviary with him, despite its size. He planned to pass through Florence, which he had never visited, on his way; and Boccaccio, having some knowledge of his plans, went out to meet him. They met on a cold afternoon just as it was getting dark; Boccaccio invited Petrarch to stay with him while in Florence, and Petrarch accepted the invitation.

Boccaccio was not Petrarch's only Florentine admirer. Bruno Casini, who had sent an *epistola metrica* to Petrarch in 1348, had died of the plague; but the schoolteacher Zanobi da Strada (who had sent an *epistola metrica* with Bruno's), Francesco Nelli, the prior of Santi Apostoli, and Lapo da Castiglionchio, a serious young man who had not yet made up his mind whether to follow the law or to devote himself to letters, formed, with Boccaccio, a quartet of enthusiasts. In Lapo's library, which he visited with Nelli, Petrarch found two treasures previously unknown to him, an incomplete copy of the *Institutes* of Quintilian, and certain Ciceronian orations. Lapo at once gave him his copy of the *Institutes*—keeping it for him, however, until he should return from Rome. In a letter written to Petrarch long afterward, Nelli gives this account of an occasion on which Petrarch read some of his own poems to the group:

> I recall (yet I can hardly "recall" what I have never forgotten) how you read some of your poems to us in that noble and reverend voice of yours, your clear enunciation revealing the emotions of your spirit; and I can still see your gentle gestures, to the right or to the left, now extended somewhat freely, now drawn in somewhat, always within modest limits: they seemed to do nothing more than suggest the grace and the emphasis that you sought.

On or about the 12th of October Petrarch started on from Florence. As a parting gift, Boccaccio gave him a finger-ring. Not wanting to undertake the journey alone, Petrarch joined or made up a party of pilgrims, one of whom was an elderly abbot. Just after they had passed through Bolsena and while the abbot was riding on Petrarch's left, the abbot's horse got out of control and kicked Petrarch's left leg just below the knee so violently that it sounded and seemed as if the bone had been broken. There being no good stopping place nearby, Petrarch, though in great pain, pressed on to Viterbo and then to Rome, which he reached three days later, on or about the 20th. Doctors were called; the wound was found to be infected; and Petrarch, much to his disgust, was kept in bed for two weeks. On the night of the 3rd of November, while he was still in bed, he wrote to Boccaccio, telling him of his mishap and of his impatience to be going about Rome again. Now, he says, he has reason to hope that before long, recovered both in body and in spirit, he will be able soon to be with Boccaccio again. He signed the letter as "Your pilgrim, whom you honored with your ring." We do not know when or to what extent Petrarch was able to go about Rome.

Before he left Rome, in all probability, he received a sympathizing letter from Nelli, written after Petrarch's letter of the 3rd of December had reached Boccaccio and had been read by or to Nelli, and doubtless by or to Zanobi and Lapo as well. This was the first of about fifty letters that Petrarch received from Nelli—many more than he received from any other correspondent.

We do not know when he left Rome. On his northward journey he stopped briefly in Arezzo, which he had not seen since his infancy. He was met outside the city by some of its leading citizens, who took him to the Vico dell'Orto and showed him the house in which he had been born. They told him that an owner of the house had wanted to restore and enlarge it, but had been forbidden to do so since it was desired that the house should remain exactly as it was at the time of Petrarch's birth.

He stopped briefly in Florence, While there he had a conference with some of the city officials, probably with regard to the possibility of his recovering the property that had been confiscated from his father. What the outcome of this conference was, we do not know; but the attitude shown by the officials was so friendly as to be very gratifying to Petrarch.

When he left for Parma he took with him the copy of the *Institutes* of Quintilian that Lapo had given him. He reached Parma shortly before the end of December.

———————— *℮* ————————

XVI. *Parma and Padua*
January - June 1351

IN PARMA, on Christmas Eve, Petrarch received the
shocking news that his kindly and generous Paduan patron,
Jacopo da Carrara, had been assassinated. The assassin had at
once been killed, and the lordship of Padua had passed to a
brother and a son of Jacopo. The son, Francesco, who soon became the sole lord of Padua, continued his father's affectionate
patronage, but for a time Petrarch felt the loss of Jacopo very
keenly. He made an appropriate note in his Virgil, just below
the note he had written in the preceding spring after he had
heard of the death of Mainardo Accursio.

On the 6th of January Petrarch, having come across the *epistola
metrica* he had written for Boccaccio in the preceding summer,
sent it on to him with a covering letter in the course of which
he tells, with deep feeling, of the death of Jacopo da Carrara.

Lapo da Castiglionchio had promised to lend Petrarch his
volume containing Ciceronian orations that Petrarch had not
known. Anticipating the receipt of this volume, Petrarch, also
on the 6th of January, sent to Lapo, as a gift, a copy of Cicero's
Pro Archia, with a covering letter.

At some time after his return to Parma—perhaps long afterward
—Petrarch wrote a letter to Quintilian. He rejoices in the acquaintance with Quintilian that his copy of the *Institutes* has
brought him, but regrets the incompleteness of that copy and
hopes that a complete copy may yet be found. He compares
Quintilian and Cicero, pointing out the special services of each
of the two men, and refers to the mutual dispraise of Quintilian
and Seneca. The letter is fictionally dated as written in Florence
at the time of Petrarch's return from Rome.

PADUA

Before the end of January, in all probability, Petrarch went
on to Padua; and there, presently, he was asked to write an
epitaph for Jacopo da Carrara, and promised to do so. He
stayed in Padua—living, presumably, in his house in the cathedral

close—until the 3rd of May. During this stay in Padua he had with him some of the sheets on which he was drafting, revising, or copying Italian lyrics, and from time to time he continued this task.

For nearly two decades Petrarch's thought on the state of the world had been dominated by two companion convictions: that Rome and only Rome was the proper seat of the papacy, and that Rome and only Rome was the proper seat of the empire. He had voiced the first of these convictions in *epistolae metricae* addressed to Popes Benedict XII and Clement VI: the second conviction he had voiced only incidentally, though it was quite as strong as the first. Only a Roman emperor resident in Rome, he had long believed, could restore Rome to its ancient glory and its beneficent imperial power, without which neither Rome nor the empire—nor indeed the world—could know peace and prosperity. In 1347 this second conviction had been modified by the prospect that the restoration so passionately desired might be achieved by Cola di Rienzo. That prospect having vanished dismally, Petrarch's conviction as to the necessity that the emperor should return to Rome had reasserted itself, with an increased sense of urgency.

By February, 1351, that sense of urgency, stimulated, presumably, by his recent visit to Rome, had become so strong that he could no longer hold his peace; and on the 24th of that month he addressed to the still uncrowned Charles IV, who seemed to be content in Bohemia, a long and very carefully written letter in which he does his utmost to persuade Charles to come to Italy without further delay.

Assuming that Charles intends to come eventually, Petrarch remonstrates with him for his failure to come promptly:

> If you have any care for your own fame, if you know the actual state of affairs, you will realize that delay is as injurious to you as it is to us. Life is uncertain and fleeting: you are still young, but life is unstable and rushes on . . . and before you know it old age will be upon you.

The task of restoration has now become so difficult that it cannot be accomplished quickly: it will take a long time, and time is therefore pressing. Much of Charles's youth had been spent, and well spent, in Italy: he should therefore be as loyal to Italy as he is to Bohemia. In Bohemia he is but a king; only in Italy can he be truly an emperor. Many tasks, indeed, confront him; but no other task can vie in importance with this task of restoration.

The rest of the letter takes the form of an imagined appeal addressed to Charles, in direct discourse, by Rome herself, pictured—as in the *epistolae metricae* to Popes Benedict and Clement—in the guise of a venerable but sadly disheveled matron. She bids Charles contrast her ancient glories, which are enthusiastically rehearsed, with her present destitution; cites the examples of Alexander and Scipio Africanus; assures Charles of divine aid; and finally introduces Charles's grandfather, Henry VII, with whose eloquent appeal to his grandson the letter comes to its end.

For nearly a hundred years the clashing interests of the two great Italian maritime cities, Venice and Genoa, both of them seeking to maintain and to expand their commerce in the Near East, had frequently led them into naval conflict. Hostilities had been renewed on a small scale in 1350; and in the early months of 1351 Venice was preparing to undertake warfare on a large scale. To Petrarch it seemed shameful and terrible that two Italian states should war against each other; and he therefore, probably in March, wrote to Andrea Dandolo, Doge of Venice, a man of great ability and of cultural as well as political interests, a long and carefully reasoned letter, urging him to desist from his preparations and to make peace with Genoa. He is writing this letter, he says, because his love of Italy compels him to do so; and he is writing to the Doge of Venice because he is himself so close to Venice: all that he has to say might equally well be said to Genoa.

Petrarch had apparently taken his son Giovanni with him, again, to Padua, and had arranged for him to have some schooling there, as he had done when staying in Padua in the preceding year. Before the end of March, however, he decided to send Giovanni back to Parma, to the school of Giberto Baiardi; and on the 26th, being still in Padua, he wrote to Giberto a letter entrusting Giovanni to his care. In this letter he expresses himself as more concerned with moral than with grammatical education —he evidently feared that Giovanni was in danger of taking "the way that leadeth to destruction" rather than "the way that leadeth unto life"—and he sets forth some of his own ideas as to educational procedures, which should vary, he says, according to circumstances and according to the individual student. There are times when a boy should be cheered and times when he should be made more serious; times for restraint and for stimulation; for friendliness and for severity; for praise and for reproof; for encouragement and for the rod; for the bridle and for the spur. He was not ready to leave Padua himself; and he presumably sent a servant to Parma with Giovanni, giving the letter to the servant to deliver to Giberto.

FLORENCE OR AVIGNON?

Boccaccio and other Florentine admirers of Petrarch were hoping to persuade him to live in Florence. A combination of circumstances might now enable them to realize their hope: Florence had never restored the property confiscated from Petrarch's father; Petrarch on the occasion of his coronation had been designated as a "magister," had been accredited as a professor of the poetic art and of history, and had been granted all the rights and privileges enjoyed by professors of the liberal and honorable arts; and in 1349 Pope Clement had authorized the establishment of a university in Florence. An offer of a professorship in this university would be fully justified by the coronation awards that were of an academic type; and such an offer, if coupled with the restoration of the confiscated property, might very possibly win Petrarch's acceptance. Boccaccio was at this time well known and well trusted in Florence: in recent months he had been sent on a mission to Ravenna, had served as one of the financial officers of Florence, and had represented Florence in negotiations that led to Florentine control of Prato. It was doubtless Boccaccio who persuaded the governing officials of Florence to give Petrarch the confiscated property; and it was certainly Boccaccio who composed the requisite letter to Petrarch.

That letter is inscribed "To the Reverend Francesco Petrarca, Paduan canon, crowned poet, our most dear fellow citizen, from the Prior of the Arts and the Gonfalonier of Justice of the People and the City of Florence." It is filled with high laudation; reports the decision to give to Petrarch the property confiscated from his father; urges him to cease his wanderings and to come to live in the city that is his *patria;* speaks of the university, the success of which only his participation could assure; and offers him a professorial chair of his own choice. This letter was to be taken to Petrarch by Boccaccio.

Meanwhile, other plans for Petrarch's future had been made in Avignon, and were in part revealed to him through a communication that probably reached him a little while before the arrival of Boccaccio. This communication was a request from the Pope transmitted by two cardinals—almost certainly Gui de Boulogne and Elie de Talleyrand—that he come to Avignon. Despite the fact that the purpose for which he was asked to come was not stated, and despite his hatred of Avignon, he felt that he could not disregard such a summons. He was doubtless influenced by other considerations as well: his relations with the Bishop of Parma were badly strained; his first Paduan patron, Jacopo da Carrara, was no longer living; he had been in Italy for nearly four years, and he was restless by nature; he longed to be again in Vaucluse, and wanted to get at the books and papers that he had left there; and three of his dearest friends, Socrates, Guido Sette, and Philippe de Cabassoles, were still living in or near Avignon.

Whether he reached his decision before or after Boccaccio arrived with the Florentine invitation we do not know; but that invitation, whenever it came, did not serve to change or to prevent his decision to go to Avignon. Happy in the prospect of being again in Vaucluse and of renewing companionship there with Philippe de Cabassoles, Petrarch, soon after making his decision, wrote a delightful epigram, beginning with the lines

> Valle locus Clausa toto michi nullus in orbe
> gratior aut studiis aptior ora meis,

and sent it to Philippe with a brief covering letter that voices his eager anticipation. The entire epigram runs thus (in an English version that inevitably lacks the fine compactness of the Latin):

> There is no place in all the world that is dearer to me than Vaucluse, or a better harbor for my labors.
>
> I visited Vaucluse as a boy; and when I returned there as a youth the lovely valley cherished me in its sunny bosom.
>
> In Vaucluse I spent happily the best years of my manhood, while the threads of my life were white.
>
> In Vaucluse, now that I am old, I desire to live out my last years, and in Vaucluse, with thy blessing, to die.

Toward the end of March Boccaccio arrived in Padua, bringing with him not only the official Florentine letter, but also letters from Nelli, Lapo, and Zanobi, a small breviary sent as a gift by Nelli, who had been troubled that Petrarch should have had to carry a book as large as the breviary that he had had with him when he went to Rome, and the volume containing Ciceronian orations that Lapo had promised to lend to Petrarch. Lapo asked for a copy of Petrarch's comedy, the *Philologia;* and Zanobi asked for a copy of Petrarch's fragment of Homer and for a copy of a portion of one of his letters to Cola.

Boccaccio stayed on in Padua for about a week. In a letter written at a later time, he recalls the pattern of the days he had spent as Petrarch's guest:

> You were devoting yourself to the study of sacred authors, and I, being eager to own copies of your writings, was making copies of them. When evening came we rose together from our labors and went into your little garden, which was beautiful with the leaves and flowers of early spring ... and we sat talking together quietly and on worthy themes until day had passed into night.

The writings copied by Boccaccio at this time probably included the letters to the ancients that Petrarch had thus far written, and some of his recent letters—especially his letters to the Emperor and to the Doge of Venice, and his last two letters to his brother Gherardo.

Among the matters that Petrarch and Boccaccio discussed there was one about which Boccaccio felt very strongly. Milan, now under the lordship of the Archbishop Giovanni Visconti, had been striving to expand its already great territorial possessions and had in consequence been at war with Florence. Both because of this warfare and because Florence, being a democracy of a sort, was antagonistic to lordships, the Florentine attitude toward Milan was bitterly hostile. Boccaccio shared this attitude, and evidently expressed it vehemently. In the letter in which he tells of his visit to Petrarch he asserts that Petrarch had assented to what he had said, that he (Petrarch) had become more and more indignant, and that, raising his eyes toward heaven, he had invoked disaster upon the Archbishop. This account may well have been exaggerated. Petrarch may have felt constrained to assent to opinions expressed by a Florentine guest; but the fact remains that he must at this time have given Boccaccio reason to believe that he (Petrarch) thought ill of the Archbishop.

While Boccaccio was in Padua Petrarch took him to the monastery of St. Justina to see the tombstone supposed to be that of Livy and to look at some of the books in the monastery library.

The two friends doubtless talked much about the Florentine invitation and the summons from Avignon. Petrarch may well have thought and said to Boccaccio that without prejudice to the possibility of his accepting the Florentine invitation he felt that he ought first to find out what the Pope wanted of him.

Petrarch's reply to the government of Florence was dated on the 6th of April: it was presumably on that day or very soon afterward that Boccaccio was to leave Padua. Petrarch's letter is devoted almost entirely to his deep appreciation of the gift of the property that had been his father's: Florence, he says, has opened for him his childhood home, to which, weary with his long wanderings, he may now return. He does not mention the offer of the professorship; but he says that Boccaccio will supplement his letter by an oral report.

When Boccaccio left he took with him not only this letter but also brief replies, all dated on the 6th of April, to the letters that he had brought from Nelli, Lapo, and Zanobi. In them Petrarch thanks Nelli for his gift and Lapo for his loan; tells Lapo that he has no copy of his comedy in Italy and that in any case he does not think much of it (it was a youthful work, and is not extant—presumably Petrarch himself destroyed it); and tells Zanobi that he will send him a copy of the Homeric fragment, if he can find it, after he gets back to Parma, but that the labor involved in making a copy of the portion of the letter to Cola that Zanobi desired would be too great.

NEWS OF GHERARDO

It may have been either shortly before or shortly after Boccaccio's visit that on a day when Petrarch was dining with Bishop Ildebrandino two Carthusian priors, one from westernmost Italy and one from Provence, came in, and were heartily welcomed: they had been sent to look into the possibility of establishing a new Carthusian monastery near Treviso. In the course of the conversation the Bishop asked them—apparently without letting them know that the man about whom he was asking was Petrarch's brother—whether they could tell him anything about a Carthusian monk of the monastery of Montrieux named Gherardo. They could indeed; and this, in substance, is the story they told:

When the Black Death first reached the monastery of Montrieux the prior advised flight, and himself fled to his own home; but Gherardo, saying that the prior's advice would be good if there were any place that was beyond the reach of death, stayed on, as did some thirty other monks. Within a few days all thirty were stricken with the dread plague. Gherardo, without any fear of contagion, ministered to the dying; received their last words and their last kisses; washed their bodies; dug their graves; carried them there; and buried them. At the last he alone survived, with a dog as his only companion. He kept watch every night, resting for a little while in the daytime; and when bandits came in the night he held them at bay by words now severe, now gentle. At the end of the summer he went to the Grande Chartreuse, and asked the Grand Prior that he be given a prior and monks whom he might choose from different monasteries, by whom his monastery might be repeopled. His request was granted; and he returned to Montrieux in great joy and in a sort of Triumph.

While the two priors were telling the story the Bishop looked at Petrarch with tears of gladness in his eyes. The priors turned to Petrarch also, and, seeing his likeness to Gherardo, realized their brotherhood and embraced Petrarch joyfully, saying "Happy are you that have such a brother!"

On or about the first of May, shortly before Petrarch was to leave Padua, he was reminded that he had not yet fulfilled his promise to write an epitaph for Jacopo da Carrara. Realizing that he must write it at once and casting about in his mind for some special inspiration, he decided to seek it at Jacopo's tomb. He went, therefore, with a few companions, to the church of Sant'Agostino, where the still unfinished tomb stood. The church was closed, but a sacristan was found and let him in—his companions waiting outside. He sat down alone in front of the tomb and began to talk, as if to Jacopo. Inspiration came; and he then and there improvised the appropriate sixteen-line epitaph that was in fact engraved upon Jacopo's tomb (which was moved to the church of the Eremitani in 1820, when the church of Sant'Agostino was torn down).

Giovanni Aghinolfi, who had been a great admirer of Jacopo da Carrara, had asked Petrarch to write something about him. This, Petrarch thought, would mean the writing of a substantial work, such as a panegyric or a tragedy, and he had not felt able to undertake it; but, apparently just before leaving Padua, he began, but did not finish, a letter to Aghinolfi, praising Jacopo and telling in some detail of the circumstances of Jacopo's death and of the writing of the epitaph, a copy of which was enclosed.

Petrarch knew that he must return to Parma before starting for Provence; but he planned to go to Parma not directly, but by way of Verona and Mantua, which he intended to visit only briefly.

He left Padua, starting toward Verona, about noon on the 3rd of May. Just before sunset he reached Vicenza. He had not expected to stop there; but a friendly group surrounded him, and engaged him in a conversation that was so prolonged that he had to stay in Vicenza for the night. The talk fell on Cicero, whom all praised. Petrarch, however, though he joined in praising Cicero's ability and eloquence, knew that Cicero's conduct had not always been upright, and he told his listeners that this was the case. They were amazed and shocked. In support of his statements he then took from his traveling bag copies of the two letters he had addressed to Cicero; and his host, Enrico Pulice, read them aloud to the company. Most of those present were satisfied that Petrarch's strictures were deserved; but one old man was entirely unconvinced, and could not brook any criticism of his idol, whom he thought almost divine. The company broke up at a late hour, with the controversy still unsettled. Before Petrarch left Vicenza Enrico asked him to make copies of the two letters at the next stop, and to send them to him; and Petrarch agreed to do so.

He did stop, on the next day, at Lonigo (which is about halfway between Vicenza and Verona); and either there or afterward in Verona he made copies of the two letters and sent them to Enrico, with a covering letter in which he recounts the conversation at Vicenza and ends by saying that only after reading Cicero's own letters could one come to a sound conclusion on the disputed point.

While at Lonigo he finished the letter to Aghinolfi that he had begun before leaving Padua.

Petrarch had intended to spend only two or three days in Verona, but he stayed there for the better part of a month, detained, no doubt, by the importunities of Azzo da Correggio and other friends.

On one of the last days of May he wrote to Boccaccio a letter in which he says that he is just leaving for Mantua, whence he will go on promptly to Parma; and that the next letter that he writes to Boccaccio will probably be an announcement of his arrival in Vaucluse, where he would always prefer to live, since there he is sure of freedom, peace, silence, and solitude. There are two things, however, that prevent perfect contentment there: Vaucluse is too far from Italy, and too close to Avignon, the infernal Babylon of the West. He cannot tell just how things will turn out. He is going to Provence in order to see the Pope; but after seeing him he will take refuge in Vaucluse and spend the rest of the summer there among his books, expecting to return to Italy in the autumn. He asks Boccaccio to commend him to the Florentine officials, and to give his greetings to Nelli, Lapo, and Zanobi.

After leaving Verona Petrarch moved speedily. He was not detained in Mantua, and he stayed in Parma only long enough to make arrangements for the care of his interests during his absence. While in Parma, or perhaps a little earlier, he decided to take his son with him to Provence, hoping, apparently, that while in Avignon he might arrange for some sort of employment for him. While in Parma, also, or perhaps somewhat earlier, Petrarch heard that Luca Cristiani had returned safely to Piacenza.

On or just before the 11th of June he and his son started westward from Parma. On the 11th they were in Piacenza, where Petrarch had the joy of seeing Luca Cristiani again; and on the 20th they reached the pass of Mont Genèvre (the next pass to the south of that of Mont Cenis).

XVII. *Vaucluse and Avignon*
Summer 1351 - Spring 1352

SUMMER AT VAUCLUSE

PETRARCH and his son reached Vaucluse on the 27th
of June. On that same day Petrarch sent word to Philippe
de Cabassoles that he had arrived, and would come to Cavaillon
after he had removed the stains and the dust of travel.

He did go to Cavaillon on that very day or the next for a joyful
reunion with Philippe. He asked Philippe to write commendatory
letters for him to two cardinals, doubtless the two who, on behalf
of the Pope, had called him back to Provence. Philippe wrote
the letters immediately after Petrarch had left, and sent them to
him so promptly that Petrarch was able to acknowledge them
on the 29th.

Within a day or two after his arrival in Vaucluse he went to
a house where he expected to find a friend of his, Matteo Longo,
archdeacon of Liége, who had been living there recently. The
house was closed; and at the door, trying to get in, was a black
dog that Matteo, who had just departed, had left behind him.
When the dog first saw Petrarch he growled, but Petrarch spoke
to him gently; the dog came to him, wagging his tail; and
from that moment they were good companions.

Although Petrarch had come to Provence in response to a
papal summons, he seems to have spent nearly the whole summer
in Vaucluse: there is no evidence that he went into Avignon
at all until late August, and it was not until early autumn that
he went there for a stay of any length.

Meanwhile he enjoyed Vaucluse to the full. He lived simply,
in his own house, with two manservants and his dog. He dressed
like a peasant and ate peasant food. He had two gardens, of which
he tells with delight: one a shaded place close to the point where
the Sorgue gushes forth from the base of the rockbound mountainside, the other, cultivated and vineclad, on an island in the
river. Near his house was a rock formation that made a cool
shelter in hot weather: he speaks of it as a place conducive
to study. He spent mornings on the hills, noontides in his rock
shelter, and afternoons in the fields or in his upper garden, where

poetic inspiration often came to him. At times he did some fishing; at times he went riding—he kept two horses, and a servant rode with him; and at times he went into the woods with his dog, "black as pitch, swifter than the wind, absolutely faithful," and a hunter at Petrarch's bidding. At midnight, after reciting Lauds, he often went out alone, wandering now in the fields, especially on moonlit nights, and now over the hills; and with a sense of fascinated awe he ventured occasionally into the blackness of the cavern from which the river issued.

Of his overseer, Raymond Monet, whose house was nearby, he has much to say in his letters. He calls Raymond a man of rock-hard physique, but very kind. He was utterly faithful to Petrarch—in the care of his books as well as in the care of his house and his fields. Though Raymond could not read, he loved the books, and had learned to know them by name. When Petrarch put a book into his hands he would press it to his heart, and sometimes, in a low voice, he would talk to its author. He reproached Petrarch for eating rough peasant fare. Whenever Petrarch left Vaucluse he scolded him, warning him of the expense of his absences, and estimating to a penny the cost of each trip.

Of Raymond's wife Petrarch writes, in substance, thus:

> Her heart is as white as her face is black; her ugliness is almost becoming to her. She is an indefatigable worker, despite her years: she toils in the fields all day long, and yet she returns toward evening, ready to take care cheerfully of the needs of her sons, her husband, my servants, and any guests that I may chance to have.

They had two sons, Jean and Pierre, and it was to them that Petrarch was to leave his property in Vaucluse, under certain circumstances, as specified in his Will.

While Petrarch reveled in the sheer unspoiled beauty of his beloved valley, its greatest charm for him lay in its provision of perfect freedom for the study and writing that were now, as always, his main concern.

One of the motives that had led to his decision to come to Provence at this time was his desire to work again with books and with incomplete writings of his own that he had not seen for a long time; and after he had opened the locked chest or chests that had contained them he plunged eagerly into the resumption of his unfinished tasks.

The particular task to which he first set his hand seems to have been the development of the *De viris illustribus*. This he had begun in Vaucluse more than a dozen years before, and by 1343 he had written a series of twenty-three biographies of ancient heroes, chiefly Roman, from Romulus to Cato the Censor. In 1343 he had been planning to extend the series to include the early Roman emperors; but he had stopped work on the *De viris* without writing any new biographies. Now, instead of beginning again at the point at which he had stopped, he decided to enlarge the scope of the *De viris* as a whole, and he began work, accordingly, on a series of pre-Romulean biographies, beginning with that of Adam. Within a few months he had written twelve such biographies, the last being that of Hercules. It seems likely that much of this work was done in Vaucluse in the summer of 1351.

In his earlier years in Vaucluse Petrarch had always known that Laura was near: now that he was again in Vaucluse, Laura being no longer near, his sense of loss took on a new poignancy, which led him to the writing of many of the poems that are included in the latter part of the *Canzoniere*. Some of them may well have been written in his upper garden, which he calls "sacer Apollini."

In several of these poems Laura is in some sense with him again. She speaks to him from heaven:

"Weep not for me, for at my death my life became eternal, and when I seemed to close my eyes I opened them to light divine."

She appears to him on earth:

I have beheld her rising as a nymph from the clear waters of the Sorgue, or walking over the green grass amid the flowers as if she were a living woman, showing in her looks that she grieves for me.

He is with her in heaven:

My thought uplifted me unto the place where she now is whom vainly I seek on earth. . . . She took me by the hand, and said to me: "Thou shalt yet be with me within this sphere, if my desire is to be fulfilled."

Before leaving Italy Petrarch had written to Boccaccio that he expected to stay in Provence for about two months, but by the middle of July his plans had changed. He had now determined to finish works, begun in Vaucluse, that he had left unfinished; and on the 19th of July he wrote to Luca Cristiani saying that he thinks it will take him about two years to do what he wants to do, and telling of the great appeal that Vaucluse holds for him, with its memories, its beauties, it solitude, and its opportunity for study and writing.

After reaching Provence Petrarch had received from Nelli a letter asking him to do all he could while in Provence to support the claim of a certain Don Ubertino to the abbacy of the monastery of Cavanna, a dependency of the monastery of Vallombrosa. This abbacy had been promised to Don Ubertino by the Abbot of Vallombrosa, who thereafter changed his mind and nominated another candidate. In a letter to Nelli (now lost) that was probably written about the end of July Petrarch promised to do what he could, but indicated that he foresaw difficulties. By September he had received a reply in which Nelli told of the efforts on behalf of Don Ubertino that were still being made in Florence.

AUTUMN AND WINTER IN AVIGNON

There were at least three things that Petrarch had to do in Avignon: he must deal with whatever proposal the cardinals and the Pope might make to him; he must do what he could for his son; and he must try to help Don Ubertino. So he went into the hated city early in the autumn, taking his son with him. During the several months of their stay in Avignon they lived with Petrarch's boyhood friend Guido Sette, now Archdeacon of Genoa, but still resident in Avignon.

There Petrarch had first of all to see one or both of the cardinals who had called him back to Provence, and find out what they and the Pope wanted of him. To his dismay he found that they had called him in the hope of getting him to accept a papal secretaryship. At some time in his last previous period of residence in Provence, the secretaryship being then vacant, Pope Clement had offered it to him, and he had refused it; and the idea of submitting himself to the limitations it would put upon him was, if anything, even more repugnant to him now than it had been then. But he could not easily resist the pressures that were brought to bear upon him, even by the Pope himself. His eventual escape came about in a curious way. He found that in the minds of those who were advocating his appointment there was just one doubt as to his fitness for the position: they were afraid that he could not lower his lofty style enough to make it suitable for the official letters that a papal secretary would have to compose. In this fear of theirs Petrarch saw a possible avenue of escape. He suggested that a trial be made to see whether he could lower his style sufficiently to meet their views. The suggestion was adopted; Petrarch proceeded to write something in the very loftiest style he could devise; and the attempt to force him to accept the appointment was dropped.

After it had become clear that he was not to be a papal secretary, he had another interview with the Pope, who then offered him a bishopric as he had done once before. This offer being again refused, the Pope, still wanting to attach Petrarch in some way to the papal court, said to him: "Tell me what you would like to have me do for you, and I will do it." Petrarch replied:

> If you desire to do anything for me, Holy Father, let not only the giving of the gift be yours, but also the decision as to what the gift should be. You know what you think of me: if there should ever occur to you anything that you might think suitable for me, please keep me in mind.

Nothing came, however, of this suggestion.

About the first of November two Florentine envoys, with a staff, came to Avignon with instructions to win the Pope to an alliance against the Visconti and to urge him to authorize the coronation of Louis of Taranto and Joan as King and Queen of Naples. One of the two envoys was Angelo Acciaiuoli (a cousin of Niccolò), who was both Bishop of Florence and Chancellor of the Kingdom of Naples; and one of the members of his staff was Forese Donati, the learned rector of a church near Florence, who was a friend of Nelli. Petrarch saw much of Angelo and Forese while they were in Avignon.

The state of things in Rome was at this time so glaringly bad that the Pope, not long before the middle of November, appointed a commission of four cardinals "to reform the government of the Roman Republic." Niccola Capocci, himself a Roman citizen, was one of the four; and it was probably after a talk or talks with him and in accordance with a request made by him that Petrarch set down his views on the subject, for the benefit of the commission, in a long and noble letter written soon after mid-November. His two main recommendations were that the Colonna and the Orsini—the two great families, neither one of Roman origin, whose incessant struggle for power was the chief cause of the plight of Rome—be excluded from the government of the city, and that membership in the Roman Senate be limited to Roman citizens. But the commission accomplished nothing.

The rift between Petrarch and Bishop Ugolino of Parma had become very grave: Ugolino had been led to believe that Petrarch had gone to Avignon out of jealousy and in order to injure him. Petrarch defended himself against this charge in a masterly letter written late in December: instead of sending this letter direct to Bishop Ugolino he sent it to his friend Don Luca, asking him to take it to the Bishop and to say what he could to help matters. But Petrarch's letter seems to have had no effect.

Less serious, but very annoying, was the circulation in Avignon of a report that Petrarch was a necromancer—because, forsooth, he read the works of Virgil! The identity of the cardinal who started this report on its way is not known, but among those who believed it was Cardinal Etienne Aubert, who held firmly to his belief even after Cardinal Talleyrand and Petrarch had ridiculed it in his presence.

In the Kingdom of Naples the years following the death of King Robert had been sorely troubled; but things had lately taken a turn for the better, and in January, 1352, a peaceful settlement with the King of Hungary was reached, and the Pope authorized the coronation of Louis of Taranto and Joan as King and Queen. This improvement in Neapolitan affairs was due largely to the skillful guidance of Niccolò Acciaiuoli, who had long been the chief adviser of Louis of Taranto. Niccolò now held the title of Grand Seneschal of the Kingdom, and was generally recognized as the power behind the throne.

Under these circumstances Petrarch felt it to be his part to provide instruction for Louis; and he therefore wrote a treatise on royal government in the form of a letter to Acciaiuoli, whom he congratulates on his successes, and bids to devote redoubled efforts to the guidance of Louis in his kingship. This letter was soon widely copied and widely admired. Barbato da Sulmona wrote an elaborate commentary on it.

Early in 1351 Petrarch had written to the Emperor, urging his return to Rome; but he had had no answer. Meanwhile the need for imperial return had not decreased, and circumstances had become more propitious for such a return: Tuscany, previously hostile to imperial claims, now desired the Emperor's coming. Early in 1352, therefore, Petrarch wrote a second letter to the Emperor, renewing and reinforcing his earlier appeal:

> For the honor of the Empire, for the salvation of Italy, for the consolation of the city of Rome—your deserted spouse—for the joy of your friends, for the welfare of your subjects, for the relief of the laboring Christian folk, for the formation of a plan for a Crusade, and in order that you may win noble and enduring fame on earth and may merit eternal blessedness after the miseries of this fleeting life, I entreat you, I beseech you, I implore you, prostrating myself in utter devotion before your knees, that you seize without delay this present opportunity for great and admirable achievement.

Shortly after this letter was written, it would seem, a report came to Avignon that Charles was intending to go to Italy very soon; and it was then planned that if he did so Cardinal Gui de Boulogne should go to Italy to meet him, and should take Petrarch and Pierre d'Auvergne with him. Charles made no move, however, and the plan for a meeting in Italy was dropped, to Petrarch's bitter disappointment.

It took Petrarch several months to bring his efforts on behalf of his son and of Don Ubertino to successful outcomes. In March the Pope granted Giovanni a canonry in Verona. In a letter to Nelli written in May Petrarch says that he had acted on behalf of Don Ubertino as he had never acted for himself, that he had been obsequious, persistent, and importunate, and that Nelli would have been moved to laughter and to pity if he could have seen him, a lover of freedom and solitude, haunting the papal palace in the midst of a crowd of courtiers.

These and other activities kept Petrarch in a most unhappy state of personal turmoil, which is reflected, in various letters, in passages such as these:

> This tempest of affairs leaves me hardly time to breathe.
> So many things press upon me and upon each other that there isn't time enough to take care of them all: there is no end of them.

> I am worn out, I am tormented, I am distressed, I am
> indignant, and I am wasting my time.

Petrarch's hatred of the papal court, intense even before this
time, increased now to the boiling point, and expressed itself in
several exceedingly violent letters and in a few pieces of Latin
verse (including the latter part of the Seventh Eclogue). Most of
these letters—too violent, in Petrarch's judgment, to be included
in the collection of the *Familiares*—were eventually gathered in
a small special collection, not intended for early release, which
he called *Epistolae sine nomine*, since in this collection (which contained certain other violent letters) the names of the addressees
were suppressed. In a typical passage in one of the letters Avignon
is characterized as a place

> in which no piety, no charity, and no faith dwell; where
> pride, envy, debauchery, and avarice reign with all their
> arts; where the worst man is promoted and the munificent
> robber is exalted and the just man is trampled on; where
> honesty is called foolishness and cunning is called wisdom;
> where God is mocked, the sesterce is adored, the laws are
> trodden under foot, and the good are scorned.

Avignon is referred to as Babylon, Pope Clement as Nimrod,
and the Countess of Turenne as Semiramis.

The Pope was taken seriously ill in December and grew worse
as time went on. Early in 1352, perhaps in February, Petrarch
sent him an oral message, urging him to put his faith not in a
multitude of doctors, but in a single doctor distinguished not
by eloquence but by learning and reliability. As this message
reached the Pope, however, it was apparently somewhat garbled;
and the Pope sent a messenger to Petrarch asking that he put
his message into written form. This Petrarch did on the 12th of
March, in a letter in which he repeats his recommendation and
asserts that doctors traffic in human life, being free to cause
death with impunity; that their disagreements are made in order
that they may seem individually authoritative; and that they go
beyond the bounds of their own proper field to indulge in high-
sounding talk, invading the domains of poetry and rhetoric.

One of the doctors concerned immediately wrote a violent
reply, attacking Petrarch, praising the art of medicine, and denying that the Pope's doctors had disagreed. He also attacked both

poets and poetry and maintained—according to Petrarch—that Averroes is preferable to Christ.

Petrarch at once, in the course of a day and a night, Pierre d'Auvergne being with him part of the time, wrote a long and scathing rejoinder, which, in an eventual revision, became the first Book of his *Invective contra medicum*. He refutes the doctor's assertions, and says that he is attacking neither medicine as such nor good doctors, but only his particular antagonist and other doctors who are similarly delirious. The most important passages of this rejoinder, however, are those devoted to the defense of poetry. One such passage, in part, reads thus:

> Open your eyes . . . and you will see that poets are lumi-
> nous with glory and with the immortality of fame, which
> they win not only for themselves but for others: for it is
> given to poets more than to other men to preserve names
> that might otherwise perish; and virtue itself needs their
> aid, not through any inherent deficiency, but in its struggle
> against time and oblivion.

In a letter written soon afterward to Pierre d'Auvergne, Petrarch says that he has heard that the doctor was excited and dismayed by this rejoinder, and that he was going about Avignon trying to find someone to help him.

During these crowded months in Avignon Petrarch can hardly have done much writing other than the writing of letters. He did, however, write a few brief *epistolae metricae*, and may have done a little more work on the *De viris illustribus*. By the end of March he was almost ready to leave Avignon. Before he did so he invited Bishop Angelo Acciaiuoli to visit him in Vaucluse, and the Bishop agreed to come: the date of May 24 was set for his arrival.

On the first of April Petrarch wrote to each of his four Floren-tine friends—Boccaccio, Nelli, Zanobi da Strada, and Lapo da Castiglionchio. The letter to Zanobi supports a request from Niccolò Acciaiuoli that Zanobi come to Naples to take a posi-tion as a royal secretary. The letter to Lapo is devoted chiefly to an imaginative account of the pleasure that Lapo's Cicero is finding in the company of other ancients assembled in Vaucluse, twenty-six of whom are mentioned by name.

XVIII. *Last Months in Vaucluse*

O N T H E first day of April or on one of the two following days Petrarch returned to Vaucluse. The sonnet beginning *Zefiro torna* was probably written soon afterward:

> Zephyr returns, and brings the beautiful season, and flowers and herbs, his dear companions, and Procne's chiding and Philomel's lament, and all the white and red of Spring.
>
> The meadows smile, and the sky is serene again: Jove delights to gaze upon his daughter. Air, sea, and land are full of love, and to thoughts of love all living things now turn.
>
> But for me, alas, there come again grievous sighs, drawn from the depths of my heart by her who has taken its keys with her to heaven;
>
> And the singing of birds and the flowering of the fields and the graces of fair and gentle ladies are as a desert and as fierce wild beasts.

(Procne and Philomel are the swallow and the nightingale, and Jove's daughter is Venus, here thought of as the evening star.)

The beloved valley was in itself as delectable and as intellectually comfortable as ever, but the sharp memory of recent experiences in Avignon, the continuance of some of the pressures that had beset him there, and the stench of the hated city combined to lessen the healing power of Vaucluse, and to turn Petrarch's thoughts again toward Italy.

Before the end of April he wrote to Laelius, who was then in Rome, a letter revealing his restlessness and asking Laelius for his opinion as to whether he (Petrarch) could now find a satisfactory refuge in Rome. There were those who wanted him to stay in Avignon, which he would not have considered; and although he had received invitations from the King of France and from Naples neither one of these two invitations appealed to him.

He had no illusions, however, as to the probability of his finding anywhere what he desired. In April, also, he wrote a long and remarkable letter to Stefano Colonna, Provost of Saint-Omer (son of a Pietro Colonna who was a grandson of Stefano the Elder), in which he surveys conditions in many different parts of Italy, in France, England, Germany, Spain, Majorca, Sardinia, Corsica, Sicily, Rhodes, Crete, Greece, Cyprus, Armenia, the Holy Land, and in Asia and Africa. He concludes that no promise of peace and freedom is to be found anywhere on earth.

In May he had the satisfaction of learning that his efforts on behalf of Don Ubertino had been successful and that Don Ubertino's claim to appointment as Abbot of the monastery of Cavanna had received papal confirmation. In May also he learned that Zanobi da Strada had left Florence and gone to Naples to take a position with Niccolò Acciaiuoli. Either the same letter that brought this word or another letter received at about the same time contained the distressing news that the long-standing friendship between Acciaiuoli and Giovanni Barrili, both of them friends of Petrarch, had been seriously strained. Friendship, to Petrarch, was the most precious of human relations, and he could not bear to think that the friendship of two friends of his should be broken: he set himself therefore to the task of mending matters. He wrote four letters, accordingly, addressing the basic letter to both men. This was a long, carefully reasoned, deeply felt, and altogether very impressive plea for the renewal of their friendship; it bore on the outside an inscription meaning "To be opened only by Niccolò or Giovanni, and only when they are together"; but instead of sending it directly to either one of the two men he sent it to Zanobi, with a covering letter in which he bids Zanobi to bring the two together to receive it. He wrote also two separate letters, one to Niccolò and one to Giovanni, pleading in each case that the friendship be renewed.

Petrarch spent the 24th of May—the day on which Bishop Angelo Acciaiuoli had promised to come to Vaucluse—expecting the arrival of his guest, for whom he had made elaborate preparations. By the ninth hour he decided that the Bishop had forgotten or broken his promise, and he then sat down and began an unhappy letter to Nelli, telling of his disappointment. But before he finished the letter he heard a great clamor at the door: the Bishop had come at last. So he added a happy postscript to the unfinished letter and gave it, doubtless, to the Bishop or to some one who was with him, to be delivered to Nelli, in Florence.

The summer, which proved to be a blessedly peaceful time for Petrarch, brought him the good news that the letters he had sent to Naples had led to the renewal of the friendship of Niccolò Acciaiuoli and Giovanni Barrili.

On the 10th of June Petrarch received from his brother a box of polished boxwood that Gherardo had made, and a letter of exhortation consisting largely of quotations from the Church Fathers. On the following day he wrote a letter of thanks, which is notable chiefly for a detailed development of the idea that men differ very greatly in respect to their dominant interests. The three main classes of their interests, Petrarch says, are pleasure, wealth and power, and meditation and wisdom, each class being extensively subdivisible. Toward the end of the letter Petrarch speaks gratefully of the three pieces of advice that Gherardo had given him at Montrieux in the spring of 1347, and says that he has heeded them all and has profited by them.

In March the Pope had granted a canonry in Verona to Petrarch's son Giovanni; and in June Petrarch sent him to Verona. While there was nothing unusual at this time in awarding a canonry to a boy of fifteen and while Petrarch had done his utmost to give Giovanni a good education and was still paternally hopeful, he evidently had his doubts as to Giovanni's qualifications. When Giovanni left Provence Petrarch gave to him, or perhaps to an accompanying servant, letters to his Veronese friends Rinaldo Cavalchini and Guglielmo da Pastrengo, asking them to do what they could for the boy—Rinaldo, who had taught Giovanni, being asked in particular to do what he could for his mind, and Guglielmo being asked to do what he could for his conduct.

The papacy at this time, regarding Cola di Rienzo as a menace even after his abdication, had made against him a charge of heresy, which, if he could have been brought to trial and convicted, might have meant death. For more than a year he had found refuge with a group of dissident monks in a sort of hermitage in the southern Apennines, and there had come under the influence of a fanatic who had convinced him that it was his duty both to persuade the Emperor to destroy the temporal power of the papacy and to serve as an adjutant to the Emperor in that undertaking. In July, 1350, accordingly, Cola had gone to Prague and had had an audience with the Emperor. Charles, however, was not to be persuaded, and had turned Cola over to the Archbishop of Prague, Arnost z Pardubic, who had ordered his arrest. The Pope had been notified, and had requested that Cola be either sent to Avignon or held as a prisoner until papal representatives should come to get him. The Emperor, unwilling to let him go, had held him as a prisoner, but had treated him with some consideration. He had done some writing for Charles; on his own account he had written a long poem on a religious theme. Early in 1352 the Pope had excommunicated him, and had sent representatives to Prague to bring him to Avignon. The Emperor had then let him go, but had evidently requested that he be treated not too severely and that in any case the death penalty should not be invoked.

Cola reached Avignon in July or early in August. Soon thereafter Petrarch, who was still in Vaucluse, received letters from Avignon telling of Cola's arrival and reporting gossip as to his chances. On the 10th of August Petrarch wrote to Nelli a letter in which he reports what he had just learned and reviews Cola's career and his own relations to it. He speaks severely of Cola's failure, but voices with intense indignation his belief that the crime for which Cola is actually being brought to trial is his attempt to restore Rome to its rightful place in the world. Of Cola's arrival in Avignon Petrarch writes:

> When he came he was not bound—he was spared that public shame—but he was so guarded that he had no hope of escape. As he entered the city the unhappy man asked whether I was at the papal court—either because he had some vain hope that I might be able to help him, or simply because he was remembering our friendship, which had begun in Avignon long ago.

He then refers to a report that the idea that Cola was a poet might save him. As far as he knew, Cola had never written any poetry; but he is glad that the Muses are held in such esteem—though he attributes it to a quite unintelligent vogue of poetry that was current just then in Avignon.

It seems likely that in the course of this spring and summer Petrarch went on with the collection of his letters; that he did some further work on the *De viris illustribus;* and that he wrote two new *capitoli* for the *Triumph of Fame,* to replace the unsatisfactory single *capitolo* beginning *Nel cor* that he had written while still in Italy.

The two new *capitoli,* beginning *Da poi che Morte triumphò* ("After Death had triumphed") and *Pien d'infinita e nobil meraviglia* (" Filled with infinite and noble wonder") are processional, as *Nel cor* had been. Together, they present about as many persons as had figured in *Nel cor;* but the doubling of the amount of space permits much more freedom of poetic treatment. A few of the persons who had appeared in the earlier *capitolo* now disappear, and a few new persons are introduced. The first of the two new *capitoli* is devoted to ancient Roman heroes, and the second to other heroes, including six moderns: Godfrey of Bouillon, Saladin, the admiral Ruggero di Lauria, Duke Henry of Lancaster, King Robert, and Stefano Colonna the Elder.

Petrarch seems not to have done any further work on the *Africa* either during this stay in Provence or at any later time.

Early in September Cardinal Gui de Boulogne, who was about to leave for an absence of a few weeks, called Petrarch into Avignon for a talk. It is likely that what the Cardinal had in mind was the possibility of securing a substantial benefice for Petrarch not far from Avignon, in lieu of a papal secretaryship, which was now clearly out of the question. Petrarch, not much interested in such a possibility, told the Cardinal of his desire to return to Italy, and received the Cardinal's assent. But soon after the Cardinal had started on his journey he changed his mind, and wrote to Petrarch, withdrawing his assent and bidding Petrarch wait for him in Avignon.

Petrarch now held four canonries—in Lombez, Pisa, Parma, and Padua. At about this time he decided to exchange the first two for canonries of lesser yield that were held by two of his friends (Socrates and someone else), but he did not at once carry out his plan. At about this time, also, he received a minor canonry in Modena, but he immediately arranged to have it transferred to Don Luca.

The fine letter that Petrarch had written in the previous December to Bishop Ugolino dei Rossi of Parma had not served to lessen the Bishop's hostility, which by the end of the summer had become so obnoxious that Pope Clement himself in September took the extraordinary action of issuing a decree releasing the archdeaconate of Parma entirely from the jurisdiction and control of the Bishop.

In the latter part of September Petrarch was still in Vaucluse.

A MONTH IN AVIGNON

In accordance with Cardinal Gui de Boulogne's desire, Petrarch went into Avignon about the first of October to wait for him.

While there and again beset by demands upon his time he was led to take what action he could with regard to certain matters of public concern. Letters and poems rained down upon him from all over the world; and the current unintelligent vogue of poetry in Avignon was so widespread that he could not go outdoors without being seized upon by frantic would-be poets.

Cola di Rienzo was now a prisoner in the papal palace, awaiting trial for heresy. There is no evidence that Petrarch made any effort to see him; but it was in all probability at this time that he wrote on Cola's behalf a long letter addressed to the Roman People. His particular purpose is to urge the Roman People to intervene by sending an embassy to Avignon to claim the right of jurisdiction over Cola as a Roman citizen, or to demand at least that he be accorded legal advice and a public trial. In this letter, as in the letter to Nelli that he had written in the summer, he takes the position that Cola's one great sin, from the papal point of view, was nothing more nor less than his perfectly proper effort to re-establish Rome as the seat of the Roman Empire. He blames Cola for having forsaken the task that he had begun so well; but the tone of the letter is much more sympathetic than that of the letter that he had written to Nelli in the summer. Cola, he says, is generally and deservedly pitied, and thought to merit reward rather than punishment. The letter culminates in this summary of Cola's efforts on behalf of Rome:

> For seven months he held the reins of the republic in such a fashion that it appears to me that since the origin of the world there can hardly have been any nobler effort; and if he had succeeded as he had begun his achievement would have seemed to be divine rather than human.

Conditions in Rome itself were as bad as ever. A series of events had raised Petrarch's friend Laelius, then in Rome, to a position of great influence. The line of action that he was following seemed to papal opinion in general to be improper and deserving of punishment: to Petrarch it seemed to be praiseworthy and deserving of lasting fame. He wrote therefore to Laelius a letter in which he urged him to persist, and to steer a middle course between passivity and excessive action.

In the spring of 1351 Petrarch had tried vainly to persuade the Doge of Venice to desist from preparations for war against Genoa; and presently Aragon and the Byzantine emperor had allied themselves with Venice. In the first major engagement of the war, however, fought in the Bosphorus in February, 1352, Genoa had been victorious, though at a heavy cost. A peace conference called by the Pope and held in Avignon in September had failed to reach an agreement. Under these circumstances Petrarch felt impelled to write to the Doge and Council of Genoa a letter urging them to use their victory for the establishment of peace, and to join with Venice in defeating the perfidious Aragonese and then in the liberation of the Holy Land. He warned them also against any renewal of the civil strife that had been so disastrous to Genoa in the past. The letter contains a vivid account of the battle of the Bosphorus, and a fine description of the beauties of Genoa and its *riviera*.

On the 8th of November, unable to endure Avignon, and unwilling to wait there any longer for Cardinal Gui de Boulogne, Petrarch went back to Vaucluse.

A JOURNEY TO ITALY ATTEMPTED

Immediately after reaching Vaucluse Petrarch wrote to the Cardinal, saying that he was very impatient to start for Italy, and that although he would still wait for a little while, in Vaucluse, for the Cardinal's return, he would not wait very long. He proceeded, accordingly, to make preparations for the journey. He had no intention of returning ever to Provence, and he therefore planned to take with him most of his books and all the manuscripts that contained writings of his own, finished or unfinished. He had not determined what his destination in Italy was to be. There was no prospect that he could now find peace of mind in Parma: Padua and Mantua, at least, were possibilities. He decided to go by the coastal road and to visit his brother Gherardo at Montrieux while on his way.

He started south from Vaucluse on the 16th of November, taking servants with him. There had been no rain in Provence for several months; but he had hardly started out when it began to rain, at first lightly and then heavily. He thought of turning back, but he kept on going until, as night fell, he reached Cavaillon.

There he would have stopped, in any case, to say good-bye to Philippe de Cabassoles. Philippe was ill; but thinking that Petrarch had come to pay him a visit he received him joyfully, his joy turning to lamentation when he found out that Petrarch was on his way to Italy. He insisted that Petrarch stay for the night, which Petrarch was glad to do, since the rain had now become a downpour, driving even through the roof as the night went on. Toward midnight there came in a rumor, soon confirmed, that near Nice a band of raiders from the mountains had descended upon the coastal road, making it impassable. Philippe urged Petrarch to give up his journey; but Petrarch by this time was thinking of going on by another route. There was little sleep, that night, in Philippe's household, and when morning came, the storm still continuing, Petrarch, fearing that his books might be ruined if he went on, decided to give up his journey. He sent some of his servants on, however, one of them being instructed to bring back a report as to the state of affairs in Italy. As soon as the servants had gone just far enough to be beyond recall, the rain stopped. In the course of the day Petrarch started back, almost alone, to Vaucluse, night overtaking him on the way.

LAST DAYS IN VAUCLUSE

Before the end of November, in all probability, Petrarch learned, with deep sorrow, of the death of Bishop Ildebrandino Conti of Padua; and soon thereafter he wrote to the Paduan clergy a *consolatoria* containing a glowing eulogy of Ildebrandino and a loving account of Petrarch's friendship with him.

Pope Clement VI died on the 6th of December, 1352. He had done much for Petrarch, and would have been glad to do more; but in spite of their personal cordiality Petrarch's judgment of Clement's conduct as Pope had been exceedingly severe. Soon after he heard of Clement's death he wrote a letter that was concerned with the evils of Clement's papacy and with the plight of the Church. He sent the letter to Philippe on the 16th of December, together with a brief covering letter and two gifts: a trout caught in the Sorgue by one of the sons of Raymond Monet, and a duck caught, also in the Sorgue, by Petrarch's dog.

Petrarch was already engaged in the making of a small and temporarily confidential collection of letters of a tenor similar to that of his letter about Clement; and in his covering letter to Philippe he asked him to let him know whether he thought that his letter about Clement should be destroyed or added to the little collection. Philippe's reply was favorable; but the letter about Clement is not extant.

On the 18th of December the College of Cardinals elected Etienne Aubert, who took the name Innocent VI, as Clement's successor. It must have been with something like consternation that Petrarch heard of this election, for Etienne Aubert had expressed the belief that Petrarch was a necromancer, and had held firmly to that belief even though Cardinal Talleyrand and Petrarch had ridiculed it in his presence. Petrarch vented his bitterness in another letter that was to find its place in his small confidential collection. It opens with the words *Ve populo tuo, Cristo Jhesu!* ("Woe to thy people, Christ Jesus!"), and is in effect a violent outburst of psalmodic lamentation and argumentative reproach. Without being irreverent in intention, it reads as if it were addressed to Christ himself rather than to any mortal man.

On or about the first of January Petrarch received a message from Cardinals Talleyrand and Gui de Boulogne, asking him to come into Avignon. He complied on the third, leaving his faithful overseer, Raymond Monet, slightly ill—or so he thought. On the next day, however, one of his servants came in to tell him that Raymond had died. He then wrote to the two cardinals asking their permission to return to Vaucluse: his letter is, in substance, a touching tribute to Raymond. The permission he had requested was evidently given.

At some time in January the servant whom Petrarch had sent forward from Cavaillon with instructions to bring back word as to the state of affairs in Italy returned with a discouraging report:

> Things would be even worse for you in Italy than they are in Avignon. You have no idea what a mass of cares awaits you; what hosts of friends have been excited by the prospect of your return; how many demands would be made upon your time; how actively you would have to bestir yourself; and what troubles you would have to endure.

Nothing could alter Petrarch's determination to leave Provence, but the report led him to postpone his departure and to settle down in Vaucluse again, at least until the spring.

Early in 1353 Petrarch's polemic with one of the doctors who had attended Clement VI became active again. To Petrarch's letter to Clement, written in March, 1352, this doctor had replied immediately; and to that reply, in that same month, Petrarch had written a long rejoinder. Now, after many months, the doctor produced an elaborate counter-rejoinder, in which he accused Petrarch of arrogance, adulation, boasting, pride, and deficiency in logic. He defended medicine as the basis for right living and maintained that the arts of speech are therefore of minor importance. He attacked poetry, saying that its purpose is to deceive by means of pleasing; that whereas science is immutable the elements of poetry are variable; and that poets delight in obscurity because they hate the common folk. Furthermore, he attacked Petrarch's exaltation of solitude, praising instead the resources of city life.

To this counter-rejoinder Petrarch, while still in Provence, wrote a counterblast, which was a substantial piece of work, divided into three parts. In the first part he refutes various charges and assertions, and insists that he is not attacking all doctors, but only those who show themselves to be unworthy. In the second he stresses the difference between the liberal and the mechanical arts; praises poetry; defends poetic obscurity, citing St. Augustine and St. Gregory; and says that his works are written for posterity. The third part is a defense of the life of solitude. At the very end Petrarch challenges the doctor to renew the argument, but no reply was ever forthcoming.

At a somewhat later time Petrarch revised his first rejoinder and his counterblast, and combined them in a work that he called *Invective contra medicum*, the revised rejoinder constituting the first Book and the three parts of the revised counterblast the last three Books of the *Invective*.

In February, having heard of the illness of the Bishop of Viterbo, Niccolò di Paolo dei Vetuli, who was a friend of his, he invited him to come to Vaucluse for recuperation. In that blessed valley, he writes, Niccolò will find no tyranny, insolence, backbiting, wrath, faction, complaining, deceit, clamor, shouting, blaring of trumpets, clash of arms, avarice, jealousy, ambition, servility, guile, or offense, but a quiet, humble, and gentle manner of life, a peaceful countryside, soft air, sweet breezes, sunny swards, clear springs, a river full of fish, flowery banks, leafy woods, dewy caverns, green meadows, the lowing of cattle, the song of birds, and the murmuring of the waters—and philosophers, poets, orators and historians who will offer him good reading.

For many years Sardinia had been under the domination of Aragon, despite Genoese attempts to set the island free. In February, after hearing that Genoa had recently made an alliance with a powerful Sardinian rebel, Petrarch wrote again to the Doge and Council of Genoa, this time to applaud their action and to urge the relentless prosecution of the new war—a war directed not against a sister Italian state but against a foreign and usurping enemy. This letter is as bellicose as Petrarch's previous letter to Genoa had been pacific.

In March Petrarch received a visit from a man, previously unknown to him, of whose intended coming he had had word from Socrates. Petrarch made his guest welcome, and showed him his house, his gardens, and his fields. The visitor then said that he would like to walk down to the Island in the Sorgue (about three miles from Vaucluse). Petrarch offered to send a servant with him, but he preferred to go alone. So he went—and never returned!

Still intent on leaving Provence, Petrarch now sent new messengers to Italy to get more information for him, presumably to help him decide to what city he should go. About the middle of April these messengers returned with a report from which Petrarch gathered that even if he could not find a place in Italy that would be perfectly satisfactory he could at least find one that would afford him something like a peaceful harbor. He decided, accordingly, to return soon to Italy and to go by way of the pass of Mont Genèvre.

Wishing, however, to see his brother once more, he made a special journey, in April, to the monastery of Montrieux. At one point on the road he met a company of Roman ladies who were making a pilgrimage to Santiago de Compostela, and had a long conversation with them about conditions in Rome in general and about Laelius in particular. They had tragic events to report; but Laelius, though he had been in danger, was safe.

Petrarch spent a day and a night in the monastery. He was received with "holy hospitality" by the entire brotherhood; and with his brother he talked long and eagerly and affectionately about many things. Gherardo asked him to send him a copy of the *Confessions* of St. Augustine, and Petrarch promised to do so. He learned that the monastery was suffering grievous depredations:

> While the monks are at Matins, in comes a weeping
> shepherd to tell them that his flock has been stolen; while

they are at Mass they hear the moans of a poor farmer whose vineyard and field and garden have been stripped by ravaging herds; while they are breaking fast or briefly sleeping the silence of the night is rent by the lamentations of a sacristan or some other servant who has been set upon and beaten.

Under similar circumstances in the past the monks had appealed to the Kings of Naples (who were sovereigns of Provence also) for protection, and had received it. Later on, such protection had seemed unnecessary and had been discontinued, but now it was very much needed again, and the monks asked Petrarch to do what he could for them. He promised that he would bring their distress to the knowledge of Niccolò Acciaiuoli, by writing about it at length to Zanobi da Strada and asking him to present the situation orally to Niccolò. When he left the monastery all the monks gathered to bid him godspeed; and Gherardo and a few others walked on with him through the woods down to the foot of the mountain. After his return to Vaucluse Petrarch began work at once on his promised letter to Zanobi.

He felt it necessary to go into Avignon once more, mainly, no doubt, to say farewell to Cardinals Talleyrand and Gui de Boulogne, and to Socrates and to Guido Sette. While he was in Avignon Cardinal Talleyrand, in accordance with the wishes of the new Pope, tried to get Petrarch to see Innocent and to say farewell to him, butPetrarch refused to do so.

Also while in Avignon Petrarch finished his long letter to Zanobi about conditions at Montrieux; and with it he sent a brief covering letter in which he vents again his inextinguishable hatred of the papal city.

Before the end of Petrarch's stay in Provence Nelli had become his chief correspondent: during these two years Petrarch had received several letters from Nelli, and had written at least sixteen letters to him. Within the same period, or possibly even earlier, Petrarch had begun to call him "Simonides"—because, like Simonides of Cos, Nelli was both a priest and a poet (no poems of his, however, are extant).

Within this period, also, the government of Florence—apparently taking Petrarch's absence in Provence as tantamount to a refusal of the offer of a Florentine professorship—revoked the action by which the confiscated property of his father had been given to him.

Petrarch started for Italy late in May or early in June, taking with him most of his books and all the manuscript sheets that contained writings of his own. He left his home in Vaucluse in the care of Jean and Pierre Monet, with instructions that any friends of his who might come there were to be made welcome.

XIX. *Transition*

As PETRARCH paused in the pass of Mont Genèvre, there came to him the idea and probably some of the phrasing of his magnificent salutation to Italy:

> Hail to thee, land most holy, dear to God!
> Land that dost shelter the good, that the proud must fear!
> More bounteous than all other noble lands,
> More fertile and more beautiful, art thou,
> Girt with twin seas, agleam with Apennine,
> Renown'd for armèd might and sacred law,
> Home of the Muses, rich in treasure and men.
> Nature and art, toiling alike for thee,
> Have given thee as mistress to mankind.
> Long absent, eagerly I now return,
> Never to leave thee more. Thou wilt provide
> Rest for my weariness, and a little earth
> To cover me at last. From the fair height
> Of Mount Gebenna I behold thee now,
> Oh Italy! The clouds are left behind;
> A gentle wind touches my brow; the air
> Rises to welcome me. I recognize
> My own dear land, and greet it joyously.
> Hail to thee, Mother, glory of the world!

In point of fact, this journey marks a main division between the earlier and the later halves of Petrarch's mature life, for in several respects his circumstances in the years that lay ahead of him were to be quite different from those of the years that now lay behind him.

Hitherto his life had been centered in Provence: he was never to see Provence again; and his life was to be centered in Northern Italy. He had left Provence repeatedly, and usually of his own accord, for journeys or absences of considerable length: he was to leave Northern Italy only thrice, only once of his own accord, and never for an absence of any considerable length.

The friends with whom he had been most closely associated had been Guido Sette, Socrates, Laelius, and Philippe de Cabassoles: he was never to see Guido, Socrates, or Philippe again; he was to see Laelius only twice, and then but briefly; and the friends with whom he was to be most closely associated were to be Italians whom he had come to know only recently, or had still to meet. In each of his last two stays in Provence he had visited his dearly loved brother at Montrieux: he was never to see him again.

Laura had died.

He had had both personal and epistolary relations with Pope Clement and with members of the College of Cardinals: henceforth his relations with popes and cardinals were to be epistolary only (except for talks with certain cardinals).

He had had no relations with the Emperor (except for the writing of two letters to which he had not received replies) or with members of his court: he was to have close relations with the Emperor and with certain members of his court. His only close association with a lord of a city had been that with Azzo da Correggio, with whom he had been associated in Parma twice, each time for less than a year: he was to be closely associated with the lords of Milan and of Padua for a total of about fifteen years. He had been mainly a dweller in the country: he was to be a city-dweller until the very last years of his life.

Petrarch's chief secular concern was still for freedom to study and to write. His most remarkable characteristic was still his unbounded devotion to his friends.

XX. Milan: Summer 1353 - Autumn 1354

WHEN Petrarch crossed the Alps he had still not decided where to settle in Italy. He had thought of Padua and of Mantua: he would certainly not go to Parma, or to Florence, or to Rome, or to Naples. The first city in which he made a stop after entering Italy was Milan, where he arrived, probably, in the latter part of June.

The Visconti had been firmly in control of Milan for forty years; they had extended their dominion over most of the cities of Lombardy; and they were now striving to extend it still farther and, in particular, to get possession of Pavia, Genoa, Pisa, and Bologna. They had thus incurred many local enmities and, in the case of Bologna, papal enmity as well. The Archbishop Giovanni Visconti, sole lord of Milan since the death of his brother Luchino in 1349, was now the most powerful ruler in Italy. His enemies called him a tyrant: there seems to be no evidence that he was such, but he undoubtedly sought territorial expansion. He had been at war with Florence (which, like Milan, wanted possession of Pisa), but that war had ended with the signing of a treaty of peace early in 1353. Three nephews of the Archbishop, Matteo, Galeazzo, and Bernabò (sons of the Archbishop's deceased brother Stefano), were the heirs apparent.

On his arrival in Milan Petrarch went to see the Archbishop, who invited him to settle there. Petrarch, apparently, was about to decline, on the grounds of his constant occupation, his dislike of crowds, and his need of quietness, when the Archbishop, anticipating such objections, promised him solitude and freedom within the city. When Petrarch asked what would be expected of him, the Archbishop replied, in effect, "Nothing but your presence here, which would honor us." Petrarch then accepted the invitation.

Soon afterward he sent to Nelli a letter written for his other Florentine friends as well, telling of his acceptance of the invitation given him by the Archbishop—whom he calls "the greatest of Italians"—and of the Archbishop's promise that he should have solitude and freedom. To friends in Florence and elsewhere, who regarded the Archbishop as a tyrant and an aggressor, the news of Petrarch's settlement in Milan came as a distressing shock. Nelli, himself perplexed and anxious, but willing to trust Petrarch's judgment, reported that other Florentine friends of Petrarch were bitter. Boccaccio, in July, wrote Petrarch a violently indignant letter, reminding him that when he had visited Petrarch in Padua two years before, Petrarch had assented to his depiction of the Archbishop as a tyrant. Many other protests arrived later in the year. An otherwise unknown Gano del Colle (probably a Florentine) wrote a sonnet urging Petrarch to leave tyrannous Milan, and sent it to Petrarch by a minstrel who sang it to him. Giovanni Aghinolfi, the Mantuan chancellor, wrote to the same effect, as did a friend in Avignon, probably Socrates. While such protests undoubtedly saddened him, they seem not to have caused him acute distress. In August he wrote twice to Nelli, telling him a little more about the Archbishop's invitation and the very satisfactory circumstances of his life thus far in Milan. He seems never to have answered Boccaccio's letter. In a note to be given to Gano del Colle he says that many men have written to him in a vein similar to that of Gano's sonnet, but that all to whom the reasons for his decision have been explained have changed their minds. In point of fact, while disapproval did not cease, Petrarch's settlement in Milan does not seem to have resulted in the loss of any of his friendships.

The Archbishop's promise was kept almost, though not quite, perfectly, both by the Archbishop himself and by his heirs; and Petrarch lived on in Milan for eight years, a longer time than he ever spent in continuous residence anywhere else. In accordance with his promise the Archbishop assigned to Petrarch a house at what was then the extreme western edge of the city, close to the church of Sant'Ambrogio. From the front of his house he looked out upon that church; from the rear he could see the walls of the city, beyond them a wide expanse of fields and woods, and, far beyond, the Alps.

He took great satisfaction in his nearness to the church, as being the burial place of St. Ambrose. He greatly admired an image of the saint—a twelfth-century *tondo* in colored stucco, which in Petrarch's time was set in the wall of a bay in the right aisle of the church (it is now in the new Museum of Sant'Ambrogio). In a letter written to Nelli in the course of the summer he speaks of it thus:

I often gaze reverently at his image, set high in the wall: it seems almost to be living and breathing. It is enough in itself to repay me for having come here. Words fail me to describe the authority of his countenance, the majesty of his expression, the tranquillity of his eyes: if he could only speak you would behold the living Ambrose.

His house had no garden; but he was invited or permitted to do some planting in the garden of Sant'Ambrogio.

The summer was uneventful. He had one undesired interview with an interminably loquacious old soldier, who met him, under a blazing sun, in a narrow and dusty street. The soldier said that he was going to Florence, and asked for a messsage that he might take to some friend of Petrarch's in that city. Petrarch tried to escape—the combination of the sun, the dust, the cicadas, and the soldier was unendurable—but his tormentor blocked the way with his horse. Finally Petrarch bade him give his greetings to Nelli; and with that the soldier let him go.

In August Petrarch added to his series of letters to ancient writers a letter addressed to Asinius Pollio, whom he censured because Asinius had censured Cicero.

SEPTEMBER

During the first half of September preparations were being made in Milan for the coming of Cardinal Gil Albornoz, who had been designated by Pope Innocent VI as Legate, and had been assigned the difficult task of re-establishing papal control in the States of the Church. On the 14th, as the Cardinal was approaching Milan, the Archbishop, with a considerable company of nobles and notables, rode out and met him about two miles west of the city. Petrarch was in the welcoming party and exchanged greetings with the Cardinal. Immediately afterward, however, he had a mishap that might have been fatal. Both he and his horse were blinded by the dust raised by the cavalcade, and his horse's hind legs slipped over the edge of a declivity beside the road. One of the Archbishop's nephews came to his aid, and helped him off his horse, which then managed to struggle back onto the road.

On the 19th Petrarch received from Nelli a petition that he wanted him to present to the Cardinal. On that same day he did so, and the Cardinal approved it, signed it accordingly, and gave it back to Petrarch. Either then or at some earlier moment in the

Cardinal's visit Petrarch presented also requests from other friends, and these also were approved. The Cardinal indicated his readiness to do something for Petrarch, but Petrarch made no request on his own behalf.

On one of the last days of August a Genoese fleet had been disastrously defeated by a combination of Venetian and Catalan fleets in the battle of Alghero, fought off the west coast of Sardinia; and by about the middle of September the Doge and Council of Genoa, dismayed by that disaster and by the factional strife that was rending the city, decided to offer the lordship of Genoa to the Archbishop Giovanni Visconti, and to send an embassy to Milan, to confer with Milanese officials and to make that offer. That embassy arrived, apparently, soon after Cardinal Albornoz had left.

On the day before the one on which the final session of the conference was to be held, the essential decisions having been reached, some of the Milanese conferees asked Petrarch to make the formal reply to the Genoese envoys on the morrow. Petrarch, however, declined, on the grounds that the time was too short for due preparation, and that one word from the Archbishop would mean more than anything that anyone else could say. Petrarch, however, was present at the final session, his account of which is in summary as follows:

> I had been requested to show attention to the Genoese envoys until the Archbishop should arrive, and I was glad to do so. We took our places in a great hall the walls and beams of which were sheathed in gold. I found myself seated next to the head of the Genoese embassy, who told me all about the battle and about the state of things in Genoa. After the Archbishop had come in and the formal session had begun, the head of the Genoese embassy declared officially that by order of the people of Genoa he entrusted to the Archbishop "the city, its citizens, its fields, its waters, its villages, its towns, it hopes, its resources, and its fortunes" from La Spezia on the east to Monaco on the west. The Archbishop then replied, accepting the proffered lordship, and promising guidance, protection, succor, and justice.

When the news of Genoa's submission to the Archbishop spread to northeastern Italy and to Tuscany it caused resentment and dismay: and both Venice and Florence set about the formation of leagues directed against Milan.

At about this same time a messenger brought to Petrarch a letter from Nelli that began with the words *Neophytum hunc*, "this neophyte," which evidently referred to the messenger to whom Nelli had entrusted the letter. But the messenger who gave the letter to Petrarch was not a neophyte—and Petrarch did not know what to make of the letter.

A few days later a monk whom Petrarch did not recognize came to his door, and on Petrarch's invitation came in and stayed to dinner. He talked incessantly about himself, his friends, his kinsfolk, and his acquaintances; about what all the neighbors were doing; and about dogs, wolves, and the Lion of Florence, the *gonfaloniere*, the priors, the drought, and many other things. Finally Petrarch realized that this man must be Nelli's neophyte; that, in spite of his monk's dress, he was also the old soldier to whom, early in the summer, he had given a message for Nelli; that it was to this man that Nelli had given the letter beginning *Neophytum hunc;* and that this man had for some reason or other given it to the messenger who had delivered it to Petrarch a few days before. The monk stopped talking only when he heard the city clock—a new invention—strike an hour that warned him that it was getting late. Petrarch and his servants then helped him onto his horse, and he rode away. In the letter in which Petrarch tells this story he calls the man "Bolanus," borrowing the name from one of the Satires of Horace. He was to reappear from time to time in later years, bringing letters from Nelli or from other friends.

In the summer of 1352 Petrarch had sent his son Giovanni to Verona to take possession of his canonry, and had written to Rinaldo Cavalchini and to Guglielmo da Pastrengo asking them to do what they could for the boy. For a time their reports had been distressingly unfavorable; but a better report came in the autumn of 1353, probably before the end of September. This report led Petrarch to write to his son a letter that is very moving in its combination of grief and reproach for the past, of faint yet affectionate hope and of exhortation for the future, and of anxiety for the years that would follow his own death.

On the last day of September and the first day of October Petrarch, with some help, planted spinach, beets, fennel, and parsley in the garden of Sant'Ambrogio; and noted the fact in his Palladius. By the end of September Petrarch had probably heard that Cola di Rienzo had won favor with the Pope and been released from his imprisonment.

In the latter part of October Petrarch spent at least a day or two as a guest in a castle belonging to the Visconti on the hill of San Colombano (about twenty-five miles southeast of Milan). At the top of the hill Petrarch admired the remarkable view, which ranges from Pavia in the west to Cremona in the east and from the Alps in the north to the Apennines beyond the Po in the south. The beauty and variety of this view reminded him of Vaucluse; he had recently learned that Guido Sette had spent a few days there; and he therefore, while still at the castle, wrote Guido a letter containing many memories of Vaucluse and a description of the view from the hill of San Colombano.

About the first of November, late one afternoon, a monk brought to Petrarch a copy of a book written by his brother Gherardo on Christian philosophy and the Christian law of life. He looked into it, thinking that he would read it on the next day; but he became absorbed and read it straight through—supper being postponed until after night had fallen. He was greatly pleased not only by the religious content of the book but by its excellence in learning and in style. On the 7th of November he wrote to Gherardo a long letter of thanks and appreciation. This letter was written in Monza (halfway between Milan and Lake Como): we do not know when or why he went there, or how long he stayed.

In February, 1351, in Padua, Petrarch had written his first letter to the Emperor Charles IV, urging him to re-establish the Empire in Italy, and to do so without further delay. A year later, not having received an answer to his first letter, he had written to the Emperor again, this time from Provence; but he had not received an answer to this second letter either. At last, in November, 1353, he received an answer to his first letter: that answer had in fact been written in 1351—the long delay in its delivery was probably due mainly to Petrarch's changes of residence. He must have been glad to see that his first letter had been received and thought worthy of an answer, but he must have been indignant at the specific contents of that answer. For in it the Emperor, though he does not say that he has given up the thought of returning to Italy, defends his present policy of inaction, ascribing it, mainly, to three causes: the existing desperate condition of Italy, far different from its condition in ancient times, is such, he says, as to make effective imperial action all but impossible; the difficulty of governing the Empire is extremely great—in this connection he quotes the remark "You have no idea what a monster the Empire is," attributing it to Augustus; and use of military force is a resort to be used only in extremity. (Curiously enough, there is evidence indicating that this letter was in some sense written for the Emperor by Cola di Rienzo—but there is no ground for thinking that Petrarch could have been aware of this.)

On the 23rd of November Petrarch wrote a long and able reply to the Emperor's letter, refuting its arguments one by one: times have *not* changed—ancient Rome was constantly at war and in peril; it was Tiberius, not Augustus, who called the Empire a monster—and, in any case, if it is a monster it should be tamed; and by this time all remedies except the use of the sword have been tried, and tried in vain.

Late in November a son, who was to be called Marco, was born to Bernabò Visconti and his wife, Beatrice della Scala, and was to be baptized before the end of the month. At the request of Bernabò, Petrarch served as the baby's godfather, held him at the font, and named him. He also gave him a golden cup; and to Bernabò he gave an *epistola metrica*, addressed in part to Marco and in part to Bernabò. Its most notable passages are one in which Marco's presumptive future realm is indicated by a listing of a dozen of the rivers of Lombardy, each briefly characterized, and one in which some thirty Latins named Marcus, together with St. Mark and an earlier Marco Visconti, are proposed for the eventual emulation of the new-born Marco.

DECEMBER-JANUARY

Toward the end of the year the Archbishop decided to send a mission to Avignon, to take part in a conference called to bring about peace between Genoa and Venice; and he suggested to Petrarch that he would like to have him serve as a member of the mission. Petrarch felt that he could not refuse to go, and would indeed have been glad to do anything he could toward the establishment of peace between the two rival states; but he was unhappy in the prospects of a winter journey over the Alps and of a return to Avignon, and the Archbishop's suggestion may well have seemed to him a breach of the promise of solitude and freedom on the basis of which he had settled in Milan. Fortunately for him the Archbishop, early in 1354, decided not to send the mission after all.

About the first of January Petrarch had the exciting pleasure of receiving a manuscript of Homer, in the Greek, sent to him from Constantinople, as a gift, by Nicholas Sygeros, whom he had met in Verona early in 1348. On the tenth of January he wrote to Sygeros a glowing letter of thanks. Of the Homer he says:

> Your Homer is dumb with me, or rather I am deaf to him. Yet I delight in the mere sight of him, and I often embrace him, sighing, and exclaim: "Oh thou great man, how gladly would I listen to thee!"

At the end of the letter he asks Sygeros to send him manuscripts of Hesiod and Euripides if he can.

MISSION TO VENICE

Early in the new year the Archbishop, after giving up his plan to send a mission to a conference in Avignon, decided to approach Venice directly and to send a mission there with Petrarch as its orator. Petrarch's agreement to serve was doubtless ready and hearty in this case: a mission to Venice offered him an opportunity to work for peace; it involved no difficult journey; it led to a pleasant destination; and it would enable him to become personally acquainted with the Doge, Andrea Dandolo, with whom he had had some correspondence.

The brief oration that he delivered before the Ducal Council is fortunately extant. In its introductory portion he expresses the hope that Christ may open the hearts of his hearers; appeals to their intelligence, and to the Doge's personal knowledge of his own good faith; prays that Christ may aid the cause of peace; and urges his hearers to listen open-mindedly. In the body of the oration he states that the Archbishop, acting for Genoa, has sent the mission to attain a peace that will benefit both parties, and indeed all Italy and all the world; assures his hearers that what is sought is peace only, and an honorable peace; quotes Cicero and Livy to the effect that the only justification for warfare lies in the attainment of peace; and warns that the desire to attain anything more than a just peace is perilous. In conclusion he cites the generosity shown by the Romans to the conquered Antiochus;

urges his hearers to win like fame by like generosity, and warns that unless they are indeed generous they will be thought unworthy of their victory.

Petrarch did not carry the entire responsibility for the mission: purely military matters were handled by another man.

While in Venice Petrarch had a private talk with the Doge and doubtless made or renewed acquaintance with three other Venetian officials, Marin Falier, Neri Morando, and Benintendi dei Ravagnani, who had just been made Chancellor of the Republic.

SPRING AND SUMMER

In the latter part of February there had been a short-lived rebellion in Verona, and those who were known or thought to have been implicated in it were dealt with mercilessly. Azzo da Correggio had fled. Petrarch's son, though probably not implicated, had left the city, perhaps expelled, perhaps of his own accord, and had been deprived of his canonry. It seems probable that he came soon to Milan, to find refuge with his father. In spite of Petrarch's paternal affection, Giovanni's presence must have been for him a constant source of trial and anxiety.

In March or April Petrarch received a letter from Socrates, telling him that Philippe de Cabassoles was trying to arrange to bring Petrarch back to Provence, there to be closely associated with him (Philippe).

Before the end of April Petrarch went to live for a time in the new Carthusian monastery, a gift of the Archbishop, which was located in or near the village of Garegnano, three or four miles west of the city. It chanced that the Prior was about to leave to attend a General Chapter that was to be held early in May at the Grande Chartreuse (near Grenoble); and Petrarch took advantage of the opportunity to send letters to Jean Birel, the General Prior of the Order, to his brother Gherardo, and to Philippe de Cabassoles. His deeply religious letter to Birel praises his saintliness, asks for his prayers, and mentions Gherardo as being a brother to Petrarch and a son to Birel. When Petrarch had last visited Gherardo at Montrieux, Gherardo had asked him for a copy of the *Confessions* of St. Augustine, and Petrarch had promised to send him one; and he did so, with his letter, at this time. Presumably he asked the Milanese prior to give the book and the letter to the Prior of Montrieux, who would certainly be attending the General Chapter, asking him to take them back with him to

Montrieux. The letter to Philippe expresses deep gratitude for the efforts that Philippe is making, and the hope that they may be successful. This letter, however, though it expresses Petrarch's desire to live and die in companionship with Philippe, does not reveal any dissatisfaction with the conditions under which Petrarch was living in Milan. Philippe's efforts were not successful.

The Venetian league against Milan, constituted in the previous December but long inactive, was formally renewed on the last day of April. Indecisive hostilities began in May and continued for several months.

On the 28th of May Petrarch wrote a long and altogether admirable letter to Doge Andrea Dandolo. He refers to his first letter to Dandolo, written in Padua in the spring of 1351, urging him to refrain from war with Genoa; to Dandolo's reply; to the two great naval battles that had been fought since that time; and to his own recent mission to Venice. He attributes the failure of that mission to the readiness of Venice to make war, to the persistence of her traditional hatred of Genoa, to pride in her victory in the battle of Alghero, and to the prospect of reinforcements from the North—in this connection he inveighs against the tragic folly of the use of mercenaries. He is now impelled to undertake once more the task of persuasion in which hitherto he has not been successful. The main arguments that he now adduces are these: war brings either defeat or victory, and the results of victory may be even worse than the results of defeat; war is contagious, and cannot be confined to the two rival cities; the only ones who can derive any advantage from a war between Italian states are the plundering mercenaries; continued war would ruin Italy, Venice included; arms should be used for defense against foreign enemies, and wealth should be used to advance the arts of peace.

Before the end of May, in all probability, perhaps considerably earlier, Petrarch had begun the writing of his treatise *De remediis utriusque fortune*, the longest of all his works, and the last of his major works to be begun. Its general character is indicated in the title of the English translation of Thomas Twyne (published in 1579):

> Phisicke against Fortune, aswell prosperous, as aduerse, conteyned in two Books. Whereby men are instructed, with lyke indifferencie to remedie theyr affections, aswell in tyme of the brygt shynyng sunne of prosperitie, as also of

the foule lowrying stormes of adversitie. Expedient for all men, but most necessary for such as be subiect to any notable insult of eyther extremitie.

To Petrarch himself excess of any sort seemed an evil: he sought to achieve and maintain a steady mean between extremes. In the *De remediis* his conviction in this regard is developed into a moral treatise in which he bids his readers to avoid excessive exultation when fortune is favorable and excessive depression when fortune is adverse. His treatise is divided accordingly into two Books, the first devoted to the perils of favorable fortune, and the second to those of adverse fortune. The form is that of a debate: in the first Book Joy and Hope, the children of Prosperity, debate against Reason; and in the second Book the opponents of Reason are Sorrow and Fear, the children of Adversity.

More will be said of the *De remediis* in later chapters; but something of its quality will appear in this passage, taken, in Twyne's translation, from a dialogue—probably one of the first to be written—on melancholy. *Sorowe* says: "The thinking of the present miserie, maketh me heavie." And *Reason* replies:

That the miserie of mankinde is great and manifolde, I doo not denie . . . but yf thou looke to the contrarie part, thou shalt also see many thinges, whiche make this lyfe happie and pleasant . . . haue not you great cause to reioyce? Fyrst, for that you are the image and likenesse of God your Creator, whiche is within in the soule of man, your witte, memorie, prouidence, speeche, so many inuentions, so many artes attendying uppon this soule of yours . . . also . . . so many sundrie shewes and kindes of thynges, whiche by strange and marueylous meanes doo serue to your delyght: moreouer, so great vertue in rootes, so manie iuices of hearbes, such pleasaunt varietie of so many sortes of flowres, so great concorde of smelles, and colours, and tastes, and soundes rysyng of contraries, so many lyuyng creatures in the ayre, uppon the lande, and in the sea . . . Adde herevnto moreouer, the prospect of the Hylles, the openness of the Valleys, the shadowie Wooddes, the colde Alpes, the warme Shoars . . . Adde lastly some Lakes, as bygge and brode almost as the Sea, and Pondes lying in bottomes, and Riuers fallyng downe headlong from the toppes of Hylles, with theyr brinkes full of flowres and pleasaunt hearbes . . . What shall I neede to speak of the foming Rockes that lye upon the soundyng shoare, and the moyst Dennes, and the Fieldes yellowe with Corne, and the buddyng Vineyardes, & the commodities of Cities, & the quietnesse of the Countrey, and the libertie of Wildernesses? And also the most glorious and bryght spectacle of all, whiche is the circumference of the starrie Firmament, that continually turneth about with incomprehensible swiftnesse, wherein are fastened the fixed Starres? Lykewyse the wanderyng lyghtes, whiche you call the seuen Planettes . . .

The Prior of the Milanese Certosa, returning—probably in June —from the General Chapter, brought Petrarch a letter from the Grand Prior, which, among other things, took Petrarch to task for flattery, saying that it was shameful to praise a living man directly, and asked Petrarch to undertake the completion of the unfinished treatise of Innocent III, *The Dignity of Man*. Petrarch wrote in reply that there had been no flattery in the praises contained in his previous letter; that St. Augustine and St. Jerome had praised each other while they were living; and that he was both too unworthy and too much occupied to undertake the completion of Innocent's treatise. He reported that he was at work on a treatise of his own on remedies against the effects of fortune, and apparently sent with his letter a copy of the dialogue on melancholy that he had written for that treatise.

On the first day of July Cola di Rienzo re-entered Rome as a Senator ruling in the name of the Pope.

In the course of the summer Petrarch did some work—we do not know what it was—on his *De viris illustribus*.

In the course of the summer, also, Petrarch received from Doge Andrea Dandolo a letter devoted chiefly to assertion of the justice of the Venetian cause. In August Petrarch wrote again to the Doge, who died, early in September, without having answered Petrarch's letter. Petrarch had regarded him as a personal friend, and in a letter written after he had heard of his death characterizes him as "a man of integrity, devoted to his republic, learned, eloquent, circumspect, affable, and gentle." He was succeeded by Marin Falier.

Even before coming to Milan Petrarch had enjoyed friendship with Gabrio Zamorei of Parma, who was now serving the Archbishop Giovanni Visconti as his vicar. During Petrarch's first year in Milan he must have made many new friends and acquaintances, including several men who will appear in later chapters. Some of them meant much to him; but there never developed for him in Milan any friendships comparable in their intimacy with some of those that he had formed in Provence and in Florence and was to form in Padua and in Venice.

He must have made acquaintance with the monks of Sant'Ambrogio soon after his arrival. From them he gathered some bits of Ambrosian lore; and with their permission he explored their library, where he found, among other things, a huge and ancient volume containing a treatise ascribed to St. Ambrose, which Petrarch, in the competence of his scholarship, believed to be the work of Palladius (an early eastern bishop, not the Palladius who wrote on agriculture.)

One acquaintance, whom he was before long to regard as a friend, was Sagremor de Pommiers, a Frenchman of noble birth, who was serving the Visconti as a trusted courier and, on occasion, as a diplomatic agent.

DEATH OF THE ARCHBISHOP

The Archbishop was taken ill in August, and died on the 5th of October. Petrarch was requested to deliver a commemorative oration, and did so on the 17th. His oration, preserved in an early Italian translation, praises the Archbishop for his devoutness, fervor of spirit, reverence, pity for the poor, loyalty toward all manner of men, pleasantness in manner, courtesy, cheerfulness, and kindly conversation; and bids his hearers devote themselves henceforth to the service of the Archbishop's three heirs.

Petrarch's delivery of the oration, however, was suddenly cut short by the court astrologer, as he reports in a letter written long afterward:

Having carefully cast a horoscope to determine the exact time at which it would be most auspicious that the symbols of office should be given to the three illustrious brothers, he interrupted me, who had been requested to speak on this solemn occasion, breaking into my oration and into the attention of the new *Signori* and of the audience, saying that the hour had come and that delay would be dangerous. Though I have no interest in such nonsense, I did not wish to stand out against the belief of the foolish majority, and stopped speaking before I was halfway through my oration. He hesitated, as if puzzled; said that there was still a little time left before the arrival of the auspicious moment; and began to urge me to go on. I replied, smiling, that I had finished; that there wasn't anything left after the end; and that I didn't think of any pretty fable that I could recite to the people of Milan. He became very much excited, scratching his forehead, while the listeners remained silent, some indignant and some laughing; but soon he exclaimed "The hour has come": and then an old soldier, to whom this duty had been assigned, took in his hands three straight and smooth white staves, such as are now used in palisades, and placed one in the hands of each of the three brothers, with joyous words and good wishes and happy omens.

XXI. *Milan: Autumn 1354 - Autumn 1355*

T H E three brothers who now shared the lordship of Milan followed the precedent set by their uncle in honoring Petrarch and allowing him his desired freedom.

Early in October Cola di Rienzo was killed by a Roman mob: the news of his death, reviving old distresses, must have reached Petrarch before the end of the month.

THE COMING OF THE EMPEROR

Through the autumn of 1354 and the first half of 1355 the main new element in the life of Italy was the presence of the Emperor, who had entered northeastern Italy early in October. He came to re-establish the prestige of the Empire in Italy and in particular to receive the imperial crown in Rome from a representative of the Pope. He had no intention of taking any part in Italian inter-state hostilities. About the middle of October Petrarch wrote him a brief and exuberant letter of greeting, in the course of which he expresses the hope that they may meet face to face.

Early in November the Emperor established himself in Mantua, where he remained until the end of the year.

By December one of the coldest winters ever known in Europe

had set in: no one in Italy could remember anything like it; and the intensity of the cold astonished even the Germans who had come with the Emperor.

Early in December Sagremor de Pommiers, who was evidently going back and forth between Milan and Mantua at this time, brought to Petrarch the Emperor's request that he come to Mantua; and Petrarch accordingly set out a few days later. The seventy-five-mile journey took four days: the roads were a glare of ice, on which the horses' hoofs would not hold; and the only safety lay in going through the snow. The first night was spent in a town on the Adda. Waking before daybreak, Petrarch insisted on starting out, in spite of the protests of his companions: the cold was so bitter that it could hardly be endured even in the daytime, in a closed room, and beside a fire—much less in the darkness before the dawn and amid snow and ice. Before they had gone very far a company of riders came toward them. It was still too dark to see their faces, but Petrarch recognized the voice of Sagremor, who, after going back to Mantua, had planned to return to Milan in time to accompany Petrarch throughout his journey: he did go with him all the rest of the way.

IN MANTUA

The Emperor received Petrarch with the utmost friendliness, and conversed with him at great length. They talked in Italian, since Charles had spent some years in Italy in his youth and knew Italian well. He asked Petrarch for copies of some of his writings, especially the *De viris illustribus*. Petrarch replied that it was still unfinished but that if he ever completed it he would send a copy to the Emperor if he lived nobly. He would judge him worthy to be treated in the work itself only if he should become famous not only through the splendor of the imperial name and crown but through his achievements and greatness of spirit. He gave the Emperor some of his Roman coins, using their likenesses of Roman emperors as a text for a further call to greatness. Then, at the Emperor's request, Petrarch told him the story of his life. A lively debate followed on the relative merits of the life of solitude, which Petrarch, of course, defended, and the life of action, defended by the Emperor. Petrarch said that he had written a little book on the life of solitude; the Emperor, jesting, replied that if a copy ever came into his hands he would burn it; and Petrarch, also jesting, said that he would take care that no copy of it should ever reach him. The Emperor asked Petrarch to go with him to Rome, but Petrarch declined.

While in Mantua Petrarch must have renewed acquaintance and friendship with members of the ruling Gonzaga family and with their chancellor, Giovanni Aghinolfi; he probably saw something of Neri Morando, who was accompanying the imperial suite, presumably as a Venetian representative; and he met for the first time Jan ze Středa, the imperial chancellor, with whom he had had some previous correspondence.

Before the end of December the Emperor, having received from the Visconti brothers the promise of gifts amounting to 150,000 florins, signed diplomas that named them vicars of the Emperor for their dominions.

IN MILAN AGAIN

Late in 1354 or early in 1355 Petrarch and Socrates agreed to exchange two of their canonries, Petrarch yielding his canonry at Lombez to Socrates, and Socrates yielding to Petrarch a canonry in a rural church in southern Italy. This exchange received papal approval at some time in the spring.

On the 4th of January the Emperor entered Milan, there to be crowned as King of Italy, on the 6th, with the ancient iron crown of the Kings of Lombardy, which had been brought from Monza. Petrarch must have been present at the coronation. The oration was delivered by Gabrio Zamorei.

While in Milan Charles proclaimed a truce between Milan and the Venetian League, the truce to last until the first of May, the expectation being that a treaty of peace would be signed thereafter. On the 12th Charles left Milan, beginning his southward journey. Petrarch rode with him to a point just beyond Piacenza. Charles again asked him to come to Rome, and Petrarch again declined. Charles continued his journey as far as Pisa, where he waited, into March, for the arrival of the Cardinal, Pierre Bertrand, who was to crown him in Rome.

Toward the end of January, perhaps, Petrarch received bad news from Vaucluse: on Christmas Day a band of robbers had attacked the village, carried off everything they could, and set fire to the rest. Fortunately one of the sons of Raymond Monet, foreseeing the raid, had taken the books that Petrarch had left there—about thirty in all, including his precious manuscript of Plato—up to the castle on the mountainside, which the robbers did not attack. They did set fire to Petrarch's house, but so hurriedly that it did not burn. After this news came to Petrarch he sent for his books.

In February Petrarch learned that Laelius, who was now an officer in the household of Cardinal Bertrand, was coming to Italy, and going directly to Pisa, in advance of the Cardinal, to make or to confirm certain preliminary arrangements; and in response to a request from Laelius he wrote to the Emperor a letter of commendation for him.

Cardinal Bertrand reached Pisa about the middle of March and the Emperor rode out of the city to meet him. When they met, the Cardinal's horse kicked the Emperor's—which seemed to Petrarch, when he heard of it, to be only natural in view of the rivalry between the papacy and the empire. Charles left Pisa for Rome toward the end of March; and in Rome, on the 5th of April, Cardinal Bertrand placed the imperial crown on his head. Keeping the promise he had made long before to Pope Clement VI, Charles left the city on that same day.

A letter written in March contains this description of an old man who was at this time a member of Petrarch's household:

> There is living in my house an old fellow who, though born at the very edge of the habitable world, is yet a man, with the spirit and the appearance of a man: but he is so alien to the common ways of men that when he wants to show affection he either growls like a bear or snarls like a boar. He is so rough and almost barbaric in his manners that when he would lick he bites; and it might be said of him, in the words of Plautus, that he "talks stones"—bare, hard stones with which he shakes and deafens the brain, afflicting the heavens with his awful thundering.

About the middle of April Petrarch received from Boccaccio the gift of a huge copy of the *Expositions on the Psalms* of St. Augustine, which delighted him both because it added to his store of the works of St. Augustine and because of the beauty of the manuscript (now in the Bibliothèque Nationale).

A little later Petrarch learned that Doge Marin Falier had entered into a conspiracy to make Venice an autocracy, that the conspiracy had been discovered, and that Falier had been beheaded before the entrance to the Ducal Palace.

In a letter to Guido Sette, in which he tells of Falier's crime and death, he paints this dark picture of conditions in Italy:

> . . . uprisings in Pisa and Siena, revolution in Bologna, Florence bearing no fruit, Rome weeping, Naples in dismay, the Terra di Lavoro too rightly named, Sicily seething in sulphureous hatreds, the actions of Genoa, preparations in Lombardy, the plots of the Emilia and the Marches, the sleepless efforts of Mantua, the fears of Ferrara, the miseries of Verona, barbaric incursions into Aquileia and the Trentino, and worst of all the ravages of the mercenaries that overrun all Italy.

The truce between Milan and Venice having expired on the first of May, delegates from Venice came to Milan to negotiate a treaty of peace. Among them was the Chancellor Benintendi dei Ravagnani, who spent as much time with Petrarch as he could, and copied some of Petrarch's letters to ancient writers.

Early in May the Emperor returned to Pisa, where he found himself beset by difficulties and even by dangers. Niccolò Acciaiuoli and Zanobi da Strada were with him; and it was doubtless at Niccolò's request that the Emperor, while in Pisa, crowned Zanobi as poet. This quite unwarranted performance seemed inevitably to belittle the significance of Petrarch's coronation in Rome many years before. Petrarch was doubtless unhappy about it: some of his friends were very indignant.

On the first of June the Milanese-Venetian negotiators completed work on a peace treaty which required ratification within two months. No ratification followed, however, and intermittent fighting, chiefly around Bologna, was presently resumed.

Early in June Cardinal Bertrand, on his way back from Rome to Avignon, spent two days in Milan, and came to see Petrarch, taking with him his secretary, Johannes Porta, who gives this account of the interview:

> There the Cardinal found a man who is not only the flower of Florence, whence he came, but is famous throughout the world—nay more, he is a unique and singular poet, than whom, it is believed, none greater has ever lived—namely, Master Francesco Petrarca, who long ago was solemnly crowned by the Senate and the People of Rome, where alone poets may be crowned without the presence of the

Pope or the Emperor. And he set forth to the Cardinal the qualities, privileges, and graces wherewith Italy is favored beyond other lands, and spoke to him about all the climes of the earth, and showed him great reverence and honor.

Laelius, who was probably traveling with the Cardinal, came to see Petrarch at or about the same time, bringing him, from the Emperor, greetings and a Roman coin bearing the likeness of Caesar.

News concerning the Emperor was now very bad indeed. Finding it unsafe to remain in Pisa, he had moved northward to Pietrasanta, where he stayed for about a fortnight. While there he granted the vicariate of Pavia to the Marquis of Monferrato, thereby incurring the wrath of the Visconti, who greatly desired to gain control of Pavia, which, though only some twenty miles from Milan, was not among their possessions.

Before the end of June the Emperor began his flight from Italy; and Petrarch, apparently while Charles was still on Italian soil, wrote him a bitterly reproachful letter:

> Having attained without toil or the shedding of blood all that your grandfather and so many others had attained with so much toil and so much bloodshed . . . you are abandoning it all, either ungrateful or witless, and returning to your own barbaric realm. . . . If your grandfather and your father should meet you on the Alps, what do you think they would say to you? I believe you can hear them speaking, even if they be not there: "Most nobly hast thou wrought, oh great Caesar, in thy long-delayed entrance into Italy and in thy hasty retreat! Thou bringest with thee crowns of iron and of gold and the sterile name of empire; thou may'st be called Emperor of the Romans: thou art in truth King of Bohemia and nothing more."

He goes on to say that if the Caesar brought to him by Laelius could have spoken, he might perhaps have prevented the Emperor's inglorious retreat.

At some time within the first half of 1355 Petrarch learned that Cardinal Jean de Caraman had been speaking ill of him in Avignon, disparaging his writings, and calling him a companion and friend of tyrants. Highly indignant, Petrarch wrote, in the spring or summer, an invective to which he gave a title meaning *An*

Invective against a Certain Man of High Status but of No Knowledge or Excellence. Its tone is stinging throughout: the Cardinal is held up to scorn and ridicule. Answering the charge that he is consorting with tyrants, he maintains that the young Visconti are not tyrants, and that he lives and moves in perfect freedom. Referring to them as "my young men," he says that they are as completely without tyranny as the Cardinal is without equity and justice:

> I am with them, but not subject to them; I live in their land, not in their house. There come to me from them only the comforts and the honors that they are continually giving me, as far as I will let them. It is to other men, born for such tasks, that they turn for counsel, for the conduct of public affairs, for financial administration: to me are assigned "otium et silentium et securitas et libertas." So while others seek the palace, I seek my woods and my solitudes . . . The depths of the abyss are no farther from the summit of the heavens than your senile and avaricious pride is from the graciousness and generosity of these young men. You may be sure, then, that they are not tyrants, and that I am completely free.

Early in the summer Petrarch received a letter, written in Genoa, in which a certain Giovanni da Parma, speaking both for himself and for Luchino dal Verme, a military officer already known to Petrarch, asked how one may best resist the summer heat. In his reply Petrarch treats their question as meaning "How may one best resist the onset of passion?" and he answers it by commending the virtues of a rare tree, which he describes at some length. It is tall, straight, and ever green; its shade is health-giving; its fruits are plentiful and sweet; it grows in difficult and solitary places. It had at first but four great branches, and weary shepherds were wont to gather around it. Then came an unknown celestial husbandman, who tended it with his hoe and watered it with dew; and the tree has now seven great branches—four dipping toward the earth and three pointing upward—and many lesser branches. Gentle breezes blow about it; white songbirds nest in it. The ground beneath is soft and decked with varied plants and brightly colored fragrant flowers. A fountain springs in its shade, giving rise to a gently murmuring stream that flows onward between confining banks.

In the summer, also, Petrarch received from Zanobi da Strada an *epistola metrica* in which Zanobi, mentioning his coronation, expressed his desire to follow in Petrarch's footsteps and professed his devotion to Petrarch. In the brief *epistola metrica* that constitutes his reply Petrarch congratulates Zanobi, belittles his own attainments, and welcomes Zanobi's profession of devotion. This was, as far as we know, the last *epistola metrica* that Petrarch ever wrote.

DEATH OF MATTEO VISCONTI

Late in September Matteo Visconti died, probably as a result of his excesses. The portions of Milan and of the Milanese dominions that had been assigned to him were now divided between Galeazzo and Bernabò; but there is no reason to think that the new division mattered to Petrarch. Although he continued on good terms with them both, he was more closely associated with Galeazzo, whom he came to admire sincerely.

───────────── ℰ ─────────────

XXII. *Milan: Autumn 1355 - December 1356*

EARLY in October Petrarch received from Barbato da Sulmona a long letter that served evidently to deepen his affection: they had corresponded frequently, but they had not seen each other for twelve years. Since Petrarch was just about to send his trusted factor, Matteo di Pietro, to Naples, on various personal errands, he now instructed him to find out whether Niccolò Acciaiuoli could provide him with a dwelling place, in the vicinity of Naples, in which he might live the solitary life that he so constantly desired to live. That inquiry, though it does imply that Petrarch was not finding perfect solitude in Milan, does not imply that he felt any great dissatisfaction with the conditions under which he was living there: it seems to have been prompted mainly by his desire to enjoy again companionship with Barbato, who was dearer to him than any of his Milanese friends. Nothing came of this inquiry.

In the course of the autumn Petrarch received from Giovanni da Parma a reply to his description of an imaginary tree. With this reply Giovanni sent two colored drawings on parchment, one representing the tree and the other the arena of human life; and he asked Petrarch for an explanation of the meaning of the tree. In a second letter, accordingly, Petrarch thanked Giovanni for the drawings, which he liked very much, and explained the allegory: the tree signifies virtue; the seven great branches signify the four moral and the three theological virtues; the husbandman signifies Christ; the gentle breezes signify pious thoughts and inspirations—and so on in complete detail. These two letters of Petrarch, taken together, constitute a thoroughly medieval piece of writing: he apparently thought them too old-fashioned to deserve inclusion in the collection of his letters.

When Boccaccio had come to visit Petrarch in Padua in 1351 he had brought with him, as a loan from Lapo da Castiglionchio, Lapo's volume containing certain orations of Cicero. Petrarch had been hoping ever since to get it copied, but he had not found a competent copyist: so at last, in Milan, he copied it himself. This done, he sent the volume back to Florence in the autumn of 1355, addressing it not to Lapo, whose present whereabouts he did not know, but to Nelli, who was asked to see that it reached Lapo safely.

On the 19th of November, after reading a Latin translation of the *Timaeus* of Plato in a manuscript that he owned, he wrote at the end a note to this effect: "Happy thou, and yet unhappy, who having all this knowledge of truth, hadst yet no knowledge of its Source."

Still another manuscript came to him late in the year as a gift from Boccaccio, who had recently been in Naples. In the monastery of Monte Cassino—then under the supervision of Zanobi da Strada, who had been made vicar for Angelo Acciaiuoli (who had been made Bishop of Monte Cassino)—Boccaccio had found an eleventh-century manuscript containing fragments from Cicero and portions of Varro's *De lingua latina*. He himself had made the copy that he now sent to Petrarch.

Late in December there came to Petrarch a man whom he had known in Avignon, who was on a pilgrimage to Rome. He was to go through Florence on his way; and on Christmas Day Petrarch wrote and gave to him a brief letter of introduction to Nelli. He told his visitor that he himself was planning to go to Rome in Lent and to visit Nelli on the way.

It was certainly before the end of 1355 that Petrarch acquired another Milanese friend, who came often to dine with him. Although fond of him, Petrarch does not mention his name. He was an octogenarian, a good man, and of noble birth, but not rich. He liked to argue endlessly about philosophical and religious questions, and always insisted that any disputant who took a view different from his was wrong—unless that disputant was Petrarch. When asked where he got all his knowledge and where he kept his books he tapped his forehead: books, he said, were only a beggarly support for human frailty, invented because of the deficiencies of memory. He usually tried to talk Latin, but his Latin was so full of errors and of barbarisms that it was hard to understand him.

At some time before the end of the year Petrarch received from Vaucluse the books left there which had been saved when robbers had set fire to his house. They had not suffered from the fire, but they apparently showed some signs of misfortune, for he says of them: "They seem still to be pale and trembling, and to show the troubled state of the place from which they had escaped."

EARLY 1356

The early months of the new year were filled with troubles for the Visconti brothers. Most of the members of the former Venetian League were as hostile as ever; rebellion had broken out in Bologna; and in January the Marquis of Monferrato began a campaign to win for himself the cities that the Visconti had been holding in Piedmont. In view of these troubled conditions Petrarch gave up his plan to go to Rome in Lent.

In March he sent word to Nelli that he would like to engage a Florentine woman as his housekeeper. In his reply to this message Nelli reported that he knew of a woman who, he thought, would give satisfaction: she was over forty-five, of good conduct, clean, and a very good cook. If Petrarch would let him know what the wages would be, he would try to persuade her to accept the position. As things turned out, however, she refused whatever offer was made to her.

At some time within these months the Visconti took Pandolfo Malatesta into their service as a military commander. Petrarch and Pandolfo had never met, but Pandolfo had long been a great admirer of Petrarch and they had probably exchanged sonnets before this time. Pandolfo had once sent a painter to make a portrait of Petrarch for him.

Ever since coming to Milan Petrarch had been working, at times, on the collection of his letters: by May he had nearly finished eight Books.

MISSION TO THE EMPEROR

Hard pressed by their enemies, Galeazzo and Bernabò decided, by the middle of May, to ask the Emperor to act on their behalf; and they requested Petrarch to go to the Emperor as their spokesman, and to do what he could "for the peace of Lombardy." Petrarch set out, accordingly, on or about the 20th, with Sagremor de Pommiers as his chief companion: Petrarch greatly enjoyed talking with him, chiefly about the Emperor and the affairs of the Empire.

He had expected to find the Emperor in Basel and went there first, but Charles was not there. Petrarch waited for him for a month: he enjoyed his stay in Basel, for he liked the city, was honorably entertained by the Bishop, and met friends whom he had not seen since they had been fellow students at the University of Bologna, thirty years before.

Finally he set out for Prague, more than three hundred miles away—a journey of some twenty days. Now, at least, another courier, whom Petrarch calls Martinus Theutonus, accompanied him. This was a dangerous journey, which Petrarch, writing to Sagremor long afterward, describes thus:

> Recall to the eyes of your mind, I pray you, that time when we covered many miles a day through German forests, attended by a band of armed men—footmen with their bows ready, riders with their swords drawn—doubtful even of our own guides, and in great danger from roving robbers . . . There were many of us, and that fact gave us some comfort, though it did not avert danger.

He remained in Prague for a month or so. We know nothing as to his efforts for the peace of Lombardy, but we do know that he held or won the esteem of the Emperor, of the young Empress Anna, of the Chancellor Jan ze Středa, of the Archbishop Arnost z Pardubic, and of Jan Očko, the Bishop of Olomouc. The Emperor made him a Count Palatine and a Councillor: his creation as a Count Palatine gave him certain "privileges, rights, graces, and immunities," as will appear in the next chapter. Writing to the Archbishop in the following year Petrarch has this to say:

I remember how last year, when I, a stranger unknown to you except by name, had come on a mission to the Emperor, you bound me to yourself by your looks, your spirit, your words, and your kindness. I remember how affectionately you used to say to me: "I am sorry for you, my friend, that you have had to come among barbarians." But I profess that no one could have been less barbarous or more humane than the Emperor and a number of highly placed men whom I will not list by name—highly placed and distinguished men, worthy of greater fame, as courteous and well-spoken as if they had been born in Attic Athens.

During his stay in Prague Petrarch saw something, also, of the court apothecary, Angelo of Florence, who was a man of considerable distinction and influence: he owned the first botanical garden in Germanic territory, a garden in which the Emperor was much interested.

Petrarch had returned to Milan by the end of August.

LATE 1356

At some time in 1356, and somewhat more probably after than before his mission to the Emperor, Petrarch began work on a new form—the third—of the *Canzoniere*. In the transcription involved in the making of this third form and of the later forms of the *Canzoniere* he had the help of copyists.

In a letter written to Nelli not long after his return from Prague he says that his experiences in the north have led him to appreciate Italy more than ever:

The more I go about the world the less I like it. If any part of it is lovable, that part, unless my own love deceives me, is Italy—whose supremacy all other regions would admit if they could speak, and in their silence do indeed admit—although, sad to say, the passions and jealousies of its inhabitants are corrupting the tranquillity bestowed on it by nature.

For some time in the autumn Pandolfo Malatesta was seriously ill. Petrarch went to see him every day; and Pandolfo, when recovering but still unable to walk, had his servants carry him to Petrarch's house, so that he might see Petrarch there, among his books.

At about this same time Pandolfo, not content with the portrait of Petrarch that he had had painted previously, employed another painter, who was a friend of Petrarch, to make a second portrait. Of this painter Petrarch writes thus:

> He came to my house without telling me why he had come; and while I was reading he sat down and began to draw, furtively. I realized then the trick that was being played on me; but I regretfully let him go ahead and finish his painting.

Petrarch did not like this portrait; but Pandolfo did, and regarded it as one of his dearest possessions.

In October Petrarch, at the request of Galeazzo, wrote three letters in Galeazzo's name. Two of them concerned the capture of King John of France by the English, in the battle of Maupertuis—a startling event that made a very deep impression on Petrarch; and the third was an abusive reply to an abusive summons addressed to the Visconti brothers by Markward von Randeck, acting as an Imperial Vicar.

On the 18th of October Basel, which Petrarch had visited so recently, was virtually destroyed by a violent earthquake. Petrarch was horrified by the news of this destruction, to which he refers vividly in a later letter and in two of his treatises.

In the first half of November Petrarch was working steadily on the third form of the *Canzoniere:* from marginal notations that he made on his work sheets we know of two *canzoni* and a sonnet in which he made revisions at this time.

At the end of the year, as at the beginning, things were going badly for the Visconti: the Marquis of Monferrato captured the city of Novara, and a rebellion, led by a local demagogue, broke out in Genoa.

———————— ࿔ ————————

XXIII. *Milan : January 1357 - October 1359*

1357, WINTER AND SPRING

EARLY in the year the Marquis of Monferrato, who already had the title of imperial vicar of Pavia, gained actual possession of the city, which was governed for him by the Augustinian monk Jacopo Bussolari.

In January Bernabò Visconti became convinced that Pandolfo Malatesta had been interfering in one of his amours. He became violently angry, seized Pandolfo, was barely prevented from killing him, and threw him into prison. Galeazzo intervened on his behalf; he was released and fled from Milan, going first to Prague. Sagremor de Pommiers, arriving from Prague about the end of February, brought word that Pandolfo had been doing his utmost there to injure the Visconti and would probably do likewise wherever he might go. Before Sagremor started back to Prague, the Visconti evidently instructed him to pursue Pandolfo and to try to counteract his influence.

At this same time Sagremor brought to Petrarch, from the Chancellor Jan ze Středa, his diploma as Count Palatine—a document of a considerable length, which states that the recipient of the award is entitled to all the "privileges, rights, graces, immunities and customs thereunto appertaining," and goes into detail as to the circumstances under which the recipient may exercise two particular rights, the right to appoint notaries and certain judges, and the right to legitimize persons of illegitimate birth (Petrarch was once to exercise this second right).

From the diploma there hung a gold seal that Petrarch describes thus:

> On one side is our Caesar, illustrious with diadem and sceptre, seated on a high throne, with the Roman eagle and the lion of his fatherland at his side; on the other is Rome, proud with its temples and its walls, and in the gleam of the gold the sacred image of the queen city delights the eyes. I was surprised and pleased to see . . . inscribed in golden letters, the words "Aurea Roma."

In his letter of acknowledgment to Jan ze Středa Petrarch tells of his great pleasure in receiving the diploma itself, but he does not feel that he should accept a gift of gold, and is therefore sending the gold seal back by Sagremor.

Early in April Petrarch planted in the garden of Sant'Ambrogio six laurel trees and an olive tree that he had had brought from Bergamo, and made an appropriate entry in his Palladius.

In May, probably, Petrarch received and answered a letter from Guido Sette in which Guido asked for information about Petrarch's manner of life. His answer, one of our fullest sources of information about Petrarch's customary experiences, contains this passage:

> By day and by night I read and write, relieving each task by the solace of the other. . . . I know no pleasure and no sweetness save in such toil; and I am so absorbed and immersed in it that I am not aware of any other labor or of any other peace. So my works grow under my hands, and new works are constantly pressing upon me. Yet the years are passing; and when I consider the brevity of life I am filled with dismay at the amount of the work that I have begun. How it will all end, God only knows. . . . Meanwhile I pant, keep vigil, sweat, seethe, and struggle onward; and the thicker the difficulties are the more eagerly I face them, excited and driven on by their very newness and hardness.

His health, he goes on to say, is good; he lives in a fortunate mean between poverty and riches; he enjoys the good will of Galeazzo and his associates and of the people of Milan in general. The fact that he lives at the edge of the city saves him from unwelcome interruptions; and when he goes into the city he is constantly being bowed to, and bowing in return. His meals are frugal, and his sleep is brief:

> As soon as I feel rested I get up and retreat to my library. I usually rise at midnight; and even if the nights are short, or if I have been keeping a long vigil, I am always up by dawn.

He prefers silence, except with his friends, with whom he loves to talk.

SUMMER AT GAREGNANO

In the spring of 1354 Petrarch had spent some time in the Carthusian monastery at Garegnano, and he now decided to spend the coming summer there—not in the monastery, this time, since he felt that the servants and the horses that he now required would cause too much confusion—but in a village house so near the monastery that he could go to it readily whenever he felt like doing so. In the course of the summer he doubtless went back now and then to the city, which was only three or four miles away. Of his manner of life at Garegnano, and of the villagers, he writes thus:

Life goes on for me as usual, except that here in the country I have more freedom. Time would fail me to tell how many city cares I escape here, what country pleasures I enjoy, and how the simple villagers vie with each other in bringing me fruit from their trees, flowers from the meadows, fish from the streams, ducklings from the marshes, birds from the nests, young hedgehogs from the fields, and hares and kids and shoats.

Of the monks he writes:

Whenever I so desire, I take part in the observances of this pious family as if I were one of them. The door is always open to me . . . I find solace in the conversation of these holy and simple friends of Christ—conversation neither learned nor eloquent, but humble and devout. I share their meals occasionally, their conversation often, and their affection constantly.

Early in the summer requests came to him from Benintendi dei Ravagnani and from Boccaccio. Benintendi wrote that the sons of Andrea Dandolo wanted Petrarch to write an epitaph for their father. Boccaccio wanted a copy of the *Invective contra medicum*. In July Petrarch sent a copy of the *Invective* to Boccaccio; but he did not feel like writing the epitaph, and he let Benintendi's letter lie unanswered until the end of the summer, when in response to a second letter he wrote and sent an epitaph.

A letter received in the course of the summer from Guido Sette contained an inquiry as to how Petrarch's son Giovanni was getting on. Petrarch replied that he was intelligent, perhaps even exceptionally intelligent, but that he hated books and all efforts to get him to make better use of his intelligence had been useless. Yet Petrarch still hoped that he might turn out to be a good man—and that, he says, is what really matters.

Not long after the writing of that reply, however, Petrarch's hope faded. Either because Giovanni's attitude and conduct had become worse or because of some particular wrongdoing, his presence became unendurable to Petrarch, who banished him to Avignon. There Guido and Socrates—and Nelli, then temporarily in Avignon—showed him friendliness.

At some time in the summer Petrarch must have heard exciting news about Sagremor and Pandolfo. Sagremor had followed

Pandolfo from Prague to London; and there he had presented himself to Edward III as a defender of the honor of the Visconti, and had challenged Pandolfo to single combat. Pandolfo, however, had not responded to the challenge, and King Edward had signed a formal document setting forth the circumstances of the case. In the course of the summer or autumn Pandolfo returned to Italy, and went to Venice, where he was honorably received.

Early in September Petrarch left Garegnano.

Before settling down again in Milan Petrarch spent at least a day or two at Pagazzano, a village about twenty miles east of Milan, on the eastern side of the river Adda. Bernabò Visconti had a castle there; and it was presumably in that castle that Petrarch stayed while at Pagazzano—on this first occasion and in later years.

A letter written by Nelli in Avignon and received by Petrarch early in the autumn opens with a diatribe, quite in Petrarch's own vein, against conditions there, and then reports that he has seen Petrarch's friends, Guido Sette, Laelius, Socrates, and Stefano Colonna, Provost of Saint-Omer; that he has visited Vaucluse; and that Petrarch's son Giovanni comes to see him often, and that he (Nelli) has enjoyed talking with him and finds him modest and well-behaved.

To this letter Petrarch wrote a reply that is so bitter in its portrayal of Avignon that he thought it wiser not to send it, since it might have gone astray:

Now you see with your own eyes and feel with your own hands what this new Babylon really is—boiling, seething, obscene, terrible . . . Whatever perfidy and fraud, whatever cruelty and arrogance, whatever shamelessness and unbridled lust you have heard of or read of, whatever impiety and immorality the whole world holds or has ever held—all this you may see heaped up there.

During the autumn and early winter Petrarch did much writing, turning now to one work and now to another. In September he was recopying and revising one of the *capitoli* of the first *Triumph;* in October or later he added to his Twelfth Eclogue a passage written after he had heard that the captive King John of France had been taken to England, and thereafter he completed a copy of the *Bucolicum carmen*. In November he was at work on the third form of the *Canzoniere*, a copy of which he was planning to send to Azzo da Correggio; in the course of the year he had made at least one long interpolation (about the Basel earthquake) in his *De otio religioso;* and by the end of the year his collection of his letters had reached its tenth Book. At some time in 1357, having revised the dedicatory poem, addressed to Barbato da Sulmona, for the collection of his *epistolae metricae*, and finding that a man whom he knew was about to leave for Southern Italy, he gave him a copy of the poem to take to Barbato. There is no evidence that Petrarch ever did any further work on the collection of the *metricae*.

EARLY 1358

About the first of the year Petrarch received from Avignon a letter written by three of his friends, probably Socrates, Laelius, and the Provost Stefano Colonna, who used three different pens and three different colors of ink. Petrarch's cordial reply was written, he says, before dawn, by the light of a dying lamp, while he was weighed down with work, sleepy, cold, and coughing, and had at hand only poor paper and a poor pen.

Petrarch's octogenarian friend was now dining with him almost regularly. One day he said to Petrarch sadly: "I am eighty-five today; how much longer do you think I have to live? Perhaps I might have twenty-five years more—that's only a short time." Petrarch replied, smiling: "Don't be troubled: you will round out thirty years." He replied, more cheerfully: "Good, that's enough." Three days later he died; and on the next day— Petrarch being present, with tears in his eyes—he was buried in Sant'Ambrogio, in the tomb of his fathers.

Early in the year Petrarch's Milanese friend Giovannolo da Mandello and some other men were planning to go on a pilgrimage to the Holy Land; and Giovannolo wanted Petrarch to go with them. He refused, however, being unwilling to undergo again the dangers and the hardships of travel by sea—in particular, he dreaded seasickness. Giovannolo then asked him to write a guidebook for the journey; and this he did.

The little book is commonly referred to as the *Itinerarium syriacum*. Petrarch's directions and descriptions—based, for the west coast of Italy, on his own voyages—begin with an account of Genoa and its southern *riviera*. He follows the coast southward, mentioning the mouths of the Arno and the Tiber and the islands (among them Caprera and Elba) that lie to the right, as far as the bay of Naples, which he describes in enthusiastic detail, referring to the many places of interest that he himself had visited there. In Naples, he says, you must not fail to see Giotto's frescoes in the Royal Chapel. His directions and descriptions for the rest of the journey are drawn from literary and Biblical sources, and from maps—in which he was greatly interested.

In March Sagremor de Pommiers brought the gold seal back from Prague, together with a letter from Jan ze Středa. This time Petrarch kept the seal, not because it was of gold, but as a symbol of the Chancellor's golden good will.

On or as of the 6th of April—the thirty-first anniversary of his enamorment, and the tenth anniversary of the death of Laura, Petrarch wrote the last of his anniversary poems, a sonnet beginning *Tennemi Amor anni ventuno ardendo*. In April, also, he was revising one of the first *capitoli* of the *Triumphs*.

In the course of the spring a letter came from Nelli expressing his detestation of Avignon and his dependence on Petrarch's friendship, and closing with this defense of Petrarch's son:

> Do not insist, I beg of you, that even in his youth he should be an old man; do not, I pray you, let your ears be open to every breath of air that is adverse to him. Unless I am mistaken, the stars will show him, if destiny permits, to be almost what you would have him be; and as he here responds constantly to my affection, so I commend him to your leniency.

Some of the several letters that Petrarch received at this time from friends in Avignon were brought to him by the monk-messenger whom he calls Bolanus.

In May Petrarch received from the Empress Anna a letter—brought, doubtless, by Sagremor—in which she announced the birth of her first child, a daughter. Petrarch replied in a long letter of congratulation, which is in effect a little treatise on famous women, celebrating many classic heroines and the Countess Matilda of Tuscany.

SUMMER

In June a treaty of peace between the Visconti and their enemies was signed in Milan in the presence of a representative of the

Emperor. By one of the clauses of this treaty Novara, which had been held for about two years by the Marquis of Monferrato, was restored to the Visconti. Galeazzo, desiring to do everything he could to secure the loyalty of the people of the city, decided to make an impressive entrance into the city, with the Emperor's representative, but without any show of force, and to have Petrarch serve as the orator of the occasion.

An assemblage of the people was convoked in the great cloister of the cathedral; and to that assemblage Petrarch delivered his very impressive oration. It opens with a text from the Psalms, reviews the recent vicissitudes of the city, exempts its people from any blame for their tolerance of the usurpation of the Marquis of Monferrato, assures them of Galeazzo's affection, bids them lay aside all fear, and closes with a prayer that God may illumine both Galeazzo and the people of Novara.

In July Petrarch finished copying and annotating a manuscript of Terence.

In July, also, Petrarch learned, with extreme distress, that two of his dearest friends, Socrates and Laelius, who had been dear friends to each other, had had a falling-out, and that their friendship had broken down. A few years earlier, when two other friends of Petrarch, Niccolò Acciaiuoli and Giovanni Barrili, had had a similar falling-out, Petrarch, by wise and energetic epistolary action, had healed the breach. He could do no less than his utmost to heal this new breach, which had resulted from Laelius' belief that Socrates had turned against him and had spoken ill of him in a letter to Petrarch. So Petrarch now wrote to Laelius, weeping as he wrote, denying that Socrates had ever spoken ill of him. This letter of Petrarch, a fine combination of reasoning, reproach, affection, and adjuration, culminates in this passage:

> For my sake and for your own sake I beg you to relieve me speedily of this distress, which weighs me down and burns me and twists me and tortures me; and if you love me, or have ever loved me, then I beg you, before this letter leaves your hands, to seek out Socrates—who is astounded by the change that has come over you and is sorely vexed by his own ill fortune—or else to bid him come to you.

This letter, like the letters Petrarch had written six years before, brought about the restoration of the broken friendship.

In September Petrarch went again to Pagazzano; and while there he engaged in some further revision of the first *Triumph*.

After returning to Milan, he learned that Zanobi da Strada had left Naples and had gone to Avignon to take a secretarial position in the papal chancery, and that he was studying a collection of model letters made for the guidance of chancery secretaries. Petrarch thereupon wrote to Zanobi very indignantly, reproaching him for going to Avignon and abandoning his literary pursuits to waste his time in an occupation that was not fit for a man of letters. Eventually Zanobi won promotion to a papal secretaryship.

Before the end of the year Petrarch finished the third form of the *Canzoniere*, which contained about 140 poems in the first of its two parts and about thirty in its second part; did some further work on the first *Triumph;* made additional revisions in his *Bucolicum carmen*, although he had supposedly finished it previously; and made some revisions in the *Secretum*.

WINTER

The winter of 1358–59 was extremely severe. In a letter written early in 1359 Petrarch says:

> The weather, wild beyond anything known hitherto, has made this year one long to be remembered. Never within the memory of man has such a mass of snow fallen between the Alps and the Apennines. Many houses have collapsed in the cities, and many trees have been blown down in the country. . . . Four years ago, at the end of 1354 and the beginning of the following year, it seemed that nothing could be colder, or, so to speak, more utterly wintry . . . but this present year has equaled that year in cold and surpassed it in snowfall.

Petrarch spent most of the winter in Padua and in Venice—in Padua, he says, for business affairs (presumably related to his canonry) and in Venice for a rest. While in Padua he looked at a manuscript of Homer that was being offered for sale, but he judged it to be inferior to the manuscript that had been given to him by Nicholas Sygeros, and did not buy it. In Padua, also, Petrarch met for the first time Leontius Pilatus, a Calabrian whom Petrarch supposed to be a Greek and a native of Byzantium. Leontius was a very disagreeable person; but his presence in northern Italy seemed to open an entrance into acquaintance with Homer, and Petrarch established relations with him on a friendly basis.

FEBRUARY 1359

Early in February Petrarch returned to Milan, worn out by the cold and the winds that had beset his journey. Among the many letters that were waiting for him was one from Laelius, who reported that as soon as he had received Petrarch's last pleading letter he had hastened to Socrates and they had embraced with deep emotion. He reported also that since the death of the papal secretary Francesco Calvo some of Petrarch's friends in Avignon had been hoping that Petrarch might be appointed in his place, and had been making some efforts to that end. He asked whether it would be all right for him to press such efforts.

To this letter Petrarch replied immediately, under difficult conditions: his fingers were numb, his ink was freezing, his pen was stiff, and his paper was rough. He expresses his happiness for the restoration of the friendship that had been broken; and he protests violently that he would not think for a moment of accepting a papal secretaryship—or even, under present conditions, a cardinalate—and requests that Laelius and his other Avignonese friends desist once and for all from seeking for him a position that he would certainly refuse if it were offered to him. His letter is notable also for its outspoken anti-Aristotelianism.

MARCH AND APRIL

In mid-March Petrarch had the pleasure of welcoming Boccaccio for a visit that was to last nearly a month. On the day on which Boccaccio arrived Petrarch was again planting laurel trees, and Boccaccio stood with him while he did so, as Petrarch's entry in his Palladius records.

We know of four matters that the two men discussed during this visit: Petrarch's continued residence in Milan, his unwillingness to release the *Africa*, the poetic merits of Dante, and the presence of Leontius Pilatus in Italy. They finally agreed that Milan gave Petrarch a better opportunity for the pursuit of his main interests than he could find elsewhere, and that there was indeed no other place in which he could live conveniently, with the single exception of Padua. He was adamant in his refusal to release the *Africa*, a refusal that he supported by many arguments.

Boccaccio evidently had much to say in praise of Dante and gained the impression—which was soon to be corrected—that Petrarch did not entirely welcome such praise. It was doubtless Petrarch's report of his meeting with Leontius in Padua that led to the formation of the plan that Leontius should be called to Florence to lecture in the university and to translate the *Iliad* and the *Odyssey*.

When the time came for Boccaccio to leave, the weather was very bad, there was a threat of floods, and Petrarch, much concerned for Boccaccio's health, did everything he could to detain him; but he started out nevertheless, taking with him copies of the *Bucolicum carmen* and of other writings of Petrarch that he had made during his visit.

MAY AND JUNE

A letter from Boccaccio received early in May brought to Petrarch the welcome news that he had reached Florence safely. In this same letter Boccaccio excused himself at some length for having said so much while in Milan in praise of Dante, pointing out, however, that since his esteem for Petrarch was higher than his esteem for Dante, his praise of Dante implied still higher praise of Petrarch. He said also that Dante had been an inspiration to him in his youth, and sent with the letter a revised form of an *epistola metrica* in praise of Dante of which he had previously sent an earlier form to Petrarch, to whom the *epistola* was addressed.

From this letter Petrarch gained the impression that Boccaccio thought that he was jealous of Dante's fame. He therefore set about the writing of a long reply. He denies vehemently that he is jealous of Dante; praises him highly, especially for his persistence in literary pursuits even under the hard conditions of exile; lauds Boccaccio for praising him; assigns Dante pre-eminence in Italian poetry; and says that while he himself in his youth, when he was writing in Italian, had preferred not to have a copy of the *Commedia*, his only reason had been his desire to avoid imitation, and that he is now glad to own a copy. In this same letter Petrarch refers to the fact that in his boyhood he had once seen Dante; and speaks very gratefully and in some detail of Boccaccio's hospitality to him when he had passed through Florence on his Roman pilgrimage.

At some time in the summer Petrarch received from Giovanni, who was still in banishment in Avignon, a letter in which Giovanni asked his father to let him come home. Petrarch replied at length, referring to the wrong attitudes and the wrongdoings that had led to banishment, blaming himself for having been too lenient, begging Giovanni to repent and to mend his ways, for his soul's sake, and saying that he may return when, considering himself in the light of this letter, he is sure that he is fit to return.

Since the volume containing the copy of the letters of Cicero that Petrarch had made for himself in Verona was very large and he wanted it always at hand, he kept it standing on the floor just by the door of his library. One day, as he came into the room, the edge of his gown caught the volume and it fell against him, bruising his left leg just above the ankle. He thought nothing of it, and put the volume back in its place, exclaiming only "Why, my dear Cicero, should you hurt me?" But the same thing happened on the following day, and at least twice thereafter. He then put the volume in a safer place, but the harm to his leg was done: the skin was broken and an infection had set in. At first he paid no attention to it, bathing and walking and riding as usual. The leg gradually swelled, however; the flesh was badly discolored; the bruised place developed a poisonous tumor; and the pain became so severe that he could not sleep. Then at last he called in doctors, who visited him repeatedly: their treatment was very painful, and they told him that the injury to his leg might be permanent. He did not believe them; but he submitted to frequent fomentations, refrained from eating his usual foods, went onto a soft diet, and kept quiet—much to his disgust. By the middle of October he was able to report that he was recovering.

OCTOBER

Early in October Petrarch left Milan to spend a few days at Pagazzano; and while there—rain and the unseasonable weather giving him quiet working days—he did some further revising of the *Bucolicum carmen*. Pagazzano was within about ten miles of Bergamo; and in Bergamo there dwelt one of the most devoted of Petrarch's friends and admirers, the goldsmith Enrico Capra. His attitude toward Petrarch had become that of a worshipper: he had filled his house with mementos and pictures of

Petrarch, and he cherished copies of many of Petrarch's writings. Moreover, despite his already advanced age, he had given up his goldsmithery and was devoting himself to study, frequenting the *gimnasium* of Bergamo. He had repeatedly begged Petrarch to honor him with a visit; and now Petrarch agreed to come. On the afternoon of the 11th of October, accordingly, he set out, escorted by Capra and accompanied by certain gentlemen who came along out of curiosity. At the gate of the city they were received by a large throng, including the governor of the province, city officials, and many friends. Petrarch was invited to stay in the city palace or in a noble home and Capra was very much afraid that he would accept one of these invitations; but he, keeping faith, dismounted at the door of Capra's house. There great preparations had been made. The dinner was fit for a king; the room in which Petrarch was to sleep was elaborately decorated; the richly covered bed, Capra swore, had never been slept in and would never be slept in by anyone else; and books appropriate for a lover of letters were abundant. Petrarch left Bergamo on the following afternoon, accompanied for a considerable distance by the governor and many others, and all the way by Capra. He reached Pagazzano as night was coming on.

The situation in Pavia had now become desperate. The city was threatened with starvation, and Bussolari ordered the expulsion of all old men, children, and women, as well as all who were not able-bodied and all the needy who could not share in the defense of the city. He ordered also that all dogs in the city should be killed. This second order, in particular, roused the wrath of Bernabò Visconti, who was a great hunter and very fond of dogs. At his request Petrarch wrote to Bussolari a scathing letter, in which he first condemns Bussolari for the wicked inhumanity of his expulsion, saying that the expulsion of Christ's poor—by one who had taken upon himself the vow of poverty—was in reality the expulsion of Christ. Then, concentrating on the order for the killing of the dogs, he ends thus:

> Not as an enemy but as a man, we ask you that before you kill all your dogs you send some of them to us, whom they will serve well. This they would themselves ask, if they could speak; and if die they must, they would rather die by the teeth of boars than by starvation or the sword.

For some time now Petrarch had been having serious trouble with his servants, who had been taking advantage of his carelessness about his belongings to steal shamelessly, leaving him little but his body and his books. Finally, on one occasion they quarreled in his presence over their spoils, menacing each other with their knives, despite his threats and his entreaties. This was too much; and he discharged them forthwith. This done, he found himself obliged to change his residence, since the house by Sant'Ambrogio was not only remote but was so large that without protection it would have been dangerously lonely. He decided, accordingly, to move to a small house close to the Benedictine monastery of San Simpliciano, just outside the city wall near the Como gate. He chose this location because his love of freedom, solitude, and quiet impelled him to get away from the city.

———————— *¿* ————————

XXIV. *Milan : November 1359 - Summer 1361*

LATE 1359

E ARLY in November Petrarch moved to his new house, which he liked very much. Directly in front of it stretched a delightful solitary region through which an unfrequented grassy path wound in and out through sun and shade in such a way, he says, that if he were not still within sight and sound of the city he would think himself in the midst of a forest.

In a letter written to Nelli in mid-November he gives an extensive account of the ways in which he is controlling and spending his time. He allows six hours for sleep and two for inevitable occupations, and claims the other sixteen as his own. He particularly grudges time spent in sleep, from which his thoughts often wake him, sometimes to the discomfort of the servant who (presumably because of Petrarch's fear of syncope) sleeps in the same room. He spends all possible time in study and composition. Like Augustus, while he is being shaved or having his hair cut, he reads or listens to readers or dictates to scribes. When he is in the country and has no guests pen and paper are always beside his bed, and sometimes, waking, he jots down in the darkness some idea that he fears may escape him if he does not make a note of it at once. When daylight comes, he often finds it hard to read what he had written. His enthusiasm for his studies is greater than ever:

> Through them I am set free from grave cares, I forget the miseries of these times, I am well content and glad to be alive, and I am hardly aware of ordinary human troubles. Let whoso will delight in riches and pleasures and honors: my studies are my riches, my honors, and my pleasures.

At one point in the campaign against Pavia, when all preparations for an assault had been made, the astrologers, in particular the astrologer who had broken into Petrarch's commemorative oration for the Archbishop Giovanni Visconti, announced that the assault must be postponed until the arrival of "the fatal hour." When that hour came the order for the assault was about to be given: but just then—after a drought of many months—the heavens opened, and the rain continued for so many days that the encampment of the besiegers was flooded, and early assault was impossible.

Petrarch, afterward, asked his astrologer-friend how it happened that he had not foreseen the disastrous rain. He replied that it was very difficult to predict weather.

Pavia finally surrendered, however, in mid-November.

Work on a fourth form of the *Canzoniere* (known as the Chigi form, since it is preserved in a manuscript, now in the Vatican Library, that once belonged to the Chigi family) seems to have begun in 1359: it continued for three or four years.

EARLY 1360

On the late afternoon of a day in January, in the midst of a deluge of rain, the old-soldier-monk-letter-carrier whom Petrarch calls Bolanus appeared at Petrarch's door, bringing several companions and a letter from Socrates. In view of the rain and the lateness of the hour, Petrarch felt that he had to ask them all to spend the night, though his house could hardly have held them. Bolanus would have accepted; but one of his companions had more sense, and the invitation, though repeated, was declined, much to Petrarch's relief.

They had just left and darkness was falling when a very different visitor, Laelius, appeared, having just arrived from Avignon, and with him came Petrarch's son Giovanni. Giovanni had good sponsorship: not only had he come with Laelius, but the letter that Bolanus had brought contained an inquiry as to what Giovanni's reception was to be. But Petrarch had suffered too long and had been too gravely hurt to pardon readily. His interview with his son was evidently one of the most painful and difficult experiences of his life. Giovanni's tearful entreaty for pardon so moved him that he too almost wept, and almost felt himself to be rather a defendant and a suppliant than an offended party. Yet he could not alter his exceedingly severe judgment of his son's character; he could not forget his son's wrong attitudes and wrongdoings; he still held to the opinion that his own leniency had encouraged Giovanni's persistence in his bad conduct; and he had no confidence in the genuineness of his son's tears, endearments, or entreaties. Nevertheless, he could not continue to resist, and at last the promise of pardon was wrung from him.

SPRING

In mid-April Petrarch went again to Padua and Venice. He was back in Milan by the second week in August: probably he had returned much earlier.

Before the end of May word must have reached Milan that on the 8th there had been signed at Bretigny a treaty between England and France, according to the provisions of which King John might re-enter Paris on payment by France of 600,000 écus, as the first instalment of a much larger total.

During the months following his visit to Petrarch in the spring of 1359, Boccaccio had been working on the plan, presumably formed during that visit, that Leontius should be brought to Florence; and by the end of the spring of 1360 Leontius was there. He was living with Boccaccio, and arrangements for his teaching had been made, or were in the making. Boccaccio undoubtedly kept Petrarch informed of the progress of his endeavors.

SUMMER

The sore in Petrarch's leg caused by repeated blows from his Cicero had not healed; and by summer he was in a really serious condition, which however he finally overcame. In a letter written in August he tells the story thus:

> For almost a year things had been getting worse and worse, and my aging days were filled with discomforts and

pains and doctors and fomentations. Finally, when it had come to be more than an annoyance, and I was getting to be sick of life, I decided to dispense with doctors, whatever the result might be, and to trust myself to the care of God and of nature rather than to these unguentaries, who were harming me by their experiments. So I dismissed them; and thanks to God and to a servant of mine—who has learned how to be a doctor from my ulcer and at my expense—now, by remembering the fomentations that had seemed to be most beneficial, and by helping nature by eating lightly, I am gradually regaining the health that I had all but lost.

But the scar, he says, will remain.

In a letter written, also in August, to Philippe de Cabassoles he expresses his longing to see Philippe again, and continues:

And perhaps God will grant this cherished desire of mine before I die, and I shall be there when you least expect me! Oh if I might suddenly appear before you among my books, or on the grassy bank of the pure stream, or at the base of the high cliff whence our king of rivers rushes forth with so loud a sound!

About the middle of August Niccolò Acciaiuoli, returning from Avignon to Naples, stopped in Milan to see the Visconti—the whole city, Petrarch says, rejoiced in his presence—and to see Petrarch. Busy though Niccolò was with affairs of state, he twice came all the way out to Petrarch's house at San Simpliciano, attended by noble companions and surrounded by an admiring crowd. He stayed for a long time, and talked with Petrarch about many things and men, including almost certainly the career of Zanobi da Strada, whose patron Niccolò had been, and probably the question of the restoration of Petrarch's Florentine patrimony.

SEPTEMBER

Early in September Petrarch was again working on the first *capitolo* of the first *Triumph*.

A letter written to Nelli in this same month records a change in Petrarch's estimation of the relative values of secular and sacred writings. Even Apollo and the Muses, he says, will approve his passing to interests that are more mature than those of his youth. Then he had been eager to win the praises of men: the praises that concern him now are the lauds of his Creator, for the recitation of which he rises at midnight. His chosen orators are now Ambrose, Augustine, Jerome, and Gregory; his philosopher is Paul; his poet is David. Yet he is not renouncing the Roman ancients he has loved so dearly: he can love both groups, turning to one group as models of style and to the other group for good counsel. The Roman ancients ask of him only that he should not forget them, and he will not do that. They do indeed offer much that is useful for right living; but he will now seek counsel rather from authors whose faith and doctrine are beyond any suspicion of error. Chief among them, for Petrarch, will be David, whose Psalms he desires to have in his hands by day, under his head at night, and in the hour of his death.

OCTOBER

About the first of October Petrarch received a very long and very remarkable letter addressed to him, ostensibly, by Homer, and actually written, in all probability, by Pietro da Muglio, professor of letters in the University of Bologna. In this letter "Homer" told of the men from whom he had learned his art; of the origin of poetry and of the earliest poets; of the variations in opinion as to his birthplace; of his travels; of the total number of his writings; and of the circumstances of his death. He then said that he had interrupted his Elysian peace in order to present certain complaints: he had suffered from imitators, ingrates, and ignorant detractors; Virgil had not deigned to mention him; his name, glorified by the jurists and physicians of his day, was despised by their modern successors; a common friend had taken him to Florence, where he felt himself to be a stranger and an exile; and he sighed for Bologna. Finally, he asked for refuge with Petrarch.

To this letter, Petrarch replied, early in October, with a letter addressed to Homer. Most of this reply is devoted to Homer's complaints, which are discussed one by one and shown to be unwarranted. Imitators, ingrates, and detractors are common pests, to be endured patiently—imitation, in particular, is an inevitable consequence of high achievement; Virgil would undoubtedly have mentioned him at the most honorific point in his poem, namely at the very end, if only he had lived to finish it; the scorn of modern jurists and physicians is in reality a proof of excellence; that a common friend should have taken him to Florence is due to that friend's love and devotion. Petrarch himself, he says, is not worthy to receive so noble a guest, yet he has cherished him in Greek, and, as far as he could, in Latin, and hopes soon to receive him completely in the translation of their common friend. The letter ends thus: "Farewell forever; and when thou returnest to thine own place, give my greetings to Orpheus and Linus and Euripides and to thine other companions."

An Anglo-French treaty, signed in May, had provided that King John might be set free on receipt of the first instalment of an immense ransom. Since France could not furnish the entire amount of that first instalment, Galeazzo Visconti came to the rescue, stipulating in return that the eleven-year-old princess Isabelle should marry Galeazzo's eight-year-old son, Gian Galeazzo. The marriage, celebrated in Milan in mid-October, was made the occasion for a series of splendid entertainments: ambassadors and other notable persons from other cities were among the guests. Petrarch doubtless witnessed some of the festivities.

The plague was now threatening Milan; and Albertino da Cannobio, a physician-friend of Petrarch, urged him to come to Cannobio (on the west shore of Lago Maggiore), promising to watch over him constantly. Replying to this invitation, Petrarch says that he would be most happy to visit Albertino as a friend, though not as a physician—but that circumstances will prevent his coming. He is not disposed to flee Milan because of any fear of the plague: he grants that medical care may conserve health and cure minor illnesses, but is sure that it could not suffice to save one from the plague. Nor does the thought of death dismay him:

To face death cheerfully is a sign of a deep-seated felicity; to face it in fear is a base weakness. To stand unterrified amid the terrible things that one beholds, and to contemplate death with unfaltering eyes, is to hold to the ideal mean and is indeed the part of a true man.

By November Petrarch had finished at least a first draft of the *De remediis utriusque fortune,* to which he refers thus in a letter written at this time to Guido Sette:

> All philosophers, all experience, and truth itself agree in this: that in times of adversity . . . the one remedy is patience . . . and that in times of prosperity the one remedy is moderation. I have had it in mind, of late, to write at some length about both these remedies, and now I have done so.

It was probably at about this same time that Petrarch wrote, as a preface to the *De remediis,* a noble letter dedicating it to his dear friend Azzo da Correggio, who had in himself experienced amazing vicissitudes of fortune and misfortune. He had known health and strength, and grievous illness and lasting frailty; he had known triumphant lordship and miserable exile; he had known happy family life, and for a time he had known that his wife and his children were held in prison by a deadly enemy. In Petrarch's prefatory discussion of the double perils of fortune he maintains—this time on the basis of his personal observations rather than on the basis of his study of the ancients—that favorable fortune is more dangerous to man than adverse fortune. His purpose in writing this treatise has not been to win praise or fame, but to be useful to those who may read what he has written.

MISSION TO PARIS

Knowing evidently that King John would soon be returning to Paris, Galeazzo Visconti decided, before the end of the year, to send a congratulatory mission to Paris, with Petrarch as its orator. Petrarch probably started from Milan late in December. He was accompanied by five men—four military officers and a civilian jurist. They took with them, as gifts from Galeazzo to the King, two rings: one that had been torn from the King's hand at the battle of Maupertuis and had eventually been recovered by Galeazzo, and a fine ruby ring of Galeazzo's own.

As Petrarch traveled through France he was shocked by the deplorable state of the country. He writes:

> It was hard to believe that this was the same realm that I had once beheld, such were now the solitude, the gloom,

and the desolation on every hand, so rough and untilled were the fields, so shattered and deserted were the dwellings—save those that had been protected by the walls of cities or of fortresses—so visible everywhere were the sad traces of the English invasion and the fresh and ugly scars of combat . . . Paris itself, the capital, defaced up to its very gates by fire and ruin, seemed to be shuddering in dismay at the fate that had befallen it.

His memories of France and Paris as he had seen them in his youth and as he saw them now are contrasted:

I recognized hardly anything, seeing a once opulent kingdom turned to ashes . . . Where now is that Paris that was once so great? Where are the throngs of students? Where is the fervid life of the University? Where the wealth of the citizens? Where the general happiness? One hears now not the voices of disputation but the din of warfare; one sees piles not of books but of weapons; the sounds of syllogisms and of lectures have given way to those of soldiers on guard and of battering rams. The rushing clamor of the hunt is no more: the woods are silent and the walls resound . . . nowhere is there such absence of security, nowhere are there so many perils.

While in Paris he evidently saw much of Pierre Bersuire, whom he had known well twenty years before in Avignon.

On the 13th of January he delivered his oration in the royal palace in the presence of the King, Prince Charles, many courtiers, and his five companions. The oration had been prepared with great thoughtfulness and skill, presumably before he left Milan. As text, he took from II Chronicles, 33:13 the words referring to the return of King Manasseh from captivity in Babylon—"and he . . . heard his supplication, and brought him again into his kingdom." In an introductory passage Petrarch excuses himself for speaking in Latin rather than in French, which, he says, he does not speak. And he knows that the King in his youth was an eager student of Latin.

In the first of the three main parts of the oration Petrarch states that many different opinions have been expressed as to the reality and the nature of Fortune, and speaks of the prayers that had been offered for the liberation of the King and would now be offered for his health and freedom, and for the freedom of the

French nation. While he was speaking of Fortune he noticed that the King and the Prince were listening intently, and were evidently very much interested. The second part of the oration is devoted mainly to Biblical quotations expressing joy after a return from captivity. In the third part the amazing reversal of fate manifested in the captivity and the restoration is taken to be a sign of the overlordship of the King of Heaven; and the experience of King John is represented as part of a celestial plan for the benefit of the King himself and of his realm. As he ceased speaking, the two rings were presented to the King, perhaps by Petrarch himself, perhaps by one of his companions.

The Prince, in particular, had been greatly interested in what Petrarch had said about Fortune, and wanted to hear more from him on that theme. Late in the evening before a day on which Petrarch and his companions and other guests, including Bersuire, were to dine at the royal table, an unnamed friend came to Petrarch and told him that the Prince was contriving that at the end of the dinner Bersuire and three learned friends of his should get Petrarch to say what he really thought about Fortune. Petrarch, therefore, though he had no desire to speak on this subject, and though he had much to do and had no books at hand, put his ideas together as best he could, expecting to say that he thought Fortune to be a vain and empty name, although he was wont to use the name in accordance with popular custom, and yet to be so careful in what he said as not to give offense to those who might believe Fortune to be an actual goddess, controlling human affairs.

At dinner on the next day, however, the King was so busily engaged in dispensing hospitality that the time when Petrarch might have been called on went by, although the Prince tried repeatedly by words and nods to remind the King of the plan that had been made—so that Petrarch did not have to speak after all.

Later, on that same day, Bersuire and his three friends came to Petrarch's room; and there they talked pleasantly, into the evening, of Fortune and of many other things.

When Petrarch was about to start back to Milan the King did his best to detain him, not only entreating him to stay but almost laying hands on him; and letters followed him, urging the Visconti—vainly—to send him back to Paris.

The journey, over the icy Alps, was very hard, and the inns

at which he stopped were unpleasant and uncomfortable. Thinking often of Bersuire, Petrarch, during one or more of his stops,
wrote him a long letter that is concerned in part with Fortune
but more specifically with the disastrous deterioration of military
discipline since the days of ancient Rome. He did not send the
letter, however, for lack of a messenger.

MARCH–JUNE

On his return to Milan, or very soon afterward, Petrarch received a letter from the Emperor enclosing copies of two documents that purported to be privileges granted by Caesar and by
Nero. Duke Rudolf IV of Austria was claiming that Austria was
a sovereign state, exempt from the jurisdiction of the Empire,
and was using these documents in support of his claim: the Emperor asked Petrarch for a confidential opinion as to their
genuineness. He also invited Petrarch to come to Prague.

Expert in ancient Roman history and in matters of classic Latin
style, Petrarch saw at once that the two documents were for-
geries; and he so informed the Emperor in a confidential letter,
reporting his findings clearly and convincingly.

In a separate letter he thanks the Emperor for the invitation to
Prague, which however he declines, since he feels himself too
strongly attached to Italy: "In the whole world there is nothing
under heaven that can be compared to Italy, in respect either to
the gifts of nature or to human worth." Then, not unnaturally,
he asserts again that it is the duty of the Emperor to return to
Italy and to re-establish the seat of the Empire in Rome. This is
the most eloquent and the most powerful of Petrarch's several
letters on this subject. Its references to the Emperor's past negli-
gence are severe but not vituperative: he is more concerned with
future action than with past inaction. The opportunity is passing,
life itself is passing. The folly of leaving undone what may then
never be done is illustrated by a series of perfectly apposite classical quotations, and the theme of fatal postponement is developed
at length. The Emperor must render an accounting of his steward-
ship—to himself, to his contemporaries, to posterity, and to the
Eternal Emperor.

In the course of these months—the last months of Petrarch's
residence in Milan, and the last of his son's life—Petrarch had the
satisfaction of realizing that Giovanni was making a serious effort

to reform, and was making progress in that effort. One of the most hopeful signs was Giovanni's great admiration for Nelli. For Giovanni there was no one else in the world who was worthy to be compared to Nelli. If in a conversation at which he was present he heard anyone spoken of as comparable to Nelli he would usually hold his peace, as being in the presence of his elders, and would merely look down and smile: but sometimes he was impelled to break his silence, and he then spoke of Nelli in such a way as to make manifest the reverence he had for him and the love he bore him.

As the spring advanced the inroads of the plague in Milan became more and more serious; and by the beginning of the summer its ravages were becoming catastrophic. Both Galeazzo and Bernabò Visconti took refuge in castles elsewhere in their dominions.

MILANESE ADDENDA

Petrarch's scorn for astrology was mingled with a real liking for the astrologer to whom reference has already twice been made. He respected the man's real learning, and pitied him for his need to support a large family; but he reproached him often for his professional practice. One day the astrologer said to him, as if waking from sleep, and sighing deeply: "My friend, my thoughts about all this are the same as yours—but this is the way I have to live." After that, Petrarch ceased his reproaching.

He contrasts thus the manners of two physicians who attended him during a Milanese illness:

One of them came quietly to my bedside, and after carefully feeling my pulse went into the next room and gave the appropriate directions to my servants: he then came back into my room, spoke encouraging words to me, and left. . . . The other sat down as soon as he came in, stayed on as if he were rooted there, and stunned me with his flow of words, doing his utmost to seem eloquent. . . . In order to get rid of him I had sometimes to pretend that something had happened to me.

Petrarch, naturally, preferred the first physician: he would have dismissed the other, but did not want to hurt the man's reputation.

It is probable that Petrarch's daughter Francesca (who would have been eighteen in 1361) came to join her father while he was still living in Milan, and that it was in Milan that she met Francescuolo da Brossano, whom she was to marry before the summer of 1362.

DEPARTURE

In mid-June or somewhat earlier Petrarch went to Padua, though expecting, apparently, to resume residence in Milan. In point of fact he never did so, though he did return not infrequently, sometimes for stays of considerable length, to Milan or to Pavia.

A MILANESE REVIEW

Petrarch's residence in Milan lasted for eight years—a longer period than he had ever spent in virtually continuous residence anywhere else since his youthful years in Avignon, a longer period than he was ever thereafter to spend in similar residence elsewhere. He was not perfectly content in Milan; but neither was he ill content. He was not living in the country solitude that he so dearly loved; yet he was close to country—of a sort—both at Sant'Ambrogio and at San Simpliciano. He had many friends in Milan; but none of cherished intimacy. He had been promised complete freedom, and the freedom actually accorded him was almost, but not quite, complete. The instances in which he served as spokesman for the Visconti were instances in which the objectives of the missions entrusted to him were consonant with his own opinions and desires. Their occasional requests that he write letters for them were doubtless less welcome; but they were infrequent. He liked to be made much of; and the Visconti did make much of him. He was enabled to come into cordial personal relations with the Emperor, and to plead with him freely and repeatedly to return to Rome. He was able to engage almost constantly in his chosen occupations of study and writing. He was steadily expanding the already great range of his knowledge, largely by means of his frequent acquisition of books that he had not previously owned. He wrote the longest of all his works, the *De remediis utriusque fortune;* he wrote a few new poems and a great many letters; he engaged in the revision of many works in verse and in prose that he had written before coming to Milan; and he made very substantial progress in the making of his two great collections, the *Canzoniere* and the collection of the *Fami-*

liares. His relations with the Visconti were constantly cordial: their cordiality, indeed, was to continue even after his residence in Milan had come to an end.

———————— ❧ ————————

XXV. *Padua: Summer 1361 - Summer 1362*

DURING Petrarch's residence in Padua he lived in the house, in the cathedral close, to the occupancy of which his canonry entitled him. This house had a small garden.

He already counted Francesco da Carrara and Pietro Pileo, the Bishop of Padua, as friends; and he doubtless had already formed, or soon formed, friendships and acquaintances with a good many other Paduans, including some whose names will appear in later chapters.

From Padua he went now and then to Venice, only about twenty miles away.

SUMMER 1361

This was to be a sorrowful summer for Petrarch. On the 14th of July he heard that his son had died of the plague in Milan, in the night between the 9th and the 10th. Soon thereafter he made this entry on the first guard leaf of his Virgil:

> Our Giovanni, born to my toiling and my sorrow, brought me heavy and constant cares while he lived, and bitter grief when he died. He had known few happy days. He died in the year of our Lord 1361, in the 25th year of his age, in the night between Friday and Saturday the 9th and 10th of July. The news of his death reached me in Padua late on the afternoon of the 14th. He died in Milan in the unexampled general devastation wrought by the plague, which hitherto had left that city immune from such evils, but now has found it and has invaded it.

In August he learned of the death of his dearly loved Socrates, to whom he refers, on the obituary leaf of his Virgil, as "my friend, my comrade, and a brother of the utmost goodness." Then, a few days later, word came to him of the death of Philippe de Vitry. At the end of his obituary note for Philippe, he adds "Woe is me, too frequent are the wounds of fate."

Early in the summer Sagremor de Pommiers brought to Petrarch, from the Emperor, a gold cup, and an urgent invitation to come to Prague. In his grateful reply he says that if Galeazzo is willing and if he can find a companion for the journey, he will come at the end of the summer, despite difficulties due to his increasing age and decreasing strength. But when the end of the summer came he made no effort to start for Prague.

About the first of September Pandolfo Malatesta, then in Padua, told Petrarch of a young Florentine, Francesco Bruni, who admired Petrarch greatly and desired very much to be admitted to his friendship. Pandolfo asked Petrarch to write to Bruni; but Petrarch refused, saying that he was not accustomed to write to men whom he did not know. A few days later, however, Pandolfo returned, bringing with him Francesco da Carrara, who seconded Pandolfo's request; and after his visitors had gone Petrarch wrote to Bruni, expressing gracefully his readiness to be a friend of his. The two men were never to meet; but the friendship thus begun, nurtured by frequent correspondence, grew to be one of the most valued friendships of Petrarch's later years.

AUTUMN AND WINTER

Early in the autumn Petrarch received from Cardinal Talleyrand a letter telling him that Zanobi da Strada had died, and that the Pope wanted Petrarch to take the position of papal secretary thus left vacant. In reply Petrarch sent word that he could not accept the position and suggested the appointment of either Boccaccio or Nelli. Petrarch's refusal, however, did not settle the matter: repeated efforts were made, without success, to persuade him to reconsider.

In October, very probably, Petrarch received from Francesco Bruni a letter in which Bruni heaped praises on him and referred to praises of him that he had heard from Pandolfo Malatesta. Petrarch's reply denies emphatically that he deserves such praises and includes this self-characterization:

> What then am I? A learner, but hardly even that; a lover of the woods; a solitary wanderer, wont to utter insipid words amid tall birches, or ply a frail pen, presumptuously and audaciously, in the shade of a tender laurel; an eager but unsuccessful worker; a lover of letters, but not expert in them; a follower of no sect, but a seeker for the truth. And because the search for truth is difficult and I am but

humble and weak in my searching, it happens often that, distrusting my own opinions, I content myself with the avoidance of error, and hold to my doubts in despair of attaining truth.

At some time in the autumn, probably rather late in the autumn, Petrarch resumed work on the *De vita solitaria*. He was interested, just then, in St. Peter Damian's love of solitude, and needed more information than he had at hand. Thinking that such information might well be available in Ravenna, believing that Boccaccio was then in Ravenna, and knowing that Donato Albanzani (a Venetian friend) was about to go to Ravenna, he sent word through Donato to Boccaccio, asking him to get the desired information, and to send it to him at Milan.

In the course of the autumn Petrarch decided that the growing collection of his *Epistolae familiares*, if increased by many of the uncollected letters that he still had on hand, would be large enough; and he decided, also, to initiate a new collection for letters that he might write thereafter—his *Epistolae seniles*. This new collection was to be dedicated to Nelli, to whom, accordingly, he addressed an appropriate dedicatory letter. He did not draw a sharp chronological line between the two collections, however: the *Familiares* contain a few letters that were written after 1361 and the *Seniles* a few that had been written before that year.

Before the end of the year Petrarch made up his mind to go to Provence, partly because he wanted to get away from Italy and to revisit Vaucluse, and partly to support one or both of his nominations for the papal secretaryship; and he planned to stop in Milan on the way.

Nelli, at some time in the year, had left Florence and gone to Naples, to enter the service of Niccolò Acciaiuoli. Late in November or in December Petrarch received letters from both men, the one from Acciaiuoli inviting him to settle in Naples, the one from Nelli seconding the invitation. In a reply addressed to Nelli (no reply addressed to Acciaiuoli is extant) Petrarch says that he cannot accept the invitation; speaks of the invitations he had received (all in 1361) from the King of France, the Emperor, and the Pope; writes with emotion of the death of his son, who had been devoted to Nelli; reports that in declining the Pope's offer of a papal secretaryship he had nominated Nelli for the position; and says that he may soon be going back to Vaucluse.

Early in January he left Padua for Milan.

The plague, by this time, was spreading eastward and southward from Lombardy.

MILAN

While in Milan Petrarch received from Boccaccio a copy of a Life of St. Peter Damian that he had found, and a covering letter containing some other information. This Life and Boccaccio's letter, however, did not serve to remove all Petrarch's uncertainties; and he therefore sent an inquiry to the monastery of Fonte Avellana, of which St. Peter Damian had been Abbot for many years. Eventually he received a helpful reply; and he then wrote the section on St. Peter Damian that appears in the *De vita solitaria*.

By about the middle of March, finding that the region to the west of Milan was overrun with warfare, Petrarch decided not to go on to Provence.

At about the same time he received letters from the Emperor and from Jan ze Středa, brought, undoubtedly, by Sagremor de Pommiers. The letter from the Emperor again invites Petrarch to come to Prague; the letter from Jan urges him to accept the Emperor's invitation, and asks him to bring with him a copy of the *De remediis utriusque fortune* and copies of other writings as well.

In his replies, written on the 21st, Petrarch promises that he will come to Prague. In his letter to the Emperor he writes: "Thou hast conquered, Caesar, and thy kindliness outweighs the hardness of the long journey and the indolence of my aging spirit." In his letter to Jan he repeats his promise to come, but warns him not to expect him too soon.

While in Milan he presumably saw something of Azzo da Correggio and his family, who seem to have been living in Milan at this time.

It was probably not before the first of May that Petrarch left Milan to return to Padua.

SPRING AND SUMMER

In the course of the spring Petrarch received from Nelli a letter saying that he would accept the papal secretaryship if it should be offered to him, and one from Boccaccio saying that he would not accept it—his decision being based on his preference for freedom and for his quiet poverty.

After hearing from these two men Petrarch wrote to Cardinal Talleyrand, definitely refusing the papal secretaryship, on the grounds of his lack of desire for riches or honors, his way of life, his literary occupations, and his age. He recommends Nelli very highly, saying that the Cardinal's messenger will supply all necessary information about him.

When Petrarch reached Padua he was expecting to go on to Prague; but he soon came to the conclusion that the warfare then current in northeastern Italy would make it impossible for him to go after all, and Francesco da Carrara refused to give him an escort. So he gave up his intended journey.

Before the end of May Petrarch received from Boccaccio a letter that was devoted chiefly to a distressed account of a recent visit from a man who had represented himself as the bearer of a prophetic message which the saintly Pietro Petroni of Siena, shortly before his death, had charged him to deliver to Boccaccio—a message to the effect that Boccaccio had only a few years to live, and that he must renounce the study of poetry. Boccaccio, credulous and crushed, had decided to give up his studies and dispose of his books, which he offered to sell to Petrarch.

Petrarch's reply is in the main a calm and searching discussion of the message that Boccaccio had received. Critical doubt is cast on the genuineness of that message; the idea that one may not have many years to live is valid for all men and is to be accepted without regret; and the position is taken that, while it might well be unfitting for an elderly man to undertake the profession of letters if he had never before followed literary pursuits, there is no reason why a man grown old in that profession should abandon it. If Boccaccio persists in his proposal to sell his books, Petrarch, believing that they ought not to be scattered, will gladly buy them and add them to his own collection, and will bequeath the joint collection to some religious institution.

It is no wonder that Petrarch was concerned as to the future of his collection of books, and did not want them to be scattered. His library was certainly by this time the largest and finest privately owned library in Europe; and from the point of view of literary scholarship it was undoubtedly larger and finer than any institutional or official library then existing. Some of his volumes, moreover, were very beautiful.

At some time in the summer Petrarch received from Pandolfo

Malatesta, whose wife had died, a request for advice as to whether he should marry again. Petrarch hesitated to reply, and postponed replying.

It was probably at some time in the summer, though perhaps a little later, that Petrarch received from Boccaccio, acting as intermediary, a letter that Barbato da Sulmona had written on behalf of three friends as well as for himself, urging Petrarch to release the *Africa* immediately, instead of holding it to be released after his death. This letter, however, had no effect on Petrarch except to renew the displeasure resulting from the fact that in 1343, after he had given Barbato a copy of the Mago passage in the *Africa* under the condition that Barbato should not release any copies of it, Barbato had soon broken his promise.

In the course of the summer the plague reached Padua.

VENETIAN PLANS

Toward the end of the summer Petrarch came to the conclusion that he would prefer to live in Venice, if a suitable house could be provided for him there: this preference was due, he says, not to fear of the plague, but simply to the belief that in Venice he could find greater peace. It occurred to him that he might combine a plan for settlement in Venice with a plan that would prevent the scattering of his books, by offering to bequeath his library to Venice if Venice would provide him with a house. He discussed his idea with his friend Benintendi dei Ravagnani, the Chancellor of the Republic, who heartily approved it. Late in August, while negotiations were still going on, Petrarch wrote to Benintendi a letter in which he says that he thinks that if his proposal is accepted his library may ultimately develop into an institution in which Venice may well glory. He wishes that the idea of the foundation of a public library—he uses the words "bibliotheca publica"—had come to him earlier, while Andrea Dandolo was still living; and he wonders that the idea had not occurred still earlier to someone else.

The document, written in Padua, in which he formulated his proposal—the earliest recorded proposal for the foundation of a public library—is not itself extant; but a minute, presumably prepared by Benintendi, that was adopted on the 4th of September by the Major Council of Venice summarizes it thus:

F. desires to institute the Blessed Mark the Evangelist, if it be to the good pleasure of Christ and of [the Blessed Mark] himself, as the heir of an unknown number of books which he now owns or may own hereafter, on this condition: that the books shall not be sold nor in any way dispersed, but shall be kept forever in a place, safe from fires and from rains, which shall be devoted to this purpose, to the honor of the said Saint, in memory of himself [Petrarch], and for the solace, such as it may be, and the convenience of those ingenious and noble men of that city who may delight in such things.

Nor does he desire this because his books are very numerous or very valuable, but in the hope that hereafter, from time to time, that glorious city may itself add other books from public funds, and that following the example thus set, private citizens—noble men who love their fatherland, or even citizens born elsewhere—may bequeath some of their books to the aforesaid Church; and thus it may readily develop into a great and famous library equaling those of antiquity: and how greatly this would redound to the glory of that Dominion no man of letters, nay, not even an unlearned man, can fail to realize. And if this shall come to pass, with the help of God and of the great patron of your city, F. himself will rejoice and will glory in the Lord that he has been in some sense the originator of so great a good. Regarding which, if the proposal is carried into effect, he will perhaps write more fully. But that it may be seen that he is ready to carry out what he is proposing, he desires now to do as he has promised, etc. [This *etc.* appears in the text of the document.]

For the time being he desires for himself and for his books a small but honorable house, so that nothing that may in the course of nature befall him may prevent the carrying-out of this plan. He himself will be glad to reside there if proper arrangements can be made, and he hopes to be able to do so, in spite of certain difficulties.

The minute of acceptance begins thus:

Considering how greatly to the praise of God and of the Blessed Mark the Evangelist, as well as to the honor and fame of our city, the offer will be that is made by Master Francesco Petrarca, whose fame today in the whole world is so great that, in the memory of man, there has never been in Christendom any moral philosopher or any poet who can be compared with him: let his offer be accepted according to the form of the following proposal, made in his own hand; and be it now ordered that there be taken from the Funds such amounts as may be needed to rent a house and habitation for him for the rest of his life, with the approval of the Signory, the Councillors, and the Chiefs or a majority thereof; provided that the Procurators of the Church of St. Mark offer to take care of the expenses necessary for a place where his books may be put and kept. And this action is taken by six Councillors, three Chiefs, thirty-two of the Forty, and finally by two-thirds of the Great Council. And the tenor of his proposal is as follows.

The minute then concludes with the summary of Petrarch's proposal that has just been quoted.

PADUAN PROBABILITIES

It was probably before the end of Petrarch's year in Padua— possibly even before he left Milan—that Petrarch finished the making of the fourth or Chigi form of the *Canzoniere*, which contained 215 poems.

It was probably in the course of this same year that he received a canonry at Monselice, a small place about fifteen miles southwest of Padua.

XXVI. *Venice*
September 1362 - December 1363

THE house provided for Petrarch, the Palazzo Molin, notable for its two towers, stood on the Riva degli Schiavoni (on the site on which the Caserma del Sepolcro now stands), just a little to the east of the Palace of the Doges, and overlooking the harbor.

Petrarch liked this house very much. One of his letters tells something of his habits while he was living there. In the summer he retired to his bedroom at midday to make up some of the sleep that he had lost [through his accustomed rising at midnight for prayer and study or writing]. To his servants—with whom he was much dissatisfied, though others thought them excellent —he gave these instructions as to the admission of visitors: if he is engaged in saying his office the visitor must wait, unless he is a "persona insignis," or comes on an errand of great importance; if he is studying they are neither to admit everyone nor to exclude everyone, but are to distinguish between cases, if they can, and act accordingly; and if he is at table or asleep they are to admit any visitor, since he grudges all time spent in eating or sleeping.

Among the Venetians whom he already knew his closest friends were Benintendi dei Ravagnani and Donato Albanzani, a teacher and man of letters. Benintendi, it would seem, sometimes took him out in his gondola. Donato used to come to his house on winter evenings and sit talking with him before a hearth fire. He was on cordial terms with the Doge, Lorenzo Celsi.

Throughout the period of his residence in Venice he went not infrequently to Padua, sometimes for a stay of several days.

AUTUMN 1362

On the 11th of September Petrarch, already in Venice, answered Pandolfo Malatesta's request for advice as to whether he should remarry. After disclaiming competence he says that while Pandolfo would have more freedom if he should remain unmarried he ought nevertheless to marry for the sake of the State, his family, and his friends. In the choice of a wife he should consider not so much dowry and wealth as birth and training, not so much elegance as devotion, not so much outer beauty as beauty of spirit.

A week later Petrarch was present at a conference held in Padua, in the garden behind the palace of Francesco da Carrara, at which a Venetian representative tried unsuccessfully to get Francesco to revoke an order to which Venice objected. The case was in itself a petty one, but a question of territorial jurisdiction was involved.

At about this same time he wrote to Jan ze Středa, and probably to the Emperor, telling why he had been unable to carry out his promise to come to Prague. This letter or these letters, however, never reached Prague.

By the end of October Petrarch must have heard of the death of Innocent VI, and of the election in his place of Guillaume Grimoard, Abbot of a Benedictine monastery in Marseilles, who took the name Urban V. This news must have delighted Petrarch, for the new pope was a man of exemplary character; he had not been a cardinal, and the election of a mere abbot to the papacy seemed miraculous; he had a personal knowledge of Italy, and his choice of the name Urban suggested at once, to Petrarch, that he regarded himself as having his proper place in Rome, which was, to Petrarch, the supreme *urbs*. The idea that Urban might return the papacy to Rome must have occurred to him at once.

Before long, word came to Petrarch that Urban wanted to have him come to Avignon, and had in mind making some sort of offer to him. Petrarch, however, thought that the offer would be that of a papal secretaryship, and was not interested.

About the first of November Petrarch learned of the death of his dear friend and sometime patron, Azzo da Correggio, to whom he had dedicated the *De remediis utriusque fortune*. He poured forth his sorrow in a deeply felt letter addressed to Moggio dei Moggi, who had been a member of Azzo's household for many years, and was himself a friend of Petrarch.

Pietro da Muglio, who for some time had been the professor of letters at the University of Bologna, and while there had in all probability written to Petrarch the letter that came ostensibly from Homer, had now been appointed to a professorship in the University of Padua, and had presumably moved to Padua before November, when his professorial duties began. Petrarch on one of his trips to Padua doubtless met him; and from this time on the two men were warm friends.

It was either in 1362 or a little later that Petrarch's first grandchild was born—a girl to whom the name of Petrarch's mother, Eletta, was given.

WINTER 1362-1363

Two Venetian ships tied up for the winter directly in front of Petrarch's house. They were as large as the house itself, and their masts rose higher than the house.

About the first of the year word came again to Petrarch that Pope Urban was anxious to have him return to Avignon, and he now learned that what the Pope had in mind for him was not a papal secretaryship but a modest canonry, apparently at Carpentras, which would not have involved any serious interference with his cherished freedom. But he was still not disposed to return to the neighborhood of Avignon.

Francesco Bruni was, on the contrary, anxious for a secretarial appointment in the papal service, and asked Petrarch for a letter of recommendation. Instead of writing such a letter, however, Petrarch asked Bruni to commend him orally to the Pope, thinking apparently that this procedure would be more helpful to Bruni than the presentation of a formal letter of recommendation.

MARCH 1363

About the first of March Boccaccio, who had spent a most unhappy winter in Naples, arrived in Padua, where he had expected to find Petrarch. After learning that Petrarch had moved to Venice he decided to stay in Padua for a while, before going on to Venice. His presence in Padua was soon made known to Petrarch.

On the 13th of March Petrarch received a visit from a young Florentine monk, who with the greatest distress—"While he was telling me all this," Petrarch writes, "his eyes flashed, his voice broke, and he was so burning with indignation that he could hardly keep back the tears"—told him that certain Florentines had indulged in criticism of the Mago passage in the *Africa* and of the *Bucolicum carmen*, and reported the specific criticisms that had been made.

Later on that same day Petrarch, highly indignant, wrote a letter of violent self-defense, including a rebuttal of the specific criticisms, addressing it to Boccaccio, who, though innocent alike of any share in the criticisms or of any share in the authorship of Barbato's letter urging the release of the *Africa*, had been at least the transmitter of that letter, and was near at hand.

Before the end of March, in all probability, Petrarch learned that a report of his death had been circulating in Avignon and elsewhere; that Pope Urban, believing the report, had assigned to other men the canonries that Petrarch was holding, as well as the modest canonry, probably in Carpentras, by the offer of which he had been hoping to lure Petrarch back to Provence; and that, while the reassignments of his present canonries were invalidated when the report of his death turned out to be a false rumor, the proposed new canonry remained assigned to someone else.

About the first of April Petrarch received from Francesco Bruni a letter telling him that he (Bruni) had been given the appointment as papal secretary that he had hoped for.

At some time in April, presumably, Boccaccio came on to Venice to begin a visit to Petrarch that was to last for about three months. We have no record of their conversations; but Boccaccio must have told Petrarch of the scurvy treatment he had received in Naples, and they must have talked of the progress of Leontius Pilatus' translation of Homer. Benintendi dei Ravagnani and Donato Albanzani joined them from time to time; and Benintendi took them out for delightful rides in his gondola.

Leontius, also, was staying with Petrarch during at least the latter part of Boccaccio's visit. He must have been a very disagreeable guest. In one or another of the letters in which Petrarch mentions him he calls him a great beast and speaks of his long and unkempt hair and beard, his slovenly dress, his bad manners, his insolence, his constant ill humor, his restlessness, and his unreliability. Boccaccio characterizes him similarly. But he was indispensable to the two friends in their effort to gain knowledge of Homer, and Petrarch did his best to be a good host to him.

Before dawn on the 9th of April, while Petrarch, though tired and sleepy, had begun the writing of a letter, he heard a sudden shouting of sailors, hurried to the top of the house to look out, and saw that the larger of two ships that had wintered in front of his house was just casting off, although the stars were hidden by clouds, the wind was so strong as to shake the house, and the sea was roaring. As the ship set sail it looked to him like a floating mountain, though much of its hull, laden with a heavy cargo, was hidden by the waves. He knew that it was bound for the Don; and in his thought he wished it a good voyage.

At some time in the spring Petrarch wrote a letter to Laelius, which he entrusted to a priest who was going to Rome, and a letter to Nelli, which he gave to another messenger.

While Boccaccio was still in Venice word came to him of the death of Laelius; but he did not tell Petrarch, preferring that this news, which was bound to distress Petrarch greatly, should come to him from some other source.

While Boccaccio was still with Petrarch, also, he received a letter written by Nelli for Niccolò Acciaiuoli, protesting his flight from Naples, accusing him of changeableness and ingratitude, and inviting him to return. To Boccaccio this letter seemed to add insult to injury, and he proceeded to write an exceedingly long and violent reply. He probably showed both letters to Petrarch, who in that case probably advised him not to send his reply to Nelli: there is indeed no evidence that it was ever sent.

At about the end of June Boccaccio, feeling that he must return to his home, left Venice, although Petrarch tried to persuade him to stay longer. Leontius, however, stayed on with Petrarch until the end of the summer.

At some time before the end of July a common friend, probably Pandolfo Malatesta, suggested to Petrarch that he write to Roberto di Battifolle, lord of the Casentino, whom he had never met; and Petrarch, though reluctantly, did so, saying that he would like very much to meet Roberto, but that his occupations would prevent him from journeying to the Casentino.

JULY–OCTOBER

Not long after Boccaccio's departure the priest to whom Petrarch had entrusted his last letter to Laelius reappeared, and gave the letter, unopened, back to Petrarch. He looked at his own writing, saw that the seal was unbroken, and exclaimed "What does this mean? Why does this letter come back to me, unopened, and without an answer? What of my Laelius?" The priest remained silent, his eyes downcast, and Petrarch understood, all too well, that Laelius had died. At almost the same time another messenger brought back to him, unopened, his last letter to Nelli, who, the messenger said, had died in his arms. Petrarch burned both letters.

Toward the end of the summer Leontius decided to go to Constantinople, although Petrarch invited and advised him to remain. He left, nevertheless, talking abusively of Italy and the Italians.

About the first of October Petrarch received letters from Pavia, from the Casentino, from Sulmona, and from Constantinople.

After the capture of Pavia by the Visconti in 1359 it had become the favorite place of residence of Galeazzo, who built a great palace there in the years 1360–1365. The letter that now came to Petrarch from Pavia was an invitation from Galeazzo to come and visit him; and Petrarch decided to accept the invitation.

Two letters came from the Casentino. One, from Roberto di Battifolle, urged Petrarch to visit him there:

I wonder that you have never visited the heights of the Apennines. Here is La Verna; here are the monasteries of Camaldoli and of Vallombrosa; and here are the sources of the Arno and the Tiber. These all join with me in desiring your venerable presence.

The same messenger who brought this letter to Petrarch evidently brought him also a companion letter from Giovanni degli Abbarbagliati, Grand Prior of the Camaldolensians, offering to come to escort Petrarch to the Casentino.

Replying to the letter from Roberto, Petrarch thanks him for his invitation, and says that he will try to come if his occupations permit; and answering the Grand Prior he thanks him for the offer of his escort, but declines it, saying that he is content in the assurance of the Prior's good will.

The letter from Sulmona, written by a man whom Petrarch had never met, brought the sad news of the death of Barbato, and asked that Petrarch write a panegyric in his memory. In his reply, however, Petrarch says that he feels unable to write such a panegyric, mainly because, though he knows Barbato's virtues, he knows almost nothing of his manner of life, of his family, of his public service, or of his writings. In point of fact Petrarch's reply, though brief, is a true panegyric in itself.

The letter from Constantinople came from Leontius, who now praised Italy, expressed his hatred of Greece, execrated Constantinople, and begged Petrarch to bid him return. Petrarch seems not to have thought this letter worthy of an answer.

Shortly before the 8th of October he left Venice to go to Pavia, stopping on the way, for a week or so, in Padua.

While there he wrote to Niccolò Acciaiuoli complaining of Niccolò's failure to fulfil a promise that he had made to Petrarch —apparently when Niccolò had been in Milan, and had come to see Petrarch there. It seems probable that this promise concerned in some way the question of the restoration of the Florentine property that had belonged to Petrarch's father.

PAVIA

Petrarch cannot have stayed in Pavia very long, on the occasion of this, the first of his several visits there: he was back in Venice early in December.

While there, on this first visit, he was probably a guest in Galeazzo's still unfinished castle.

Pavia is only about twenty miles from Milan; and in the course of his visit Petrarch doubtless found opportunity to go to Milan, to see his daughter Francesca and her husband, Francescuolo da Brossano—and perhaps to see his little granddaughter, Eletta, for the first time.

DECEMBER

On his return to Venice he found the city excited and distressed by bad news from Crete. A rebellion against the domination of Venice had been simmering for some time among Venetians resident there; but Venice had been temporizing; and a disastrous outbreak had now occurred. A Venetian merchant fleet on its way to Cyprus and Alexandria had put in at Sitia to get water; when permission to get water was refused, two bands of Venetians from the ships had attacked the place; and the attackers had been killed or driven into the sea. This may have been a matter of common report in Venice; but Petrarch knew of it directly through a letter he had received—presumably he had found it waiting for him on his return—from his Venetian friend Paolo de Bernardo, who had watched the fray from the afterdeck of one of the Venetian ships.

In a letter written later in the month he speaks vividly of the ravages of the plague in Venice: "Everywhere you hear weeping and lamentation; everywhere you see corpses that are still warm; everywhere you see the carrying of coffins." Toward the end of the month, apparently, he received from Roberto di Battifolle a letter in which Roberto greets with delight the prospect of a visit from Petrarch, and assures him of a hearty welcome.

At some time in 1363 or early in 1364—certainly before February 19, 1364—Petrarch served, in Padua, as godfather at the baptism of Pietro da Muglio's son Bernardo.

It was presumably either in 1363 or not long thereafter that Petrarch became acquainted with Philippe de Mézières, Chancellor of King Peter I of Cyprus. In each of the years 1363–1368 Philippe was in Venice—usually for a brief stay—on missions related to King Peter's proposed crusades.

———————————— ❧ ————————————

XXVII. *Venice and Pavia: 1364 - 1365*

THE Venetian government, determined to put down the Cretan rebellion, was now seeking a commander for the land forces that were soon to be sent to Crete. A possible commander was Giberto da Correggio, one of Azzo's sons; but Giberto was at this time a captive in Modena, having fallen into Modenese hands while leading troops of the Visconti. On the 15th of January it was voted that if the command should be offered to Giberto, Petrarch should be sent to procure his release. It was decided, however—perhaps at the suggestion of Petrarch —that the command should be offered to Luchino dal Verme; and Petrarch was asked to write to him, conveying or seconding the official request. Petrarch did write to him; and Luchino accepted.

In January and again in February Petrarch was working on the *Triumph of Fame.*

It was probably late in February or early in March that Petrarch went to Bologna to pay his respects to the Papal Legate, Cardinal Androin de la Roche, planning also to go on from Bologna to visit Roberto di Battifolle in the Casentino. His interview with the Cardinal is recorded in a later reminiscent letter:

> Three years ago, when I went to see that excellent man, who had just begun his service as Papal Legate, he received me with glad embraces, more honorably than I deserved, and we talked of various things. When I asked him about the state of affairs in Bologna he replied, jokingly, as was his wont when speaking of troublesome matters: "This, my friend, used to be Bologna, but now it is Macerata"—playing on the name of the city in the Marches.

From Bologna Petrarch went on to the Casentino, probably by way of Forlì. His account of his visit, contained in a grateful letter written to Roberto soon after his return to Venice, may be summarized thus:

> It was a joy to be with you. I praise the seriousness, the affability, and the dignity of your household, in which

frugality and ancestral manners persist; and I praise your own alertness and zeal. Who would not be refreshed, rejoiced, and moved to contemplation by a region where there are green and dewy hills and well-nigh a thousand sunny fields, and where amid dark woods, the haunts of the Muses, and gently flowing streams one may find sweet peace and sweet silence. No less delectable are the sacred hermitage, the marvels of Mount Alvernia, and many other venerable sites. I was much impressed by your little son—by his singing, his conversation, and the excellence of his Latin. Nor can I fail to mention the convent, known for your generosity. I cannot easily say what sweetness and what depth of devotion came to me there at the celebration of the Mass, when the singing of the nuns seemed a celestial harmony. Knowing that in the past there had been trouble between your brother and yourself I was thankful to witness your reconciliation; and I urge you both to continue in fraternal affection.

On the first day of April Petrarch dated a long letter to Luchino dal Verme, whose expedition was about to leave Venice for Crete. The letter, which opens with an assertion of the justice of the Venetian cause and prophesies that Luchino will be successful, turns presently into a learned treatise, based on Ciceronian statements and Roman experiences, of the qualifications necessary for a good military commander.

SPRING AND SUMMER

In the course of the spring and summer Petrarch made a series of insertions in his Tenth Eclogue, most of them composed while walking back and forth on the shore of the lagoon.

In the summer Petrarch had as a house guest Bartolomeo Carbone dei Papazurri, a friend of long standing, who had been promoted from the bishopric of Chieti to the archbishopric of Patras, and was to proceed to Patras at the beginning of the autumn. Early on the 4th of June, as the two men were talking together at one of the front windows of Petrarch's house, looking over the lagoon, they saw a galley decorated with green branches, its sails trimmed, being rowed swiftly in. They stopped talking as they watched, hoping that the ship bore good tidings. As it approached, they could see sailors moving about briskly and at the prow young men, with joyous faces, who were wearing garlands of leaves and waving banners over their heads; and as it came still nearer, they could see banners of the enemy hanging downard from the stern. They knew, therefore, that the ship came from Crete with news of a victory.

On this same day or immediately thereafter, services of thanksgiving were held in San Marco and throughout the city; and around San Marco and in the Piazza there was a great procession of clergy and laymen. A series of games and spectacles began presently, and continued for more than two months. These games culminated in two major equestrian events, a display of horsemanship and a tournament, both held in the Piazza di San Marco. Tommaso Bombasi of Ferrara, a friend of Petrarch, had been employed as master of ceremonies for the first of these events. The tournament began on the 4th of August. The Piazza was crowded with spectators; a special grandstand had been erected for ladies; and the Doge and his official party watched from the loggia of the four bronze horses on the façade of San Marco. The Doge had invited Petrarch to sit on his right hand, and he did so on two days: he then asked to be excused, on the ground of his occupations.

Before the end of the summer Petrarch took into his service the brilliant young Giovanni Malpaghini of Ravenna, who had been a pupil and protégé of Donato Albanzani. Giovanni, who was about eighteen at the time, helped Petrarch in various ways with his work, most especially by copying the collection of the *Familiares*.

AUTUMN AND WINTER

Early in the autumn Petrarch had a serious attack of scabies, and went for relief to the baths of Abano (about six miles southwest of Padua). He was there in October: how long he remained there we do not know. His illness certainly lasted into the early part of 1365: he could then hardly feed himself, or write. His doctors could do nothing for him except to say that the coming summer might bring relief.

Late in 1364 Petrarch received a visit from Sagremor de Pommiers. They talked naturally of the Emperor and of the possibility of his coming to Italy again. Sagremor told Petrarch of the many causes for the Emperor's delay, and hinted at preparations in the making. Probably while Sagremor was still with him,

Petrarch wrote again to the Emperor, renewing his previous exhortations. He would not have written this letter, he says, had not Sagremor's visit revived his hopes and stimulated his sense of duty. His earlier letters had failed to produce the desired results; the present effort, he says, will be his last.

Petrarch's sight had hitherto been very keen; but beginning in or shortly after 1364 he had to use glasses, much to his disgust.

SPRING AND EARLY SUMMER 1365

By early March Petrarch was back in Venice. Wanting, just then, to know how Homer had described certain regions, he wrote to Boccaccio, asking him for a copy of a passage—which he did not define very clearly—from Leontius' translation of the *Odyssey*.

Petrarch's Florentine friends, who in 1351 had failed in their effort to bring him to Florence as a lecturer in the University, now tried—Boccaccio doubtless the prime mover—to have him brought there as a canon, and they obtained governmental cooperation. At the end of March an envoy was to be sent to Avignon, primarily for another purpose; but one of the items in the instructions drawn up for him reads in part thus:

> Item, while you are in Avignon . . . we desire that you go to see the Pope, and . . . that you say to him that the celebrated fame and excellence of Master Francesco Petrarca, our fellow citizen, has led us and leads us to desire greatly to bring him to live in Florence, both for the honor of our city and for his own repose. . . . And since he has no property in Florence, nor any means of obtaining property there, and does not wish to live as a layman, may the Pope, in order that he [Petrarch] may have ecclesiastical income, deign to grant to him the first canonry that shall fall vacant in Florence, regardless of previous commitments.

Pope Urban acted favorably and promptly, conditioning his approval on Petrarch's relinquishing his canonry at Monselice. Petrarch, however, refused the offer, presumably because of unwillingness to settle in Florence, which had withdrawn its restoration of his Florentine patrimony: he was well content with his relations with Venice, with Francesco da Carrara, and with Galeazzo Visconti.

Before the middle of the summer Petrarch received from Boccaccio a copy of what Boccaccio mistakenly thought to be the Homeric passage that Petrarch wanted. In a covering letter, moreover, Boccaccio said that he was sending Petrarch a complete copy of the *Iliad:* Petrarch could not understand why he was not sending the *Odyssey* also.

Perhaps in the first half of 1365, perhaps in an earlier year, Petrarch had formed friendships with four men who were then living in Venice: Leonardo Dandolo, a son of the late Doge Andrea Dandolo; Tommaso Talenti, a wealthy merchant of Florentine origin; Zaccaria Contarini, a Venetian noble; and Guido da Bagnolo of Reggio, an eminent physician. It is probable that two of the four had studied at the University of Bologna and that one of the others had studied at the University of Paris: all were convinced Aristotelians. They came often to see Petrarch —sometimes just two of them, sometimes all four together— courteously, happily, and with affectionate greetings. They did not take kindly, however, such comments on their Aristotelian lore as were, for Petrarch—an Augustinian Platonist—inevitable.

In July the Doge Lorenzo Celsi died. He had honored Petrarch highly, and his death must have brought Petrarch real regret. There is no evidence that his successor, the octogenarian Marco Corner, ever paid any attention to him.

Petrarch had now finished—as he thought—his revision of the *De vita solitaria;* and he commissioned a Paduan priest to make a copy of it.

PAVIA

Before the end of the summer Petrarch went to Pavia for a visit that lasted into December. While there, both at this time and on later visits, he presumably occupied a house rented for him by Galeazzo. He liked Pavia. In a letter to Boccaccio written during this visit he gives an enthusiastic account of the city, telling of its history, describing its situation—rising a little above the level of the plain, lifting its many towers toward heaven, viewing the Alps and the Apennines, watered by the gently flowing Ticino. He speak in particular of an ancient equestrian statue that stood in the main piazza, of the marble bridge over the Ticino, and of Galeazzo's great palace, which was now just finished or just nearing completion.

Another letter to Boccaccio written at this time contains one of Petrarch's several diatribes against the majority of physicians.

He inveighs against medical pronouncements that one should not eat fruits, herbs, or vegetables, that bloodletting is bad for the system—he says that he could not get along without being bled once every spring and once every autumn—and that young people do not need to drink water except in cases of acute illness. Certain physicians are indeed friends of his, and when he is ill he is glad to have them come to see him as friends; but, trusting to the curative powers of nature, he pays no attention to their directions unless he happens to approve them himself.

A third letter to Boccaccio concerns Leontius and his translations, which Petrarch was eager to receive.

Being unable to find a messenger to take these three letters to Boccaccio, Petrarch entrusted them to a man in Pavia who promised to send them to Boccaccio—but instead of doing so held onto them for himself.

From Pavia Petrarch went occasionally to Milan or its vicinity —as he did also on his later visits to Pavia.

Once, during his visit in 1365, Petrarch was at supper in Milan with Galeazzo, when a courier brought word of the approach of a healer from the Canton Valais, called in by Galeazzo in the hope of gaining relief from the gout. The courier brought also the healer's orders that a certain concoction of eggs and other ingredients should be prepared immediately and taken by Galeazzo. Galeazzo sent a company of knights and servants to meet the healer, taking with them a fine white horse for him to ride; and he rode into the city in the midst of a marveling crowd. Petrarch returned presently to Pavia, where before long he learned that Galeazzo's gout was worse than ever, and that the healer now said that the only remaining hope of cure lay in consulting certain books of magic, for which search was to be made.

It was probably not before the latter part of December that Petrarch left Pavia to return to Venice.

Rumors that Petrarch had died circulated again and again in the course of his life. At some time in 1365 such a rumor reached the Emperor, and led him to cancel a plan of some sort from which Petrarch had expected to derive substantial benefit.

XXVIII. *Venice and Pavia: 1366*

LATE one night, about the first of January, Petrarch reached Venice. Early on the next morning Donato Albanzani came to see him. They talked of Boccaccio, and Donato told him that the promised copy of Homer had not arrived, although word had come from Boccaccio that he had sent it. Donato told him also of the tragic death of Leontius Pilatus: he had started back to Italy; after his ship had entered the Adriatic a storm arose; all was confusion on the ship; Leontius clung to the mast; he was struck and killed by a bolt of lightning; and he was buried at sea. Some books that he had with him were brought to Venice.

It was very possibly in this same interview that Donato reported that Petrarch's four Aristotelian friends had decided that he (Petrarch) was a good man but uneducated, and that their verdict had become widely known in Venice. Donato wanted Petrarch to reply; but Petrarch, though much offended, was not disposed to do so, at least immediately.

By the beginning of 1366 Petrarch's daughter Francesca and her little daughter Eletta were living in his house in Venice, and presumably Francesca's husband, Francescuolo da Brossano, was living there with them. When they had come to Venice we do not know: possibly as early as the latter part of 1363. In January or February, 1366, their second child, a boy named Francesco, was born in Venice. Donato Albanzani served as his godfather. In the spring of 1367 Francescuolo was absent on business for a month or so: he may have been absent at other times, earlier or later.

Toward the end of the spring the Paduan priest who had been copying the *De vita solitaria* finished his task, and Petrarch was at last ready to send the book to Philippe de Cabassoles, for whom it had been written twenty years before. The messenger who took it to him was Sagremor de Pommiers.

PETRARCH'S FIRST LETTER TO URBAN V

By the spring of 1366 Petrarch had received letters from Philippe de Cabassoles and from other men in Provence praising Urban highly for his saintly spirit, his active mind, his resolute piety, his ardent study, his memory of the past, his foresight for the future, his love for good men, his hatred for evil men, his devotion to justice, and his maintenance of ecclesiastical discipline. It was reported, moreover, that the name of Rome was constantly on his lips. He had said that even if there were no other reason for a return to Rome the need for arousing the devotion of the faithful would be reason enough; and in 1365, after Avignon had been forced to pay 200,000 florins to be rid of a powerful band of mercenaries, he had said that all such troubles were due to the abandonment of the See of Peter.

Urban had now been pope for more than three years; but in spite of his repeatedly expressed opinion that the papacy should return to Rome, he had not returned. Petrarch, whose conviction of the necessity of that return was so intense, now felt that he could no longer hold his peace; and at some time in the spring, therefore, he began work on an exceedingly long and important letter to Urban.

The letter opens with reasoned and specific praise of Urban, then demonstrates the necessity of the return to Rome, then discusses the difficulties that must be overcome, and ends—as first drafted —with an impassioned entreaty. At one point Petrarch writes thus of the dire plight of Rome, a plight due to the absence of the papacy:

> In your absence . . . peace is exiled; civil and external warfare rages; dwellings are prostrate; walls are toppling; churches are falling; sacred things are perishing; laws are trodden underfoot; justice is abused; the unhappy people mourn and wail, calling with loud cries upon your name. Do you not hear them? . . . Must the Queen of Cities be forever widowed? . . . How can you sleep, under your gilded beams, on the bank of the Rhone, while the Lateran, the Mother of all churches, ruined and roofless, is open to the wind and rain, and the most holy shrines of Peter and of Paul are quaking, and what was once the Church of the Apostles is but a ruin and a shapeless heap of stones?

Return to Rome would bring perennial glory to Urban's name. It was in Rome, not on the Rhone, that Christ had established his Church. The very election of Urban to the papacy had been manifestly a miracle designed to bring about the return to Rome. What account will Urban be able to render to God if he fails to fulfil the task allotted to him? It will avail him nothing, as the poor widow once said to Trajan, if he leaves that task to be fulfilled by another.

The great difficulties in the way of the return arise from the fact that the French cardinals are unduly hostile to Italy and unduly attached to Avignon. Hostility to Italy is due mainly to ignorance, as a result of which it is said that Italy is out of the world, beyond an unnavigable sea and impenetrable mountains; that the air, wines, waters, and foods of Italy are unhealthy; and that Italian hostility would make it dangerous for the Pope and the cardinals to live in Rome. These charges Petrarch refutes effectively, saying that mistaken impressions of Italy would disappear if only those who hold them would visit that fair land. In praise of Italy Petrarch quotes the remark once made to him, near Lake Garda, by Cardinal Gui de Boulogne, who had said: "It is clear, I confess, that your fatherland is much more beautiful and productive than ours." For his own part, Petrarch asserts, "There is nothing under the stars that can be compared with Italy." The attachment of the cardinals to Avignon is due to the fact that they have built there, as it were, a paradise of pleasure, a celestial habitation in which they dwell as if they were to continue to dwell there forever.

The letter thus drafted is a masterpiece in content, in structure, and in eloquence. But when Petrarch had come to the end of this draft he was not satisfied that he had said all that he wanted to say, and so he laid it aside for a little while.

Toward the end of June he resumed work on it, writing a supplement that is about as long as the main portion of the letter. This supplement is not a unity in itself: it consists of a series of distinct elements, some of them being in effect addenda to particular passages of the original letter.

He begs the Pope to persuade the French cardinals that Italy, far from being such as they think it to be, is in fact "the best, the most illustrious, and the most famous part of the world," lacking solely in peace, which would follow if only the papacy would return to Rome. There follows a glowing passage in which Italy is praised for its noble and beautiful cities, its salubrious air, its even temperature, the sagacity of its southerners, the vigor and stoutheartedness of its northerners, its lakes, its rivers, its two seas, its defending Alps, its hills, valleys, and fields, its metals, its flocks, its shipping, its grains, wines, oils, fruits, game, fish, birds, and its foods of every sort.

To the causes of the hostility of the French cardinals he now adds their frequent complaint that Italy has no wine of Beaune (the Côte de Beaune, in Burgundy): "a dreadful shame, indeed, and a just cause for keeping away from Italy!" They could have their Beaune sent to them in Italy, if they so desired; but once there they would soon be content with Italian wines.

Petrarch is writing, he then says, on the very day and at the very hour when Peter and Paul had suffered martyrdom in Rome: what holy joy would be Urban's if at such an hour he could be present at service in the basilica of Peter—properly his own basilica! Nowhere save in Rome is such joy to be experienced in all its fulness.

At the end of the supplement Petrarch begs Urban to pardon him for any offense he may have given, and entreats him to return to a place whence, on the Last Day, he may rise not in company with the sinners of Avignon but in company with Peter and Paul, Stephen and Lawrence, Sylvester and Gregory, and Jerome and Agnes and Cecilia and thousands of other saints. The last sentence of all is this prayer: "May the omnipotent Christ prolong the days of your life; and may He open your heart to counsels that may not be bland and pleasing, but are sound and faithful."

The completed letter was dated in Venice on the 29th of June. But Petrarch was not yet ready to send it, and decided to take it with him to Pavia, whither he was about to go.

PAVIA: JULY–DECEMBER

In July Petrarch returned to Pavia.

While there he had the pleasure of renewed association with Pandolfo Malatesta, now reconciled with the Visconti and again in their service.

In the previous winter, when he had been about to leave Pavia, he had entrusted three letters for Boccaccio to a man who had promised to transmit them to him. On his return in July he found that this man was still holding the three letters. When Petrarch asked for them he swore that he had already given them back; and he would have continued to hold them if Petrarch, becoming angry, had not notified him that he would no longer endure his misconduct. Then at last he gave the letters back to Petrarch —who sent them, a little later, to Donato Albanzani, asking Donato to send them on to Boccaccio, with whom Donato was in correspondence, as Petrarch knew.

Since ancient times the 63rd year of a man's life had been regarded as the grand climacteric, a year that was liable to bring disaster, peril, and death. At dawn on the 20th of July, his 63rd birthday, Petrarch wrote to Boccaccio, saying that he faced the year without belief in its peculiar character, and with entire acceptance of the prospect of death whenever the allotted day should come for him. But since he did not want to alarm Boccaccio he did not send this letter until long after he had written it.

Before the end of the summer Petrarch received a letter from Philippe de Cabassoles, telling of his receipt of his copy of the *De vita solitaria*, and saying that he was delighted with it; that the Pope and Cardinal Gui de Boulogne wanted copies of it; and that the Archbishop of Embrun and the Bishop of Lisbon had read it eagerly, and vied with each other in praising it. It was customary, in churchly houses, to have the Scriptures or some other holy work read aloud while the members of the household were at table: Philippe frequently made such use of the *De vita*.

During the first months of this stay in Pavia Petrarch's main literary undertaking was the completion of the *De remediis utriusque fortune*.

THE LETTER TO URBAN SENT TO AVIGNON

Petrarch was extremely anxious that his letter to Urban should not fall into hostile hands; and it was not for some weeks after his return to Pavia that he found an absolutely reliable messenger, and entrusted the letter to him.

He was extremely anxious, also, as to the effect the letter might have on Urban, his anxiety being due primarily to the intensity of his conviction that the Pope ought to return to Rome. He instructed his messenger, accordingly, to deliver the letter not to the Pope himself, but to the papal secretary, Francesco Bruni, to whom Petrarch sent, by the same messenger, precise written instructions as to the way in which Bruni was to handle the letter. First of all, Bruni is himself to read the letter, alone, unhurriedly, and without advisers; and if he finds anything in it that seems to him objectionable he is not to give the letter to the Pope, but is to send it back to Petrarch without showing it to anyone else. If he does not object to anything that he finds in it, he is to call in, as advisers, Philippe de Cabassoles and Agapito Colonna (Bishop of Ascoli) and submit the letter to them; and if there is anything in it that seems objectionable to them, Bruni is to send it back to Petrarch without showing it to anyone else. If it should be approved by Bruni, Philippe, and Agapito, Bruni is then to give it to the Pope, quietly, and without making any ado about it.

Bruni followed Petrarch's instructions exactly; approval of the letter was unanimous; and Bruni accordingly gave it to the Pope, whose reception of it was all that could have been desired. He even asked Bruni to write some comments on it.

Urban actually left Provence for Rome in the following spring: it seems probable that Petrarch's extraordinary letter had some influence upon him as he came to the making of his momentous decision.

OCTOBER–DECEMBER

On the 4th of October Petrarch finished his work on the *De remediis*, and dated the end of his manuscript thus: "Pavia. In the year of our Lord 1366, on the fourth day before the Nones of October, at the third hour."

In its completed form the *De remediis* consists of the dedicatory letter addressed to Azzo da Correggio; a first Book, containing more than a hundred chapters, each devoted to an aspect of favorable fortune; and a second Book, which opens with a prologue devoted mainly to exposition of the idea of the constancy and the ubiquity of conflict in all forms of animate life, and continues with more than a hundred chapters, each devoted to an aspect of adverse fortune. Among the topics treated in the first Book are bodily beauty, health and speed, eloquence, noble birth, banquets, personal adornment, fragrances, singing, dancing, ballplaying, dice and chess, hunting, palatial abodes, furniture, jewels, books, the title of Doctor, wealth, gardens, elephants, camels and monkeys, dowries, wives, children, teachers, students, fair weather, travel by sea, release from prison, popular favor, high office, warfare, vengeance, alchemy, and soothsayers. Among those treated in the second Book are ugliness, weakness, illness, base birth, poverty, servants, importunate neighbors, shipwreck, theft, overcrowded houses, imprisonment, exile, old age, gout, sleeplessness, bad dreams, earthquakes, toothache, blindness, deafness, the seven deadly sins, and the fear of death. In its massive entirety the *De remediis* is tedious; but it is rich in human understanding, and contains notable reflections on many varieties of human experience.

By late October Giovanni Malpaghini, who had now been in

the service of Petrarch for two years, had virtually completed the enormous task of copying the collection of the *Familiares* from Petrarch's exceedingly difficult revised drafts. As finished, the collection consists of twenty-four Books, which contain a total of three hundred and fifty letters.

In his great satisfaction at Giovanni's achievement, Petrarch wrote to Boccaccio a letter in which he says that he has come to love Giovanni as a son, and gives this account of his qualities and remarkable abilities:

> His moderation and his seriousness would be laudable even in an old man, his intelligence is keen and quick, his memory is rapacious, capacious, and, what is more, tenacious. . . . He has a marked gift of invention, a noble urge to write, and a heart devoted to the Muses. . . . The common folk does not love and seek money as much as he hates and rejects it; one tries in vain to give him coins; it is all one can do to make him accept what is necessary for the maintenance of life; he vies with me, and often surpasses me, in his desire for solitude and in fasting and keeping vigil.

Now that Giovanni had finished his work on the collection of the *Familiares*, Petrarch turned to the making of a fifth and enlarged form of the *Canzoniere*, with Giovanni to do the transcription. This form was to preserve the division into two parts—the second part beginning with the *canzone I' vo pensando*—that had appeared in each of the three preceding forms; and Petrarch's plan was to begin each of the two parts of the fifth form with most or all of the corresponding part of the fourth form, and to enlarge each part by the addition of poems that had not previously been included in the collection: the poems that were thus to be added were to be selected from a stock of some two hundred poems that he had on hand.

He provided Giovanni with a supply of parchment quaternions, and gave him first, as ready to be transcribed, the first 163 poems of the fourth form, and two other poems. Giovanni's transcription of this first block of poems probably began in October and was probably completed at about the end of the year.

While Giovanni was engaged in the transcription of these poems, Petrarch was deciding what poems he should add to the collection, revising them if they seemed to him to need revision, and planning the order in which he wanted them to stand.

At about the end of the year Petrarch returned to Venice. Immediately after his return Donato Albanzani came to see him, bringing him the long-awaited copy of Leontius' translation of Homer, and showing him a letter in which Boccaccio expressed his fear that Petrarch's long stays in Pavia were restricting his freedom.

----------------------------- ❧ -----------------------------

XXIX. *Venice, Padua, and Pavia: 1367*

PETRARCH took great delight in his grandson, the little Francesco. He speaks of him as "the chief solace of my life, and the hope and joy of the house," and as being of remarkable intelligence and beauty. Of his own affection for him he says: "the love of that little boy so filled my heart that it would be hard to say whether I had ever felt such love before." And he refers to him again as "the one sweet solace of this so-called life of mine, the one joy of the increasing burden of my age, the one light of my eyes."

VENICE

Not long after his return to Venice Petrarch wrote to Boccaccio a letter in which he seeks to calm Boccaccio's fears. His statement as to his "freedom," as to his association with men called "tyrants," and as to the relative desirability of government by one man and government by a whole people runs thus:

Lay aside your fear on my behalf, and be assured that hitherto, while I might seem to have been subject to a yoke, I have always been the freest of men, and as far as I can see I shall continue to be so. I shall endeavor . . . to be free in spirit wherever I may be, even if it be necessary for me to be subject, bodily and materially, to rulers—whether to a single ruler, as in my own case, or to many rulers, as in your case. I believe it easier to stand a man than a tyrannous people. If I had not been able to live in freedom [of spirit] either my life itself or at least my tranquillity and contentment would have come to an end. Nor would I ever serve

anyone [even bodily and materially] save of my own free
will and as affection may command.

The letter ends with thanks for the Homer:

Your Homer has at last reached us, and has filled me, and
all the Greeks and Latins who dwell in my library, with
joy and marvelous delight.

About the first of the year, in all probability, Giovanni Malpaghini had finished his transcription of the first 165 poems of
Part I of the *Canzoniere*. When he had reached this point Petrarch had not yet decided what poems should come next in Part
I. He was satisfied, however, that Part II should begin with the
41 poems that had constituted Part II of the fourth form; and he
therefore told Giovanni to transcribe these poems, beginning on
a new quaternion. By the time Giovanni had finished this second
task, Petrarch had twenty-four poems ready to be added to Part
I; and by the time Giovanni had transcribed those poems Petrarch had fourteen ready to be added to Part II. It was at some
time before mid-April that Giovanni finished the transcription of
this fourth block of poems.

Before the middle of a March that may have been either that
of 1367 or that of 1368 Petrarch received from Sagremor de
Pommiers a letter telling him that he had become a Cistercian
monk, and asking for copies of Petrarch's *Penitential Psalms* and
De vita solitaria. Petrarch replied promptly, expressing his pleasure in the news of Sagremor's entrance into the monastic life, and
exhorting him to persevere in his holy vocation. He is sending
Sagremor a copy of the *Penitential Psalms*, but he has now only
his own copy of the *De vita:* he will have a copy made for
Sagremor if he can find a copyist.

PADUA

Not long after mid-March, apparently, Petrarch went to Padua
for a stay that lasted for a month or more.

He had come to love Giovanni Malpaghini as a son, and he had
reason to think that Giovanni was well content. On the 21st of
April, however, Giovanni came to him, with a look on his face
that Petrarch had never seen before, and told him that he wanted
to leave his service and go elsewhere.

When he recovered from his first speechless amazement he

asked Giovanni whether he or any member of the household had offended him. This Giovanni denied, adding, with tears in his eyes, that he knew there was no other place in the world where he could live in so much honor and tranquillity. This dialogue then followed:

"Unhappy youth, if all this is so, if you lack nothing that you need, if there is nothing here that offends you, what is it then that drives you away?"

"Nothing except that I cannot write any more."

"What is the trouble? Do your hands tremble? Or have your eyes grown dim?"

"No. But my passion for writing has not merely cooled: it has turned to ice. Nothing could induce me to write any more."

Petrarch then reminded him that he had often advised him not to work so steadily, and suggested that a temporary cessation of work might be all that he needed. But he replied:

"No, by Hercules! Never again will I write for you or for anyone else."

Petrarch then bade him give up writing entirely, and remain with him not as a copyist but as a son. But Giovanni answered:

"You are wasting your time. I could not endure living in a house in which I was of no use. I could not bring myself to eat bread that I had not earned."

After some further discussion Giovanni exclaimed:

"You are not getting anywhere, and you shall not hold me by any set of words."

And with that he dashed to the door, and would have run away but for the walls and moats that surrounded the city.

VENICE

Very soon thereafter, perhaps immediately, Petrarch and Giovanni returned to Venice. Giovanni's determination to leave was unshaken, but he had not made up his mind where to go. He spoke now of Naples, now of Calabria, and now of Constantinople, indicating a desire to learn Greek; but when he left, very soon after the return to Venice, he said that he was going to Avignon.

Soon after the middle of May Petrarch received a letter from his son-in-law, Francescuolo da Brossano, who was then in Pavia, telling him that Giovanni Malpaghini had arrived there after a considerable series of hardships and perils; and that he had sought out Francescuolo, who at first had not recognized him in his sorry state, but after realizing who he was had taken pity on him, and had bidden him to stay in Petrarch's house and await his coming.

TO PAVIA

Within a few days Petrarch started for Pavia, doubtless in response to an invitation from Galeazzo. He made his journey to Pavia by barge, via the Po and the Ticino—the first stage being presumably from Venice down the lagoon to Chioggia, and the second from Chioggia down the Adriatic coast to one of the mouths of the Po. It may be, however, that he went first from Venice to Padua, and thence, perhaps by canal, to a point on the Po. On his way he finally wrote his reply to the four Aristotelians who more than a year before had declared that he was "a good man, but uneducated." To this reply, the most brilliant of his several invectives, he gave the brilliant title *De sui ipsius et multorum ignorantia*. The little book is addressed to Donato Albanzani.

PAVIA

When his barge reached Pavia, he found at the landing-place, waiting to greet him, a group of friends—and, among them, Giovanni Malpaghini, his eyes downcast in shame. Petrarch embraced him, but with less than his wonted affection.

It was perhaps on that very night or on the next day that Giovanni told Petrarch his pitiful story. He had made his way over the Apennines, in a deluge of rain, to Pisa; there he had waited in vain for a ship that would take him to Provence; then, amid hardships and dangers, he had recrossed the Apennines; he had nearly been drowned in an attempt to ford the Taro; he had made his way to Pavia, knowing that Petrarch would soon be there; and in Pavia Francescuolo da Brossano had received him kindly and had bidden him to stay in Petrarch's house there and await his arrival.

Before the end of June, presumably, Giovanni had resumed his work as copyist—perhaps helping Petrarch with his correspondence, but doing no more work on the *Canzoniere*. Petrarch, however, had now little confidence in Giovanni—and what confidence he still had was shaken when he learned that during Giovanni's peregrinations he had told inquirers that he was traveling at Petrarch's behest. Thinking that Giovanni would be leaving him again before long, Petrarch put aside a sum of money that might serve him on his travels; and he resolved to be a friendly employer to him as long as he might stay.

In June, presumably, Petrarch lost the pleasure of association with Pandolfo Malatesta, who had left Pavia and the Visconti before the end of the month.

THE RETURN OF THE POPE

In May and June Petrarch must have rejoiced to hear of the Pope's decision to return to Rome, and of the progress of that return. Urban left Avignon at the end of April, spent some time in Marseilles, embarked there, on a Venetian galley, and reached Italy early in June, going to Viterbo, where he remained through the summer.

Certain cardinals, following him by land, passed through Pavia about the middle of June: among them was Pierre Roger, who had a very friendly talk with Petrarch.

BOCCACCIO IN VENICE

Meanwhile, Boccaccio had been in Venice. The story of his visit is told in a delightful letter that he wrote to Petrarch after returning to Florence. Desiring to visit Petrarch again, he had left Certaldo late in March; but he had stopped in Florence for a long time, partly because of the continuing bad weather, partly because of the solicitousness of his friends, and partly because of fear of the dangers of the journey, as reported to him by recent travelers. After hearing that Petrarch was going to Pavia, he decided nevertheless to go on to Venice, since he had matters to attend to there for some of his friends, and since he wanted to become acquainted with Petrarch's daughter and son-in-law. He traveled with Francesco Allegri, apparently a Florentine who had a house in Venice. At a point near Venice he chanced to meet Francescuolo da Brossano. Arriving in Venice, he accepted the hospitality of Francesco Allegri, declining offers from other friends and the hospitality that Petrarch had offered him by letter. As soon as he had rested somewhat, he went to pay his respects to Petrarch's daughter Francesca, who received him with a becoming affectionateness. She entertained him and other friends in the garden, and renewed her father's offer of hospitality. Presently in came her little daugher Eletta, who, though she did not know who Boccaccio was, looked at him and smiled. She reminded Boccaccio instantly of the little daughter that he had loved and lost, and, deeply moved, he took her into his arms. Before many days had passed Francescuolo returned to Venice, and showed all possible courtesy and kindness to Boccaccio. While in Venice, also, Boccaccio was received with particular honor by Guido da Bagnolo.

A year earlier, on his 63rd birthday, Petrarch had written to Boccaccio, saying that he faced the traditional "grand climacteric" without fear. Now, having survived his 63rd year, he wrote again to Boccaccio, reporting that he could not remember any period of his life in which he had enjoyed better health. No personal disaster had befallen him, and two events of public importance had rejoiced him: the capture of Alexandria by King Peter of Cyprus and Urban's return to Rome.

Writing to Pietro da Muglio toward the end of August, Petrarch says that things are going well with him, but that he is saddened by the departure of Pandolfo and by the death of Galeazzo's chief minister and counselor, Giovanni de'Pepoli. He asks that Francesco da Carrara be assured that he (Petrarch) would not under any circumstances take Giovanni's place.

Either in the summer or somewhat later Petrarch's son-in-law was appointed to a position in the government of Pavia, and his wife and children joined him there.

Between mid-October and mid-November Petrarch spent some time in the country near Milan—perhaps at Pagazzano, perhaps at Garegnano, perhaps elsewhere. There Petrarch's friend Stefano Colonna, Provost of Saint-Omer, who was on his way from Avignon to Rome, spent a few hours with him. They had not seen each other for a long time, and each of them had much to tell. Petrarch asked him to give Pope Urban a message assuring him of his devotion, a devotion he had never felt for any of Urban's predecessors.

RETURN TO VENICE

Leaving Pavia about the middle of November, Petrarch returned to Venice without stopping in Padua for any length of time on the way.

After reaching Venice he was shocked to learn from men who had been with the Venetian fleet that had brought Urban to Italy that immediately after they had set sail from Marseilles certain cardinals—to the amazement of the sailors and of others on board—had broken out into wailing, crying out "Oh the bad pope, oh the heartless father, where on earth is he taking the poor sons that he has torn from their home?" Either from these same men or else from other sources he learned that shortly before Urban had left Avignon the King of France, Charles V, had sent an embassy to Avignon, with Ancel Choquart as orator, to endeavor to dissuade Urban from leaving France, and that Choquart, not content with exalting the claims of France, had heaped scorn on Italy.

The news from Rome was bad also. The bitter hostility of the French cardinals to Rome and to Italy continued. The heat in Viterbo had been intense, and a clash had occurred there between some of the citizens and some of the servants of the cardinals. No supply of the wine of Beaune had reached Rome. The air of Rome was called unhealthy. A cardinal who was taken seriously ill had sent word to the Pope that his doctor said that the only hope for his recovery lay in a return to his fatherland, and he therefore requested permission to return to France.

From such tidings Petrarch inevitably drew the conclusion that there was a real danger that Urban might be unable to withstand the pressure, and might be forced to return to Avignon.

Not long after Petrarch's return to Venice he received from Pietro da Muglio a letter which, though worded cautiously, indicates clearly that Petrarch's Paduan friends were worried lest his association with the Visconti should interfere with his freedom of movement, though not with his mental freedom. And one friend had reported to Pietro that Francesco da Carrara, on hearing of Petrarch's return to Venice, had complained repeatedly, presumably because Petrarch had made no stay in Padua, and that he had asked eagerly when Petrarch was coming to Padua again.

After reaching Venice and before the end of the year Petrarch wrote his last letter to Guido Sette—a long and famous autobiographical letter reviewing much of the course of his life. But Guido died before this letter reached its destination.

XXX. *Venice, Padua, and Pavia*
January - July 1368

T H E news that had reached Petrarch regarding the Pope's
return to Rome had troubled him greatly. He was angered
by the fact that an orator sent to Avignon by the King of France
should have dared to disparage Italy; and he realized that there
was danger that the continuing hostility to Rome and to Italy
shown by the French cardinals might force Urban to return to
Avignon. Under these circumstances he felt constrained to write
to Urban again, his main purpose being to fortify Urban's intention to remain in Rome.

This new letter, written probably soon after the first of the new
year, opens with the quotation "In exitu Israel de Egypto, domus
Iacob de populo barbaro"—Egypt meaning France and the barbarian people meaning the French—and congratulates Urban on
his actual return to Rome. To this first accomplishment the Pope
is then exhorted to add a second, equally great and equally difficult: a reform of the Sacred College that would imbue it with a
truly apostolic purity and fervor. The letter contains bitter criticism of the French cardinals, in particular for their addiction to
life in Avignon and to the wine of Beaune: consideration of
wines would be proper in selecting a site for a bacchanalian fes-
tival, but is shameful in selecting a site for the papacy.

A portion of the letter that was to have noteworthy repercus-
sions is devoted to a comparison of Italy and France in terms of
intellectual achievement, the palm being given to Italy. All four
of the Doctors of the Church were Italian, two by birth, and the
other two by study or residence: "Nullus est gallicus. Nullus
doctus in Gallia." Civil and canon law are Italian in origin and
development. The great Latin orators and poets were all Italian by
birth or study. The Latin language and Latin literature are the
foundations of all the arts and sciences. France has nothing comparable to offer.

Referring to the anti-Italian oration that had been delivered by
Choquart, Petrarch offers himself as a duelist, on behalf of Italy

and of truth, in a contest of writings—a written contest, because "spoken words are fugitive; written words remain."

This letter, however, was not dispatched immediately; and when it was sent forward, a little later, it was sent to Bruni, under safeguarding conditions virtually identical with those under which Petrarch's earlier letter to Urban had been sent in the previous summer. It was well received by Urban, but it gave great offense to the French cardinals to whom it became known. A "duelist" was found to reply to it; but it was several years before Petrarch even knew that such a reply had been written.

PADUA

Early in the spring, probably in March or early April, Petrarch went to Padua. At this time he was still expecting to resume residence in Venice; but he never did so.

In Padua, Giovanni Malpaghini began the making of a fine copy of Leontius' translations of the *Iliad* and the *Odyssey*.

At about the same time Petrarch, who no longer had any thought of requiring Giovanni to do any further work on the *Canzoniere*, decided to go on with the work himself, taking it up at the point at which Giovanni had left it. Before the middle of May he had made legible copies, on his work sheets, of ten poems that he had written long before. In one case, while making a copy of a sonnet beginning *L'aura serena*, he became so much interested in it that he then and there drafted on the same work sheet two companion sonnets, beginning *L'aura gentil* and *L'aura celeste*, which represent Laura as living: these are probably the last sonnets that Petrarch ever wrote. By the month of May he had transcribed all twelve of these poems into the unfinished series of quaternions. He was to go on with such work, preparing and copying one or two or a few more poems at a time, to the end of his life.

Late in April Charles IV entered Italy with a considerable body of troops, in agreement with the enemies of the Visconti; and Francesco da Carrara, taking Petrarch and Bishop Pietro Pileo with him, went to Udine to greet the Emperor. Jan ze Středa, the Imperial Chancellor, coming in advance of the Emperor, reached Udine on the 24th of April; and the Emperor arrived on the 27th. He was received with elaborate ceremonies, and remained in Udine for about a week. Petrarch must have been glad to meet the Emperor and Jan ze Středa once more. From Udine the Emperor moved slowly southward to Padua, where Petrarch, who had presumably returned earlier, doubtless met the Emperor and the Chancellor again.

While in Padua Petrarch received an urgent request from Galeazzo Visconti that he should come at once to Pavia, where his presence was desired in order that he might participate in the negotiation of a treaty of peace. He hesitated to go, both because of the approach of summer heat and because the roads were infested by robbers. But the summons to help in the peace negotiations prevailed; and he asked the Emperor for permission to go, and received that permission, coupled with the command that he return to Padua.

It is probable that during this stay in Padua Francesco da Carrara brought pressure on Petrarch—pressure of kindness, pressure of argument, and pressure of insistent request—to resume residence in Padua, and that he asked him, in particular, not to stay long in Pavia. It is probable, also, that Petrarch agreed to return fairly soon from Pavia, but that he was not ready to commit himself to a resumption of residence in Padua.

PAVIA

Petrarch reached Pavia at the end of May. There a great sorrow awaited him: his dearly loved little grandson had just died. He wrote for him a touching epitaph in Latin verse, and had it incised in golden letters on a marble slab that was placed on an inner wall of the church of San Zeno, above the point of burial.

At some time in June Petrarch went to Milan, called there, probably, to attend the festivities celebrating the wedding of Galeazzo's daughter Violante to Lionel, Duke of Clarence. While in Milan he was confined to his bed, for at least much of the time, by an ulcerated leg. On the 3rd of July he rode back to Pavia; but the riding was bad for his leg, and he had to go to bed again. He was up, but only partially recovered, a few days later.

In Pavia Giovanni Malphaghini came to the conclusion that he could not remain in Petrarch's service, after all. Having finished his copying of Leontius' *Iliad*, and of all but the last Book of the *Odyssey*, he now copied that last Book in a hurried script very different from his usual beautiful script. He told Petrarch of his decision to leave, saying that he was planning to go first to Rome and then to southern Italy, where he hoped to learn Greek, and asking for letters of recommendation. Petrarch gave him two kindly letters, one to Bruni, in Rome, and the other to an officer in the royal service in Naples. Giovanni then left, without any emotional outburst, and with Petrarch's consent. Sooner or later he found a position as an assistant to Bruni.

XXXI. *Padua: July 1368 - December 1369*

TO PADUA

LEAVING Pavia by mid-July, Petrarch went by barge down the Ticino and the Po. The Po was within the area of warfare; armed boats were everywhere; troops were on the banks of the river; and Petrarch's boatmen and servants were pale with fright. He, however, was unafraid, and was not only unharmed, but honored. His barge, indeed, was so laden with wine, fowls, fruit, and other gifts brought to him by the soldiery that his voyage proceeded slowly.

PADUA

A hearty welcome awaited him in Padua. He reached the city toward evening, in a hard rainstorm. His arrival had been expected: Francesco da Carrara himself had come to the city gate to meet him, but because of the rain and the approach of night had gone back to his palace, leaving some of his men to serve as an escort for Petrarch. Furthermore, Francesco sent servants, bearing various gifts, to Petrarch's house, and later in the evening he came himself, with a few companions; sat down to supper with Petrarch; and after supper stayed on talking, among Petrarch's books, until bedtime.

Soon after Petrarch's arrival in Padua, Donato Albanzani brought him two letters, one from the Pope and one from Bruni, that had come during his absence in Pavia: these letters had been written before Petrarch's second letter to Urban had reached Rome.

The Pope's letter expressed his appreciation of Petrarch's (first) letter, and his desire to see Petrarch and to extend favor to him: in his reply Petrarch voices his gratitude for Urban's "urbanity," and says, with reference to Urban's invitation, that in spite of his age, the heat, and a recent illness, he will try to come.

Bruni's letter included a message of greeting from Coluccio Salutati, who had recently become his assistant; and Petrarch, in his reply, sends a gracious greeting to Coluccio. This exchange of greetings marked the beginning of a cordial epistolary friendship between Petrarch and Coluccio, who had never met, and were never to meet.

THE "DE VIRIS ILLUSTRIBUS"

It was generally known that Petrarch had begun the *De viris illustribus*, and that he had not finished it. The only portions of it that he had certainly completed before 1368 were the 23 biographies, chiefly of Roman heroes, that he had written by 1343, and the twelve biographies of early non-Romans that he had written in the years 1351–53. He had done some work on the *De viris* while in Milan, but that work probably did not include the writing of any new biography. It is possible that he had begun a biography of Caesar in or after 1361.

Probably while Petrarch was in Padua in 1368 Francesco da Carrara requested him to complete the *De viris*, and to dedicate it to him. Petrarch of course agreed to do so; and he soon wrote an appropriate dedicatory preface. It is highly probable that Petrarch now planned to complete his series of biographies by adding, to the original twenty-three, thirteen more, all of Romans, ending with Trajan. It may well be that he began or continued his biography of Caesar as part of his undertaking to complete the *De viris:* there is no evidence that he ever did any work on any other new biography.

THE "SALA VIRORUM ILLUSTRIUM"

Francesco da Carrara desired also to have the great hall of his palace decorated with a series of frescoes of illustrious men, and having in mind Petrarch's writing of the *De viris* he asked his advice as to the selection of the men who should be represented. The hall in question was and is an oblong room, with long walls on the north and south, and short walls, broken by windows, on the east and west. It is now called the "Sala dei Giganti." It is highly probable that Petrarch's list of the heroes to be portrayed included the same thirty-six men for whom he had already written or was planning to write biographies; that the series of frescoes began with a portrait of Romulus in the north-west corner, continued in chronological order clockwise around the hall, and ended with a portrait of Trajan in the southwest corner; that below each portrait there was an appropriate historical scene; and that below each historical scene there was an inscription. It is probable also that Petrarch advised the (unknown) painter or painters with regard to certain details of Roman architecture, his advice being based on his exact knowledge of such matters—a knowledge gained on his archaeological peregrinations in Rome.

The frescoes painted at this time were irremediably damaged by fire about 1500; but a new series, painted about 1540, retains some of the features of the original series.

Not long after Petrarch's return to Padua, Boccaccio arrived for a visit that continued into September, when Boccaccio went on to Venice. Late in 1367 Boccaccio had been in Rome as an envoy sent by Florence to give the official greetings of the city to the newly returned Pope, and while there he had seen something of Bruni and of Coluccio Salutati. Now, doubtless, during his visit in Padua, he told Petrarch much of what he had seen and heard in Rome: Petrarch must have been keenly interested. During this visit also—or, with Petrarch's permission, in Venice—Boccaccio made for himself copies of some of the works of Petrarch that he had not previously possessed.

Not long after Boccaccio's departure Petrarch's health began to fail—though no serious illness developed for another year.

Early in September Petrarch must have heard that a treaty of peace not unfavorable to the Visconti had been signed in Modena, under the auspices of the Emperor. In view of his own probable participation in the preliminary negotiations this news must have brought him much personal satisfaction.

In the course of the summer or early autumn Petrarch finally decided to resume residence in Padua. The probabilities are that he came to this decision mainly because of the kindly pressure brought to bear on him by Francesco da Carrara; but it may well be that other considerations had some weight with him.

His tenancy of the house in the cathedral close had never ceased; he had spent some time there occasionally during his Venetian years; and his relations with the Paduan clergy, including the Bishop, had been uniformly happy. Francesco da Carrara had already made much of him, and had just taken him as a companion on the mission to Udine to greet the Emperor: he could therefore look forward to continuance of the friendliest patronage, and to new opportunities for service of a public nature. It is quite possible that Petrarch still longed for a home in the country, and that there was already present to his mind the possibility of finding such a home as he was soon to find at Arquà.

Petrarch's resumption of residence in Padua does not preclude the possibility that he went to Venice now and then, though there is no evidence that he did so. He probably brought many, at least, of his books to Padua, or had them sent there; but if he did so it was presumably without prejudice to the carrying-out of his part of the agreement made when he had moved to Venice in 1362.

It was probably not very long after Petrarch had decided to remain in Padua that he received from Francesco da Carrara a gift that was to determine happily the location of the home of his last years—a gift of land at Arquà, about ten miles southwest of Padua, in the lovely Euganean hills.

At some time in the autumn, probably in October, Petrarch was rejoiced to learn that Philippe de Cabassoles had been made a cardinal and was now in Italy.

Before the end of 1368—perhaps even much earlier—Petrarch had formed additional warm friendships in Padua: with the brothers Bonaventura and Bonsembiante Badoer, both Augustinian monks; with Giovanni Dondi, an eminent physician; with Lombardo della Seta, a minor humanist who was to be devotedly helpful to Petrarch in many ways; with Manno Donati, a Florentine *condottiere* resident in Padua; and with some other men.

About the first of February, 1369, there came to Petrarch from Coluccio Salutati a letter reporting that the Pope had received his (Petrarch's) second letter benignantly, but that it had made the French cardinals very angry. It is their intention, Coluccio says, that someone should reply to the charges contained in that letter, exalting the excellence of France in its great cities, in music, in theology, in the flourishing condition of the University of Paris, in skill in the mechanical arts—and even in its wine of Beaune, which they claim to be conducive to temperance—and deriding Italian boastfulness based on ancient glories, and such local traits as "Roman incivility, Genoese pride, Florentine avarice, Venetian weakness and Lombard voracity." Decision lies with the Pope; but Petrarch should gird himself for the defense of Italy.

Another letter from Coluccio, received somewhat later, urges Petrarch to come to Rome, to see for himself what Urban has already achieved: Rome is rising from its ruins; St. John Lateran, St. Paul's and St. Peter's are being restored; the license of Italian clerics is being repressed; and the ceremonies of Holy Week have been attended by an unprecedented multitude, the papal benediction being given and received with profound emotion. The Pope desires Petrarch's presence; winter is past; the roads are open; and peace prevails.

In the course of the spring Petrarch was having a house built in Arquà, on the land given to him by Francesco da Carrara, and was having trees and bushes planted around it—his Paduan friend Lombardo della Seta overseeing the actual planting. Some of the trees were gifts from Petrarch's son-in-law. Not all the tree-planting was successful; but the planting of vines and bushes went well, except for nibbling by animals that frequented the place while the building was going on. All this Petrarch recorded in his Palladius. During the spring he doubtless went out to Arquà occasionally, to see how the building and the planting were getting on.

About the first of June Petrarch went to Pavia, for a brief and uneventful visit that was to be his last visit there. By mid-August, and perhaps considerably earlier, he had returned to Padua.

In the course of the summer he must have learned, presumably with little or no surprise, but doubtless not without a lingering disappointment, that the Emperor was returning to Prague.

Early in the autumn he was taken with an exhausting fever. In the course of the month his illness became so severe that he could not go even to the cathedral unless his friends or his servants supported him. Up to this time his health had usually been good; but he never fully recovered from the illness that had now come upon him.

Invitations from the Pope kept coming to him. To one such invitation, transmitted by Philippe de Cabassoles, he replied, by the hand of an amanuensis, begging Urban to hold him excused because of his illness.

At some time in the autumn he received from Boccaccio a copy of an invective that he (Boccaccio) had written against the four

Aristotelians who had spoken disparagingly of Petrarch, and an accompanying letter, in which Boccaccio said that he had heard that when Petrarch had first learned of the pronouncement of his adversaries he (Petrarch) had been furious, and had started at once to write his own invective.

In his reply Petrarch speaks of his loss of health, and thanks Boccaccio for his invective, which he praises for its style, its judgment, and its affection. He says, however, that the report of his own fury is baseless, and that he had begun the writing of his own invective only after a year had passed, and even then only on the continued urging of Donato Albanzani. The pronouncement of the Aristotelians, he asserts, had moved him not to fury, but to laughter because of their ineptitude.

Before the end of the year Petrarch received a letter from Urban himself, desiring him to come to Rome, and indicating that he had it in mind to do something generous for him.

Petrarch in his answer says that he had hoped to come, but that his illness has left him so weak that he could not possibly get himself onto a horse. His physicians, however, are bidding him hope that he will be better in the spring. He is planning, therefore, to come then, and he is already beginning to get the necessary horses that he will need—two horses, he says, are usually enough for him, but for this journey he will need more than two. Turning finally to the Pope's proposed benefaction he does his best to make it clear, within the bounds of courtesy and of reverence, that a great benefaction would burden him by distracting him from his desired quiet freedom, but that a lesser benefaction that would increase such freedom would be gratefully received.

———————— ❧ ————————

XXXII. *Arquà: 1370*

PETRARCH'S HOUSE

EARLY in 1370 Petrarch's house was ready for him, and he moved into it before the end of March. It was built partly of masonry and partly of wood; on each of the two floors there were four rooms; the window-arches were pointed; and above the front door there was a wooden pensile balcony. The house still stands. It has recently been restored, as far as possible, to its original state: complete restoration, however, was found to be impossible—in particular, the relatively modern masonry projection at the front of the house could not be removed.

There are in the house two pieces of furniture that were probably used by Petrarch in his study: an armchair, and an upright chest with four compartments, presumably for books lying on their sides. We know of two other possessions of Petrarch that have now disappeared, but were certainly in the house in his time: his lute, and a Madonna that he describes, in his Will, as "a work of that excellent painter Giotto, the beauty of which the ignorant do not comprehend, while masters of the art find it wonderful."

There was much planting around the house. It stands on a southern hillside, facing south, and commands a fine view.

Francesco da Carrara, who was fond of Arquà, came there from time to time to see Petrarch, as did other friends; and Petrarch went occasionally into Padua, where his house in the cathedral close was still available for his use.

PETRARCH'S WILL

As the spring of 1370 approached, Petrarch felt well enough to try to go to Rome. It seems probable, however, that he faced the journey with some trepidation: it was at this time that he decided to make his Will.

He wrote it on the 4th of April, in Padua. After appropriate opening reflections and a commending of his soul to Christ, he deals with the matter of the burial of his body, listing seven places—Padua, Arquà, Venice, Milan, Pavia, Rome, and Parma —and indicating in each case the church in or near which he desires to be buried if he should die in the place in question. In his statement as to Arquà he says that he is hoping to build a small chapel there in honor of the Blessed Virgin, and that if he dies in Arquà after building it he would wish to be buried there, but otherwise in or near the parish church (he never built the chapel). He then specifies his several bequests: to the Cathedral of Padua; to the church in or near which he may be buried; to Christ's poor; and to several individuals, among them Francesco da Carrara (his Madonna by Giotto), Donato Albanzani (a remission of indebtedness), Lombardo della Seta (horses, and a silver cup), Boccaccio ("fifty gold florins, for a warm gown to be worn when he is studying or meditating on winter nights"), Tommaso Bombasi (his lute, to be played "not for worldly vanity, but to the praise of the eternal God"), Giovanni Dondi (fifty ducats for a finger-ring), his servant Pancaldo (twenty ducats, that are not to be used for gambling), and his brother Gherardo (a hundred florins at once, or five or ten annually, as he may prefer). Francescuolo da Brossano is named as his residuary legatee, and is referred to "not only as an heir, but as a very dear son." He desires that his property at Vaucluse be used for the benefit of Christ's poor, or, if that should not be legally feasible, that it go to the heirs of his faithful overseer, Raymond Monet.

SYNCOPE IN FERRARA

Soon after the writing of his Will Petrarch set out from Padua for Rome. His account of what happened to him, as reported in a later letter to Pope Urban, may be summarized thus:

I started out with such alacrity as had never, I believe, marked the beginning of any other journey. But my alacrity was of the spirit only. My body was still weak and ill, and I put my faith in the help of Heaven. And so it happened that on the way my desire to reach your presence led me to make greater haste than was fitting for my lack of strength and for my age; and suddenly death halted me. . . . Nor was it merely illness, but true death. Others may say that only through poetic fiction or through undue exaggeration could one give the name of death to a malady or a syncope. . . . All I can say is that for more than thirty hours I was unconscious. . . . There was no thought in my mind and no feeling in my body; I knew nothing of the many and drastic remedies that were being tried . . . everyone said and thought that I was dead. . . . I was lying in the palace of the lords of Ferrara, who were greatly distressed. . . . The report of my death spread widely, reaching Padua, Venice, Milan, Pavia, and other places where there are friends of mine. . . . When consciousness returned I desired as much as ever to continue my journey; nor would I have been deterred by the menaces of the physicians, who all with one accord affirmed that it would be impossible for me to reach Rome alive. . . . But what prevented me from coming was not fear, but my weakness, which would have kept me not only from coming to Rome, but even from returning to Padua, were it not that I was taken thither by boat, lying flat on my back.

Of the care and affection shown him in Ferrara, especially by the young Marquis Ugo d'Este, Petrarch writes thus, in effect, in a letter sent to the Marquis Niccolò later in the year, after the death of Ugo:

> Never shall I forget how kindly you received me, as if I were a member of your own family, doing everything that could possibly be done for me—or how your brother, now a blest soul, came to see me three or four times every day, showing his sympathy in his words, his manner, and his looks, and bringing me—in that kind and gentle voice of his—such consolation, such generous offers, and such soothing that I was hardly aware of my condition.

After his return to Padua he remained there for some time, ill, and grieving over the failure of his hopes. Messengers from Ugo kept coming to him, bringing him letters and gifts.

SUMMER

By mid-June, probably, Petrarch, though still in poor health, returned to Arquà; and at about the same time he heard the news —distressing news for him—that the Pope was planning to return to Avignon.

It was probably before the end of June that Petrarch received a letter of advice from his physician-friend Giovanni Dondi, who was evidently much worried about Petrarch's physical condition: Petrarch calls the letter faithful and solicitous. Giovanni's general premise was that for the sake of his health Petrarch should consider his advancing age, and should modify his manner of life, and in particular his habits in respect to eating and drinking. With regard to these habits Giovanni made six definite recommendations: (1–3) that Petrarch cease eating salted meat, salted fish, and raw vegetables; and (4–6) that he give up his habits of fasting, of eating fruit, and of drinking water.

Petrarch wrote promptly a long reply, which is fundamentally serious but in part jocose, and friendly in tone but strenuous in argument. He agrees, in general, with Giovanni's premise that he should consider his advancing age and should modify his habits accordingly; and he agrees, in particular, with Giovanni's recommendations that he refrain from eating salted meat, salted fish, and raw vegetables. But he disagrees emphatically with Giovanni's three other recommendations. He defense of his lifelong habit of fasting is based both on religious and on sanitary grounds. His defense of the use of fruits, based on the provision by nature of foods so inherently attractive, relies largely upon the attention paid by classical authors to agricultural matters. His most elaborate and most sarcastic defense is devoted to the justification of the use of water rather than of wine as his normal beverage. He cites the longevity of our earliest ancestors, the prowess of Roman warriors born of mothers who touched no wine, the prowess of ancient Gauls who knew no wine, and the devotion of Brahmans and Gymnosophists to the drinking of water; attacks the use of wine as a source of shame; and protests that neither the dicta of Hippocrates nor anything else could shake his conviction that it is good for him to drink water. Underlying his whole argument is his willing acceptance of old age and of the prospect of death. Old age is neither good nor bad in itself: it may indeed be bad, but it may be good if it is devoted to the cultivation of truth and wisdom. Death comes irresistibly and to all the works of nature and of man; and Petrarch himself has lived long enough, longer already than Virgil or Cicero or Caesar or Scipio. The authority of Hippocrates is belittled.

On a morning in early August word came to Petrarch of the death of the young Marquis Ugo d'Este, who had shown him such affectionate kindness while he had lain ill in Ferrara only a few months before. Though his continuing illness made it difficult for him to write, he wrote to the Marquis Niccolò, on that same morning, a deeply felt *consolatoria*.

At some time in the summer Petrarch, hoping that Pope Urban might still be induced to remain in Italy, began work on what was doubtless intended to be another long and carefully reasoned letter: he actually wrote, however, only an introduction, which contains this plea, supposed to be addressed to Urban by a personified Italy:

> When I was afflicted with deadly sores you came to me, to heal them; but now, before they are bound up or healed, you are departing. So now you desert me: but who knows whether Christ and Peter might not enable you to complete the healing process? You would be leaving us in dire peril, and peril would beset you even upon your journey: in the forests there are fighting men, in the fields there are plunderers, in the roads there are robbers. . . . Stay, then,

most blessed Father: for if you should not be persuaded by this exhortation He will meet you on your road, who met the retreating Peter, and when Peter said to Him "Quo vadis, Domine?" replied: "Vado Romam iterum crucifigi."

Petrarch's discontinuance of work upon this letter was presumably due to receipt of word that the Pope's decision was irrevocable—or perhaps that he had already left Rome, as he did about the first of September.

In August Manno Donati, after winning a major victory at Reggio over troops employed by Bernabò Visconti, returned to Padua in a state of exhaustion. At the end of the month Petrarch received from Lombardo della Seta, writing in Padua, a letter telling him that Manno had died, and asking him to include Manno in his *De viris illustribus*. Such inclusion was of course out of the question; but Petrarch did write for Manno, probably at once, an appropriate and laudatory epitaph in Latin verse, most of which was in fact inscribed on the tablet that marks Manno's tomb. Within a few days, however, Petrarch must have learned that Manno was alive and recovering: apparently he had suffered a syncope similar to that which Petrarch had suffered at Ferrara.

AUTUMN

Before the end of September Petrarch must have heard that Pope Urban had left Rome to return to Avignon; and he must have realized that this would necessarily mean that Francesco Bruni, as Urban's secretary, and Philippe de Cabassoles, as well as the cardinals in general, had also left for Avignon.

In the course of the autumn Petrarch, despite continuing weakness, was busy building an addition to his house and planting fruit trees. Before many months had passed he was to invite his daughter and her husband and their daughter to come and live with him: it is likely that the addition to his house was being made with a view to their coming.

Toward the end of October Giovanni Dondi wrote and sent to Petrarch a long rejoinder to the reply that Petrarch had written to him in the summer. He notes that Petrarch accepts the first three of his six specific recommendations, and says that he will plead again the soundness of the other three. He refuses to accept Petrarch's dismissal of the dicta of Hippocrates, arguing vigorously that just as one should respect the authority of Priscian, Cicero,

d Virgil, Aristotle, Archimedes and Euclid, and Ptole-
respective fields, so also one should respect the author-
rates in medicine. Acceptance of the first three of
tions is not enough: they are parts of a unified
t must be accepted in its entirety if the desired results
e attained. Partial change of habit is better than sudden
ge; but partial change should be made in the whole area of
habit. Petrarch may say that his physical nature, as he has grown
older, has changed not completely but partially, and that while
he will not entirely give up his habits in regard to fasting, eating
fruit, and drinking water, he will modify them slightly. If Petrarch will indeed take this position, agreement is in sight, for it
was modification rather than the complete abandonment of these
habits that Giovanni had urged in his previous letter. The letter
then develops into a carefully reasoned discussion of the three
habits concerned, arguing at length for moderate change in each
case.

Within a week or two Petrarch wrote a long reply to this rejoinder. He disposes at length of Giovanni's claim that one should
give to the authority of Hippocrates respect comparable to that
given to Priscian and the other ancients mentioned by Giovanni;
renews effectively much that he had said elsewhere in criticism
of physicians in general; and refers to physicians who do not
themselves follow the rules that they themselves set forth. He
trusts in nature rather than in medical lore; he is already moder-
ating his habits in certain respects (he is eating less fruit than for-
merly); and he agrees with Giovanni that in respect to the eating
of fruit and the drinking of water moderation is indeed desirable.
But he will not yield in the least in the matter of fasting. The letter is enriched by passages of classical learning and by modern
instances and anecdotes. It ends on a note of warm friendship,
and with the statement that he will soon be coming to Padua,
where Giovanni and he can meet face to face.

All in all, the debate carried on in the two letters of Giovanni
Dondi to Petrarch and in Petrarch's two replies is very notable
in form and content, in its vigor, and in its manifestation of a
deep underlying friendship.

At some time in November Petrarch received from Lombardo
della Seta a request for a statement of Petrarch's opinion as to the
nature of mortal life. In response, Petrarch wrote a *tour de force*
that consists mainly of a series of nearly two hundred epithetic

characterizations of mortal life, most of them combinations of just two Latin words. A few of these combinations may be rendered thus:

A performance of mountebanks, steaming caverns, a river of tears, a pleasing frenzy, helpless strength, sweet poison, rich poverty, beautiful ugliness, a leaking sack, stinging desire, a sticking burr, a fading flower, blind prudence, a black whirlwind, a pit of hatred, a chain of habits, a Siren song, Circean goblets, circling wheels, serious folly.

Before the end of the year Petrarch went into Padua, expecting to stay there for some time.

XXXIII. *Arquà: 1371 - 1372*

1371

WHILE still in Padua, and probably in January, Petrarch heard of the death of Pope Urban V and of the election of Gregory XI, who, as Cardinal Pierre Roger, on his way to Rome in 1367, had come to see him in Pavia.

About the first of the year Petrarch received a letter from Matteo Longo, Archdeacon of Liége, a friend of his young manhood, whom he had not seen since 1347 (in 1351 he had become the owner of the black dog that Matteo had left in Vaucluse). This letter reported that Matteo was in good health, and asked for news of Petrarch.

Petrarch's reply expresses his great pleasure and relief on hearing from Matteo, and gives a succinct account of his present state of spirit and body and of his main experiences in recent years. His spirit, he says, is now satisfactorily calm and tranquil. His bodily health had long been good, but in the last two years he has been ill and often thought to be dead. He has not changed in his general ways of life since he and Matteo had parted, twenty-four years since. He might have had high positions, but he has refused them, remaining thus in a more useful and a happier humility. He has nothing more than he had so long ago, except many years and a few books, and nothing less, except his health and the many friends that he has lost. He had lived for a time in Venice, but is now in Padua, at his church. He has built a house in the Euganean hills, small, but pleasant and respectable, and there he spends much of his time, reading, writing, and thinking. He has no fears, except for those he loves; he has no desires, except for a holy death; he regrets the necessity of keeping servants; he cannot escape a stream of visitors, but the task of entertainment is an honorable one. The Pope, the Emperor, the King of France, and other princes have called him to their courts, but he has refused, cherishing his liberty.

We do not know just when Petrarch returned to Arquà.

No springtime weather came to the region of Padua in 1371: bitter wintry cold was followed immediately by burning heat. In February or March Petrarch received from Philippe de Cabassoles a letter inviting him urgently to come to Avignon. Despite his ill health Petrarch made up his mind to undertake the journey, going as far as he could by barge, and then overland by slow stages; and he even set about packing.

Early in May, however, Petrarch, again in Padua, suffered one of his attacks of high fever. Doctors gathered at once, some of them sent by Francesco da Carrara, some of them coming out of friendly concern for Petrarch. They thought death imminent— one of them, at least, proclaimed that Petrarch could not live through the night—and declared that the only hope of keeping him alive was to bind him with cords in such a way that he could not sleep. This was not done, however: Petrarch's servants had standing orders either to pay no attention to directions given by doctors, or else to do exactly the opposite of what the doctors directed. The doctors came back in the morning, expecting to find Petrarch dead: they found him writing. He was so weakened, however, that he gave up the idea of going to Avignon.

In May, also, Petrarch received letters from the Pope and from Bruni. The Pope's letter and Petrarch's reply to it are not extant; but it is clear that the Pope's letter invited him to come to Avignon and that it indicated a disposition to confer some benefaction on him, and we know that Petrarch's reply was brief, and closed with a statement that he was writing to Bruni in full detail.

In his letter to Bruni he endeavors to make his feeling about a possible benefaction as clear as he can. His present income is such as would be adequate for a single canon, but he is compelled to maintain a household that is so large as to strain his resources. He would therefore welcome a benefaction, but he will be content with whatever Gregory may or may not do for him: "Whether he does much, or nothing, or just a little, I shall be content." Nor will he make any specific request. He recalls the conversation he had had with Clement VI in which Clement had said to him "Tell me what you would like to have me do for you, and I will do it"; and he had replied: "If you desire to do anything for me, Holy Father, let not only the giving of the gift be yours, but also the decision as to what the gift should be." It would be easier for him to say what he would not want than what he would want. Specifically, he would not want any appointment that would involve the cure of souls—the care of his own soul, he says, is enough and, he fears, more than enough for him.

The most interesting portion of this letter is that in which he tells of his household and his stables. He has servants; he keeps at least two horses; he usually has five or six copyists, but they are hard to find, and at the moment he has only three; a venerable priest is living with him; and dinnertime often sees the arrival of visitors. Furthermore, he is eager to build a small oratory dedicated to the Blessed Virgin, even if he has to pledge or sell his books in order to do so. Toward the end of the letter he speaks of his failing strength.

In the spring and summer the plague was raging in Venice and the Venetian territory, whence it spread to Padua; and Pandolfo Malatesta—who may not have known of Petrarch's move to Arquà—wrote to him, inviting him to come to Pesaro.

In his grateful reply Petrarch says that he would be very glad to pay a friendly visit to Pandolfo were he not prevented by his ill health, and bids Pandolfo not to worry about the possibility of his exposure to the plague, since he is living not in Venice or in Padua, but in a delightful and salubrious retreat in the Euganean hills.

Before the end of the year, in all probability, Petrarch went into Padua, planning to spend some time there, as he had done a year before.

It was probably in 1371, though possibly before the end of 1370, that Petrarch was visited in Arquà by Giovanni degli Abbarbaglia-ti, the Grand Prior of the Camaldolensian Order, with whom he had exchanged letters in 1363. Giovanni told him that while in Venice, recently, he had seen in the house of Donato Albanzani the copy of the *De vita solitaria* that Petrarch had given to Donato;

that he had been shocked to find that no mention was made therein of St. Romuald, the founder of the Camaldolensian Order, who had been a great lover of solitude; that he had asked Donato about this omission; and that Donato had replied that he knew of no cause for it. Giovanni then asked Petrarch about the omission: Petrarch replied that it was due simply to the fact that he had not known of St. Romuald's love of solitude, and asked Giovanni to send him a life of the saint. This Giovanni did, sending the life written by St. Peter Damian; and Petrarch then—still probably in 1371—wrote a passage of some length about St. Romuald's love of solitude, and inserted it in the *De vita*.

Probably at some time in 1371, though perhaps not until the following spring, Petrarch asked his daughter and her husband and their daughter Eletta, now about nine or ten years old, to come and live with him in Arquà; and they came.

After they had come Petrarch wrote to his brother, Gherardo, from whom he had not heard for four years. He tells of his ill health, of the invitations he has received, of his attempt to go to Rome, and of the house he has built, in which, though sick in body, he is living with a tranquil mind, without tumult or wanderings or cares, always reading and writing and praising God. He wishes that there were a Carthusian monastery near by, and that Gherardo might be there. The other members of his family are with him, and he has many friends in the region, including the lord of Padua, who has a filial affection for him. He is well satisfied to be neither rich nor poor. He has enough for his needs, and has made provision for Gherardo in his Will. He is content that he has not much longer to live on earth: "there is no faithful servant who, however fortunate in respect to the goods of this world, does not desire to behold the face of his Lord."

At some time in 1371, in all probability, Petrarch and two friends of his, Manno Donati and Tommaso del Garbo, an eminent physician, served as godfathers at the baptism, in Padua, of a boy, Francesco degli Alberti, who was of a branch of the Florentine Alberti family.

1372

Early in the year Petrarch learned, with great pleasure, that Philippe de Cabassoles had been sent to Italy as papal legate, and that he was stationed in Perugia, and acting as governor of that recently turbulent city.

He soon wrote to Philippe a letter in which he speaks with much enthusiasm of Philippe's coming to Italy, not only for public reasons, but also because he hopes that it may make it possible for him to fulfil his one and only remaining desire, which is to see Philippe once more. He mentions the failure of his attempt to go to Rome to see Pope Urban; but now, he thinks, unless contrary fortune pursues him to the end, he may at least be once more with Philippe. He imagines their being together and talking of the times they had spent together in Vaucluse, sometimes wandering in the woods, forgetful of food, until the evening, sometimes staying up all night, among Petrarch's books, until the coming of dawn. He refers to his writing of the *De vita solitaria* for Philippe, and of Philippe's custom of having the *De vita* read aloud to him, in preference to almost all other books, while he sat at dinner. He hopes for two final mercies: that his sufferings may be accounted to him as trials tending toward the forgiveness of his sins, and that he may be given health and strength enough to see Philippe once more. If even that hope should fail, may God grant that they be together in Paradise.

We do not know just when Petrarch returned to Arquà.

At some time in April the intensity of Petrarch's desire to see Philippe once more led him to try to ride for a mile, to see whether he could undertake the journey to Perugia. But the experiment proved to him that he could not do so.

Early in May he wrote to Philippe, telling him first of the failure of his attempt to ride for a mile. The letter then becomes a new nostalgic reminder of the tranquil solitude and the leisure that he and Philippe had enjoyed at Vaucluse, with its murmuring waters and its bird song; of the days they had spent there together wandering in the woods, beyond the searching of servants come to call them at dinner time; and of their surprise, when the sun set, to find that the day had passed so quickly. The latter part of the letter is one of Petrarch's finest statements of the value and power of friendship—friendship that can survive in absence, even after the death of a dear friend.

In June, not having received any reply to the letter that he had written to Bruni about a year before, Petrarch wrote to him again, stating his belief that Bruni's silence was due to his inability to send him any favorable news. He says again that it will not trouble him if Gregory does nothing for him: he is satisfied that Gregory wishes him well, and infers that Gregory's favorable intentions may have been blocked by hostile cardinals. The letter concludes with a lengthy review of Pope Urban's unsuccessful effort to re-establish the papacy in Rome, and with a bitter diatribe against the current state of the world. Bad as his century has been hitherto, the prospects for the future are even worse. He is grieved and ashamed to have lived his life at such a time: he would far rather have lived in some other time or place—even in India or China—or to have died years ago. At the very end of the letter he bids Bruni to make no further request of any man on his behalf, but to pray that Christ grant him a calm spirit and a happy passage from the life that is death to the life eternal that is life indeed. The letter is dated as written in the Euganean hills, but with a phrase that indicates his fear that warfare may make it impossible for him to remain there.

In Padua, during the preceding winter, Petrarch must have heard much of the dangerous tension between Padua and Venice. Such tension, caused mainly by boundary disputes, was nothing new; but it had been increased recently by certain Paduan actions that Venice regarded as aggressive. Efforts to reach an agreement had been made during the spring, but had failed; and by summer war was imminent.

In August Petrarch had the profound sorrow of learning that Philippe de Cabassoles had died, in Perugia; and thereafter, probably soon thereafter, he made in his Virgil an entry—the last of his obituary entries—ending with the exclamation: "Alas, I am now all but alone!"

The expected warfare between Venice and Padua began on the 3rd of October, when a considerable Venetian force captured a Paduan border fort and town. Early in November Rainiero Vasco, the *condottiere* commanding the Venetian troops, penetrated so far into Paduan territory that the male citizens of Padua were called to arms, some being stationed at the gates of the city and some in the *piazza*. Vasco did not attack the city, but his penetration of Paduan territory continued.

Petrarch now felt that the time had come for him to leave Arquà; and on the 15th of November he went into Padua, taking many of his books with him. His family followed presently, with the result that the house in Padua was overcrowded.

Vasco's westward advance reached a point about halfway between Padua and Arquà; but he did not go on to Arquà.

XXXIV. *Padua and Arquà: 1373*

V ENETIAN-PADUAN warfare continued for several months. Padua itself was never in immediate danger, but Paduan territory suffered greatly.

THE LAST INVECTIVE

Early in January Uguccione da Thiene, a legist in the papal service, arrived in Padua as a papal nuncio commissioned to endeavor to bring about a settlement between Padua and Venice. Soon after his arrival he came to see Petrarch and gave him a copy of a document that amazed and angered him.

In his second letter to Urban, written just before Petrarch had left Venice, he had offered himself as a duelist, in a contest of writings, on behalf of truth and of Italy; and early in 1369 he had received from Coluccio Salutati a letter telling him that it was the intention of the French cardinals that someone should reply to Petrarch's letter. As far as Petrarch had known, no such reply had ever been written; but in point of fact a reply had been written, before Urban had left Rome, by Jean de Hesdin, a member of the household of Cardinal Gui de Boulogne. It was a copy of that reply that Uguccione now brought to Petrarch, who seems not to have known who wrote it, and to have received the impression that it had been written only recently.

Petrarch's letter had begun with the quotation "In exitu Israel de Egypto, domus Iacob de populo barbaro," Egypt meaning France and the barbarian people meaning the French. Jean retorts with the quotation "Homo quidam descendebat ab Hierusalem in Hiericho et incidit in latrones," Jerusalem meaning Avignon and Jericho meaning Rome. He justifies his own initial quotation and repudiates Petrarch's by means of assertions of French excellences and Italian deficiencies, or by quotations, taken chiefly from classic authors. He then attacks Petrarch on four counts: for congratulating Urban on his most unfortunate return to Rome; for preaching virtue to the Pope and the cardinals; for slandering Avignon and the wine of Beaune; and for his scornful disparagement of France and his glorification of Italy. Jean's attack, relatively moderate in temper, varies from occasional effectiveness to patent absurdity and misrepresentation. He gives no consideration at all to the religious idea developed by Petrarch in his first letter to Urban, but treated only in passing in his second letter, that Rome is the true home of the Church, since Christ had chosen to establish it there: he is concerned with the purely mundane question of the relative merits and demerits of France and Italy.

His worst misrepresentation consists in taking Petrarch's words, "Nullus doctus in Gallia" out of their context, and treating them as meaning "there are not and have not been any learned men in France"—whereas Petrarch's four words, in their context, had meant only that no one of the four Doctors of the Church had been educated in France—and he then offers a quite unimpressive list of fourteen Frenchmen whom he rates as notably learned.

By temperament, by conviction, and by the terms of his own duelistic offer, Petrarch was bound to write a rejoinder to this document. His rejoinder, the *Invectiva contra eum qui maledixit Italie*, was dated in Padua on the 1st of March; but Petrarch had probably begun work on it much earlier. It is in general strong in its argumentation, it is impressively learned, and at its best it is eloquent; but its argumentation, its learning, and its eloquence are shot through with contemptuous and exclamatory vituperation. He characterizes the French scornfully; emphasizes the enduring glory of Rome; says that Avignon cannot fall, since it is already prostrate; recalls the fact that Gaul had once been enslaved by Rome; and dwells upon the sanctity of the Holy City. He takes the French writer to task for his extraordinary misrepresentation of the meaning of the words "Nullus doctus in Gallia," and ridicules his list of supposedly learned men. Mistaken statements of fact are corrected, and untenable assertions are demolished. Praise of France and dispraise of Italy are countered by praise of Italy and dispraise of France

A brief and feeble reply to this *Invectiva* was written before long by an unidentified Frenchman; but there is no reason to think that it ever came to Petrarch's notice.

Pandolfo Malatesta had died in January: Petrarch presumably learned of his death soon afterward.

GRISELDA

While Petrarch was in Padua, and probably early in 1373, there came to him, without his knowing from whom or how it had come, a copy of the *Decameron*. Seeing that it was lengthy, in

Italian prose, and intended for the commonalty, he looked through it only casually, stopping to read a little here and there. He noted with interest and sympathy the passage in the Introduction to the Fourth Day in which Boccaccio speaks of the biting attacks of hostile critics. He judged the book to be a work of Boccaccio's youth, and was disposed to excuse its lascivious character as being due both to the author's youth and to the nature of those for whom it was written. He liked the book in general, and he read with particular attention the beginning and the end. The introductory account of the plague seemed to him to have been admirably written; and the final *novella*, the story of the patient Griselda, pleased him greatly—partly because he remembered having heard it many years earlier. Boccaccio's version pleased him so much, indeed, that he committed it to memory, repeated it frequently to himself, related it to friends when it seemed appropriate to do so, and found that it pleased them also.

Toward the end of the winter or at about the beginning of spring, apparently, it occurred to him that it would be a good thing to make the story of Griselda available to readers who did not know Italian; and he therefore—probably in March—made a free Latin translation of Boccaccio's version.

His translation is an admirable piece of work. Many of Petrarch's letters contain passages in which anecdotes or short accounts of experiences are excellently presented; but his *Griseldis* is his main achievement as a narrator. Boccaccio's narrative verve is replaced by a less attractive rhetorical style; but there are respects in which Petrarch's version is superior to Boccaccio's. Certain features of the story that in the *Decameron* retain the uncompromising starkness of their ultimate folk origin are humanized, and the story as told by Petrarch is therefore pleasanter, more plausible, and more impressive as a story of extraordinary patience. Petrarch's characterization is more painstaking; and his additions, omissions, and alterations serve in general to improve the story. Very notable, in particular, is Petrarch's extensive and effective use of direct discourse.

The first reader of the translation, a Paduan who was a friend of both Petrarch and Boccaccio, was moved to tears by the time he was halfway through, and had to get a companion to go on with the reading; and a similar episode occurred somewhat later. Many people praised the story, and sought copies of it.

Under such circumstances Petrarch felt that he ought to send a copy of his translation to Boccaccio; and he therefore set about the making of a copy and the writing of an introductory statement. While he was engaged in this work, despite his ill health, and was copying from a draft that was full of corrections, a friend took pity on him and finished the copying for him.

(Chaucer was in Italy in 1373; but it is highly improbable that he went to Padua.)

ADVICE FROM BOCCACCIO

At some time in the winter or spring Petrarch received from Boccaccio a letter in which, after saying that he suffered in the knowledge that Petrarch was suffering from bad health, he reminded Petrarch of his exact age, attributed his suffering to old age, and went on to advise him to desist from his labors. In support of this advice he asserted that Petrarch had already attained greatness, his works being known far and wide, and argued that the time had come when Petrarch should cease his writing and leave it to others to write what they would, lest it should seem that he desired that he alone should write everything. He then reproached Petrarch for having spent a good part of his life in the service of princes. In conclusion he tried to persuade Petrarch to preserve his own life for the sake of his friends, and begged Petrarch to forgive him for venturing to advise him and to prescribe a new manner of life for him.

Petrarch knew that Boccaccio's advice was motivated by friendship, but he disliked the letter, and put it aside, intending not to answer it. Later on, however, when he had his translation of the Griselda story ready to send to Boccaccio, he decided that he must send also a reply to Boccaccio's letter. In this reply he expresses his appreciation of Boccaccio's concern for his health, and agrees with much that Boccaccio had said about old age. But he rejects Boccaccio's advice, which he characterizes as a recommendation of sleep and idleness. He dismisses as absurd Boccaccio's assertions of his greatness and of the world-wide extent of his fame, saying that even if these assertions were valid they would only spur him on to greater achievements. Of his relations with princes he has this to say:

> Apparently I have dwelt with princes, but in reality princes have dwelt with me. Never have I taken part in their councils; very rarely have I been at their tables. No manner of life would ever suit me that interfered in the

least with my liberty and my studies. So while everyone else sought the palace, I sought the woods, or sat quietly in my own room among my books.

Length of life on earth is not a thing to be desired for oneself, or for anyone by his friends. He thanks Boccaccio for his letter, and asks Boccaccio to forgive him if, instead of taking his advice, he continues to work as much and as long as he can. There follows this noble conclusion, which is in a sense Petrarch's valedictory:

Constant toil and application are the food of my spirit. When I begin to seek rest and to work but slowly I shall soon cease to live. I know my own strength; I am not now fit for other kinds of labor, as I used to be. This reading and writing of mine, from which you bid me to desist, is but a light task, or rather it is a welcome respite that enables me to forget tasks that are heavy. No burden is lighter than the pen, none more delightful. Other pleasures are fleeting and injurious: the pen brings joy as one takes it up and satisfaction as one lays it down; and it serves not only its owner but many others, often those who are far away, sometimes those who will live a thousand years hereafter. Confidently I declare that of all earthly pleasures none is nobler than literary activity, none more enduring, none sweeter, none more faithful, none that he who engages in it can obtain so readily, or with so little trouble. . . .

On this, therefore, my mind is fixed; and the following letter will show you how far I am beyond the reach of advice to be inert. Not content with the long works that I have begun, and for the completion of which neither my life nor twice the span of my life would suffice, I am looking every day for new and different tasks—such is my hatred of sleep and languid idleness. Have you not heard the saying of Ecclesiasticus: "When a man hath done, then he beginneth; and when he leaveth off, then he shall be doubtful"?

To me, indeed, it seems that I have just begun: however it may seem to you or to others, that is my judgment of myself. If in the midst of all this the end of my life should come—and it cannot now be far away—I could wish, I confess, that it might find me with my life complete. But since, things being as they are, I cannot hope for that, I do hope that death may find me reading or writing, or, if it should so please Christ, in tearful prayer.

Good health to you; remember me; live happily; and persevere manfully.

In April there came to trial in a Paduan court a case of which Petrarch, though not personally involved, must have heard with interest. Among the rights that he had acquired when the Emperor had made him a Count Palatine was the right to legitimize persons of illegitimate birth. At some time thereafter he had exercised that right on behalf of one Giovanni di Bartolommeo of Vicenza, who had now brought suit against a Paduan citizen for repayment of a loan. One of the points raised by the defendant was that Giovanni, being of illegitimate birth, had no legal competence; but Giovanni produced a copy of the document whereby Petrarch had legitimized him and a copy of Petrarch's diploma as a Count Palatine, and won his case.

On the first day of May the Paduan army, reinforced by a large body of Hungarian troops, defeated the Venetian army in the first major battle of the war.

It was probably soon after this event that Petrarch and his family returned to Arquà.

In a second major battle, fought in July, the Venetian army, reinforced by a large body of Turkish troops, won a decisive victory. The Paduan cause was now hopeless, and peace negotiations began in August. Desultory fighting continued into September; but on the 18th of that month the conditions of peace required by Venice were presented to Francesco da Carrara, who could do nothing but accept them. One of the conditions was that Francesco should either come to Venice himself or send his son, Francesco Novello, in his stead, to make submission and to ask forgiveness for all injuries and offenses committed by Padua to the detriment of Venice.

MISSION TO VENICE

Francesco da Carrara decided to send his son to Venice in his stead; and he asked Petrarch to accompany him, and to deliver an introductory oration. Petrarch, despite his ill health, could not refuse this request: he may indeed have been genuinely glad to serve, in a sense, as a messenger of peace.

Francesco Novello and Petrarch went to Venice, with a noble company, on the 27th of September, and were honorably received. The official ceremony was held five days later, in the Ducal Palace.

Petrarch's brief introductory oration begins with a quotation of Terence's dictum that lovers' quarrels lead to a renewal of love. This principle is then generalized and applied to the recent warfare; and Francesco Novello is then formally introduced as having come to make satisfaction in accordance with the conditions of peace. In a contemporary chronicle it is said that while Petrarch was speaking his voice trembled a little, because of his age and an illness from which he had not fully recovered.

In the evening the company left Venice. The night was spent in Oriago, a halfway point, and Padua was reached on the next day.

At some time in the year, probably in the autumn, Petrarch learned, certainly with much interest and pleasure, that the Augustinian monk Luigi Marsili had been sent by his Order to Padua to study theology there. Petrarch's acquaintance with him had begun some twenty-five years earlier, when Luigi was but a boy; and even then Petrarch had received a very favorable impression of his ability, and had accepted him as a friend.

After hearing of Luigi's arrival in Padua Petrarch wrote him a letter in which he speaks of their earlier association, congratulates him on having attained a good reputation, and exhorts him to persevere in the way of life he is already following. Having in mind the fact that Luigi had been sent to Padua to study theology, Petrarch urges him not to let himself be dissuaded from carrying on literary studies as well. The theologian, Petrarch says, needs wide, almost universal, knowledge. All knowledge is indeed one body, and derived from God. He bids Luigi, after finishing his course in theology, to write a treatise "against that rabid dog Averroes, who, driven by an abominable madness, barks against Christ his Lord and the catholic faith"—thus carrying out a project that Petrarch had once thought of carrying out himself.

TREATISE ON PRINCELY GOVERNMENT

Francesco da Carrara had often expressed his desire that Petrarch should write something just for him; and in November Petrarch at last complied with that request, by the writing of an exceedingly long letter which is in effect a treatise on princely government, with specific reference to conditions in Padua, and to Francesco da Carrara himself.

His first general thesis is that the prince should be lovable: the one sure way to win love is to love; and the ruler, then, should love his citizens as truly as he loves his own son. The second general thesis is that the prince should be just. The treatment of these two general theses is followed by a series of discussions of several particular matters.

The prince should promote public works: he should restore churches and public buildings that are in need of restoration; he should build city walls; he should see to it that city streets be properly tended and used; and Francesco, as lord of Padua, should see to it that the swamps around the city be drained. Of the streets of Padua Petrarch has much to say. Long neglected, they have suffered from constant use by men, by horses, and by wheeled vehicles, of which he heartily disapproves. Particularly obnoxious, in the case of Padua, is the disgusting extent to which the streets are infested by roving pigs. Responsibility for repair and maintenance of the streets should be entrusted, as an honorable charge, to some worthy citizen.

The prince should be extremely careful not to allow the use of public funds for projects that are useless or superfluous. He should make sure that ample stocks of food are available: "There is nothing more terrible than a famished mob."

When new taxes are necessary, the necessity for them should be made clear to the people; the prince himself should contribute something of his own; and the taxes should be as light as possible and collected with as much consideration as possible.

Other means of winning the affection of one's people—means abhorrent to haughty men, but already generously employed by Francesco—are personal consolation, visitation, and conversation.

Cruelty and rapacity on the part of a prince or of his officials are sure sources of hatred and of disaster. Care must be taken not to entrust power to officials to such an extent that they rather than the prince should seem to be the real rulers of the state. The prince's gratitude toward officials may be expressed by gifts other than the gift of power. The prince should cherish friendships that are unrelated to the cares of state. The prince should be generous, but his generosity should be its own reward: no gifts should be expected in return. Benevolence may well be extended to the poor. The prince should be free from vanity, overweening pride, and self-exaltation, and should be humble in spirit and modest in manner, speech, and dress. The prince should honor men who are of uncommon excellence in respect to justice, sanctity, military experience and skill, literary activity, or learning.

Finally, the popular Paduan custom of funeral processions and ceremonies made unseeemly by noisy lamentations should be corrected.

XXXV. *Continuations: 1370 - 1374*

THE "CANZONIERE"

T H E transcription of the quaternions that constituted the master manuscript of the final form of the *Canzoniere* had been begun by Giovanni Malpaghini in the years 1366 and 1367, and had been continued afterward, a little at a time, by Petrarch himself. When Petrarch moved from Padua to Arquà the manuscript contained about 300 poems, about 230 in the first Part and about 70 in the second Part. From time to time thereafter Petrarch continued to work on the collection—selecting, from a stock of a hundred or more remaining poems, those that he thought suitable for inclusion, deciding which ones should come next in one or the other Part, revising them carefully, and finally transcribing them into the master manuscript. This process of occasional addition to the collection continued into 1374. When Petrarch for the last time laid down his pen, Part I contained 263 poems, and was still incomplete, while Part II, containing 103 poems, was complete.

In addition to selecting, preparing, and transcribing poems that had been written long since, Petrarch, who held the conviction that the final element in any literary collection should be especially impressive, felt the need to write a worthy terminal *canzone* for the *Canzoniere*. The collection as a whole contained a few religious poems, but only a few: now, when he knew that his death could not be far distant, he naturally thought it appropriate that his terminal poem should be religious. His Christianity had been and was still Christ-centered; but he had lately developed a special devotion to the Virgin Mary—a devotion made manifest in his Will, both in its preamble and in its statement of his intention to build a chapel in her honor. He determined, accordingly, that his final *canzone* should likewise honor her; and he wrote at some time before the end of 1373—perhaps considerably earlier —the stately and beautiful prayer to the Virgin, beginning *Vergine bella, che di sol vestita,* with which he sealed the collection of his Italian poems.

It is a deliberate rather than an impulsive poem, most carefully constructed, learned, even, in its use of concepts derived from the Fathers of the Church, and yet vibrant with deep feeling. He must have toiled over its composition for many hours. Each of its first six stanzas opens with an invocation consisting of the word *Vergine* followed by a characterizing adjective, and similar invocations appear at other points in the poem. Among the characterizing adjectives or phrases are these: *bella, saggia, pura, santa, d'ogni grazia piena, sola, chiara, benedetta, gloriosa,* and *dolce e pia.* Each stanza closes with a petition for some special form of help. The final petition is for mediation with Christ on his behalf:

> Raccomandami al tuo figliuol, verace
> omo e verace Dio,
> ch'accolga 'l mio spirto ultimo in pace—

> Commend me to thy son, true
> man and true God,
> that he may receive my last breath in peace.

THE TRIUMPHS

Long before 1370 Petrarch had written four *Triumphs,* those of Love, Chastity, Death, and Fame; but how they stood in his mind at the time of his move to Arquà is quite uncertain. For the *Triumph of Love* he had written four *capitoli;* but there is one of the four that he may have decided to discard. He may or may not have decided to discard the *capitolo* of the *Triumph of Death* that tells of Laura's appearance to him in vision. The first *capitolo* that he had written for the *Triumph of Fame* had been replaced by two *capitoli,* and for this *Triumph* he had written a third *capitolo,* with which, however, he was not satisfied. Even the *capitoli* that he intended to retain were still subject to revision. He doubtless thought of the four *Triumphs* as constituting a series; but there is no reason to think that he had thought, before 1370, of writing any additional *Triumphs*. He had never lost interest, however, in the *Triumphs* that he had written: many marginal notes made on his work sheets before 1370 indicate retouching or re-reading or recopying of one or another of the first four *Triumphs*.

Retouching of these *Triumphs* continued in the years 1370–1373; and in 1371 he began the writing of a new *capitolo* designed to take the place of the unsatisfactory third *capitolo* of the *Triumph of Fame*—but he never finished it.

In the course of his last years, while his thoughts were directed more and more toward the passing of earthly values and to a life beyond life, he wrote two more *Triumphs*, on the closely related themes of Time and Eternity.

The underlying idea of the *Triumph of Fame* had been that Fame conquers Death. Fame, through much of Petrarch's life, had seemed to him to be something ultimate; but now, as his weakness increased and the thought of his own death became familiar, he realized that even Fame must yield to Time. His *Triumph of Time* is therefore, in a sense, a corrective of his earlier assumption.

The two first *Triumphs* and that of Fame had been of a processional character: neither of the two new *Triumphs* is processional. The *Triumph of Time* tells of a sun revolving with such fearful speed that a human life is seen to be an affair of a single day: "this morning I was a child and now I am old." Time itself is but a moment: the *Triumph of Eternity* endeavors to reflect the peace of a timeless Heaven. The thought of Heaven still carried with it, for Petrarch, the thought of Laura; and this final *Triumph* closes with his imagination that he will behold her in Heaven. The last two lines read:

> If he was blest who saw her here on earth,
> What will it be to see her again in Heaven!

The first draft of this *Triumph*, begun in January, 1374, was finished on the 12th of February. Soon thereafter he rewrote the last line without changing its meaning, but finding words that carried that meaning in greater rhythmic beauty:

> *Or che fia dunque a rivederla in cielo!*

Beside this line, on his work sheet, he entered the words "hoc placet"—recording thus his last poetic satisfaction.

He never assembled the *Triumphs* in a final form; but he gave them, at least, a perfect ending.

Petrarch's decision to make a separate collection of his later letters had been reached in 1361; and from that time to the end of his life he worked now and then upon the making of the collection. The main processes involved were, as in the case of the *Familiares*, selection, revision, arrangement, and transcription. The considerations that seem to have been dominant in his mind as he made his decisions as to selection were considerations of literary quality and of moral value or other public value.

Having decided to include a given letter in the *Seniles*, Petrarch was concerned to see that it could stand therein as a satisfactory work of epistolary art. In most cases, presumably, this involved a fairly considerable amount of revision, which might be so drastic as to be in effect a rewriting of the letter in question. The order of the *Seniles*, like that of the *Familiares*, is roughly, but only roughly, chronological. The transcription was undoubtedly done by copyists.

Much of Petrarch's work on the collection had been done before 1370; but a considerable amount was done in the years 1370–1374. By July 1374 the collection consisted of seventeen Books, containing a total of 127 letters, and was complete except for a final Book, which was to contain a single letter. Petrarch, who had closed the *Familiares* with his letters to ancient writers, had decided to close the *Seniles* with his letter to Posterity.

That letter, as it stood before 1370, was a straightforward autobiographical narrative, beginning with a statement of the time and place of his birth. It covered at least the portion of his life that ended with his return to Provence in 1351, and probably much more, but whatever he may have written about the latter part of his life is lost. The extant portion of the narrative is well told, but it contains little that is not known from other sources.

When he came to put the letter into a form that would make it appropriate as the terminal element of the *Seniles*, he decided to prefix a self-portrait to the narrative; and that self-portrait is in fact the most interesting part of the letter. Unfortunately he drafted this portrait in a confusing fashion, on the margins of his working copy of the letter. No fair copy of the letter having been made during his lifetime, his literary executors did not know what to do about it, and left it out of the collection, entering, after Book XVII, a note that reads, in part: "Rerum senilium liber XVII explicit. Amen. In originali sequitur: incipit XVIII. Posteritati."

Thus, the collection of the *Seniles* was never quite finished. Several modern attempts to edit what remains of the letter have been made; but it is only very recently that a thoroughly reliable edition has become available.

In his introductory self-portrait Petrarch speaks first, briefly, of his physical make-up. His body, in his youth, had been agile but not exceptionally strong. He had been good-looking, but cannot claim to have been handsome. His complexion was neither pale nor dark. His eyes were bright, and his eyesight had been very keen until he reached his sixtieth year. His health had been excellent until old age brought him its usual train of troubles.

He has much more to say of his mental and moral disposition and experiences. He has always scorned wealth, because of the labors it would necessarily impose. He has never cared for rich foods or elaborate meals, but he had always liked to have companionship at table. He had had one single love, intense and pure, that might have continued even longer had it not been that, at a time when it was already fading, death brought it to an end. In his youth he had yielded to incontinence, which, however, he had overcome while still in his forties. He does not think himself to have been guilty of pride, or of injurious wrath: he has been ready to forget offenses and constant in the memory of benefits. He has always been exceedingly desirous of worthy friendships, and has cherished them with the utmost fidelity: the greatest of the sorrows of old age is the frequent loss of those who had been dear. He has enjoyed association and friendship with princes and kings and noblemen, but he has always preserved his personal freedom. His mind is well balanced rather than acute. Interested in all good and worthy studies, he has concerned himself chiefly with moral philosophy and with poetry. In later life his preference has been for holy writings, in which he has found a sweetness that had been hidden from him. His special interest has been the ancient world: he has always thought so ill of his own time that if it had not been for those who had been dear to him he would have preferred to live in any other age—as indeed he had endeavored, in spirit, to do. For that reason he has had a particular interest in the historians; and when he has found discrepancies in their statements he has accepted the version that has seemed to him to be the most verisimilar or to be best certified by the authority of the writer. His speech has been called clear and effective, though he himself has felt it to be weak and obscure. In ordinary conversation he has never made any effort to be polished in his diction; but when circumstances have seemed to him to call for it he has endeavored to attain excellence. If only he has lived aright, he is not concerned about the quality of his words.

In the narrative that begins at this point he traces the course of his life, mentioning Arezzo, Incisa, Pisa, Avignon, Carpentras, Montpellier, Bologna, Avignon again, Lombez, his journeys in France and Germany and to Rome, Vaucluse, Naples, his coronation, Parma and Selvapiana, Verona, and Padua. He refers gratefully to members of the Colonna family, to Philippe de Cabassoles, to King Robert, to the Correggio brothers and to Jacopo and Francesco da Carrara. The extant portion of the letter ends abruptly with a statement of his return to Provence after the death of Jacopo.

THE "DE VIRIS ILLUSTRIBUS"

Francesco da Carrara had requested Petrarch to complete the *De viris illustribus;* but by about 1371 or 1372 Petrarch had worked on only one of the thirteen biographies that remained to be done, and he was carrying that biography, the Life of Caesar, to a length that was so far beyond that of any of the other biographies as to make it seem that he was treating it rather as an independent work than as one of several sections of a composite work. Under these circumstances Francesco, apparently anxious to get Petrarch to write something, at least, about each of the heroes who according to the existing plans were to receive biographies in the *De viris* and fresco portraits in the "Sala virorum illustrium," requested him to write a series of *short* biographies for the thirty-six men concerned.

Petrarch set to work, accordingly, on this new series, and for it he wrote biographies for the first fourteen of the twenty-three men for whom he had written his original series of biographies. He seems however to have been more interested in revision than in abbreviation: only one of the new biographies—that of Romulus—is much shorter than its predecessor, while several of them show improvements of one sort or another. When he had finished the fourteenth new biography he presumably intended to complete the series; but he never did so.

After his death both series were completed, at the request of

Francesco da Carrara, by Lombardo della Seta; and fresco portraits of Petrarch and of Lombardo, were painted, probably by Altichieri, in spaces on the west wall of the "Sala virorum illustrium." The portrait of Petrarch, though it has suffered greatly, is the least unsatisfactory portrait of him that has come down to us: it shows him as an old man, keen-eyed, but otherwise not impressive.

———————————— ℰ ————————————

XXXVI. *Arquà: January - July 1374*

DURING the last months of his life Petrarch lived and wrote quietly in his home in Arquà. His main new achievement, an appropriate and worthy one, was the writing of the *Triumph of Eternity*. He doubtless continued his work on the collection of the *Seniles*. The epitaph, consisting of three rhymed hexameters, that is inscribed on Petrarch's tomb may or may not have been composed by Petrarch himself. If it was written by him, it was probably written in the course of these last months.

Letters kept coming to him, and calling for answers. In January he received from the young Augustinian monk Luigi Marsili a letter in which Luigi spoke very gratefully of Petrarch's past kindnesses and asked Petrarch to send him—apparently as a loan—his copy of the *Confessions* of St. Augustine. That copy had been given to Petrarch, some fifty years before, by another Augustinian monk, Dionigi da Borgo San Sepolcro, and had become one of his dearest possessions. Now, however, he felt moved to give it to his young Augustinian friend; and he therefore sent it to him, with a letter about it. It was a small book, written in a script so minute that it was hard for Petrarch to read, and it was now badly worn. He had carried it with him wherever he went, in Italy, in France, and on a northern journey. It had come to be almost a part of his hand. It had shared many accidents that had befallen him; once it had been in peril with him on the sea. He is glad now to have the book return to an Augustinian, and foresees that it will accompany Luigi on his journeys.

A conspiracy against the life of Francesco da Carrara, fomented by Francesco's brother Marsilio, had been discovered and suppressed early in the year; and Francesco, sorely troubled, said or wrote to Petrarch that at one and the same time he was amazed and yet not amazed at the ways of the world, and asked Petrarch to comment on his perplexity. Petrarch replied, by letter, saying that goodness is rare, and is therefore to be wondered at, yet it is derived from God, and is therefore not to be wondered at; and that it is indeed amazing that a brother should become an enemy to his brother or a servant to his master or a beneficiary to his benefactor, yet such enmity is manifested so frequently that it is not to be wondered at.

Writing to Luca da Penna, a legist in Avignon, who had asked Petrarch to send him, at his expense, copies of any rare works of Cicero that he might possess, he says that the Ciceronian works of which he has copies are all well known, and goes on to tell at length of his own early devotion to Cicero, and of various experiences related thereto. Thus he tells of the interference of his boyish reading of Cicero with the legal studies that his father had made him undertake; of his father's throwing the boy's books into a fire; of his distress and of his father's rescuing of a Virgil and a Cicero; and of Convenevole da Prato's pawning of a manuscript containing the *De gloria* that he had borrowed from Petrarch.

A brief letter from Pietro da Muglio, written in Bologna, told of the raging of the plague there in such virulence that many were fleeing the city and that fear prevailed among those that remained: Pietro, however, had learned from Petrarch to be courageous, and had neither fled nor given himself up to fear. He expressed his regret at his long separation from Petrarch, and his desire to have a portrait of Petrarch and a collection of his writings. In his reply Petrarch writes of his pleasure in hearing from Pietro again; refers to the good times he had had in Bologna in his youth; praises Pietro for his courage; regrets their separation; and wishes that Pietro might visit him in his home in the Euganean hills, where he and his family are living happily.

Petrarch's last letter was written to Boccaccio. He had heard in some way that Boccaccio had never received the letters that he had sent to him a year ago. He now sent him copies of those letters, together with a new covering letter that contains some further information about Petrarch's translation of the Griselda story. This new letter, as it stands in the collection of the *Seniles*, ends with a general farewell to friends and to the writing of letters:

"Valete amici, valete epistole." It may be that these words appeared at the end of the letter as sent to Boccaccio, but it is also possible that they were added when Petrarch prepared the letter for inclusion in the *Seniles*. In either case, they may be the last words that Petrarch ever wrote.

On the 18th of July Petrarch suffered one of the attacks to which he had been subject for some years. This time, after midnight, death came to him.

The only reliable account of his death is given in a letter written on the 19th by Giovanni Dondi to another physician, Giovanni dall'Aquila. That letter begins thus:

> Alas, my dear friend, you will now be reading a sad and mournful letter that will tell you of the sudden death of a very great and very famous man, our common friend: for the ill-starred night, now spent, that preceded the light of the day on which I am writing this, took from us our illustrious and admirable Petrarch, who had been seized, only a few hours earlier, by an attack of the illness from which, as you may recall, he was suffering when you and I went to see him in his pleasant retreat in the Euganean hills—an illness by which he had often been attacked, and has now been overcome.

The funeral service, held on the 24th, was attended by Francesco da Carrara and a large company of clergy and laymen. The eulogy was given by Bonaventura Badoer. Burial was in the parish church of Arquà, in accordance with the desire expressed by Petrarch in his Will. After the erection of a marble tomb, commissioned by Francescuolo da Brossano, Petrarch's body was transferred to that tomb, which still stands beside the church.

————————— ❧ —————————

XXXVII. *Portrait of Petrarch*

THE dominant trait in Petrarch's nature was a constant desire to love and to be loved, a desire that manifested itself not only in his love for Laura, but also in his love for members of his family, and, most distinctively, in his love for his friends.

It was in his love for Laura that this desire reached its highest intensity. That love was not returned, but it continued, though eventually fading, until her death, after which it remained as a cherished memory and as an element in Petrarch's thought of heaven.

His mother and he loved each other dearly: in his reminiscent letter to Guido Sette he speaks of her as "the best mother I have ever known of, a mother to me in love as well as in blood." His brother and he loved each other with a love passing the usual strength of fraternal affection. In his last years he brought his daughter and her little family to live with him, first in Venice and later in Arquà. In his Will he refers to his son-in-law as being not only his heir, but a dearly loved son. Nor is there anything that enables one to come closer to him than his love for his grandson, and his grief when the life of that little Francesco came to its untimely end.

Never did any man form and cultivate a richer store of friendships; never did any man draw deeper devotion from his friends, or maintain a deeper devotion to them. Repeatedly he sought to have one or more of them share home and life with him. He wanted friends of his to be friends of each other. Twice he learned that two of his friends had fallen out with each other; and in each case he so wrought that the broken friendship was made whole again. Nothing short of proven unworthiness could lead to a withdrawal of friendship—not the blows of a cruel fortune, not even the rare wounds given him in friendly faithfulness, not even the rare necessity faithfully to wound his friends. He rejoiced when actual companionship with friends was possible; but through the powers of his memory and his imagination he felt them present even in absence, even if they had never met. The death of a friend brought him deep distress—as the notes he made in his Virgil testify—but that distress found relief in the confident hope that even death meant nothing more than a temporary separation. Petrarch could not have been Petrarch without such friendships as those he had with Guido Sette, with Giacomo Colonna, with his Socrates, with his Laelius, with Philippe de Cabassoles, with Azzo da Correggio, with Barbato da Sulmona, with Nelli, with Boccaccio, with Donato Albanzani, with Francesco da Carrara, with Lombardo della Seta, with many others whose names are written in this book, and with many others still.

A second desire, which during his youth and early manhood was nearly or quite as strong as the first, was his desire for fame —a desire closely related to the creative urge that drove him to his activities as a writer. Of this desire he speaks thus in the *canzone I' vo pensando* (in a passage quoted more fully in Chapter X):

This thought has been growing in me ever since I slept in swaddling clothes, and I fear that it will go down with me into the tomb.

This desire, however, lessened its hold on Petrarch during his later years. He had achieved the fame that he had sought, only to find that it brought him more envy than satisfaction. In his Letter to Posterity he speaks sadly of his coronation. He was ready, before he died, to write of the triumph of time over fame.

His love for Laura and his desire for fame were never in conflict with each other: indeed they reinforced each other, their alliance finding confirmation in the similarity of the name Laura and the word laurel. But in the years when Petrarch was writing the *Secretum* and the *canzone I' vo pensando*, he felt both his love for Laura and his desire for fame to be in conflict with his hope for salvation—not that they were sinful in themselves, but that they distracted him from the living of such a life as would most surely qualify him for salvation—and the sense of this conflict brought him a deep distress, from which he gained some measure of relief by achieving, in the *Secretum* and the *canzone*, a thorough analysis of his own plight.

This special conflict was in fact a phase of a still more comprehensive and fundamental conflict: a conflict between the manifold enjoyment that Petrarch found in earthly life and his whole concept of the nature and function of religion.

He greatly enjoyed the sights and sounds of nature, from mountain grandeur, seen close at hand or from afar, to the intimate charms of Vaucluse, where he could wander freely through unfrequented woods and over fields and hillsides, or visit, even at night, the cavern of the Sorgue, or rest quietly by the riverside, aware of the rippling of the stream and the song of birds—perhaps reading, perhaps writing, perhaps fishing, perhaps just thinking—or toiling happily among the trees and shrubs of his garden. And he reveled in the endlessly new sights and sounds that came to him with travel and with changes of residence.

He took delight also in human beauty and intelligence, in the marvelous reflective and creative powers of the mind, in history and in philosophy, in poetry, in eloquence, in conversation, in music (he played the lute, and he had heard, in Laura's voice, *il cantar che ne l'anima si sente*), and in art (his references to Giotto and to Simone and to the *tondo* in Sant'Ambrogio are such as to prove his sensitiveness to artistic qualities).

For these values, both in nature and in man, Petrarch gives thanks in one of his *Penitential Psalms*, in a passage that has been quoted in Chapter VIII; and he writes of them, with deep awareness and appreciation, in the *De remediis*, in a passage that has been quoted in Chapter XX.

And yet, though these values were God-given, and although, above and beyond them, man had also the prospect of eternal life, that very prospect involved not only the possibility of eternal bliss but also the possibility of eternal woe; and the earthly values carried with them the danger of an absorption that might lead to eternal fatality.

Petrarch's personal religion consisted essentially in acceptance of the beliefs and the observances then held and prescribed by the Church. He never questioned any article of the creed; he never explored the field of theology; and after his youth he conformed regularly and willingly with the practices of confession, of fasting, and of daily and nightly prayer. His religion was for him less a spiritual experience, less a consciousness of divine love and a response thereto, than a pattern of belief and observance which, if followed faithfully, would greatly increase his prospects of avoiding Hell and winning Paradise. And he felt that a thoroughly faithful following of this pattern would involve a renunciation of very much that made life seem good to him. Thousands of men in his time were making such renunciation by entrance into monastic orders. Petrarch knew many members of many orders—Augustinians, Benedictines, Camaldolensians, Carthusians, Celestines, Cistercians, Dominicans, Franciscans, Vallombrosans—and found them content in the life they had chosen. His own dear brother had made such renunciation; but though Petrarch recognized its rightness, he could not bring himself to do likewise. His constant contacts with monasticism embrowned his concept of religion. The last line of the *canzone I'vo pensando* is

> E veggio 'l meglio et al peggior m'appiglio—
>
> And I see the better course, and cling to the worse.

Petrarch's fears are most vividly expressed, and his pleas for rescue are most urgent, in his relatively early *Penitential Psalms;* but similar fears and pleas are voiced in the terrified *epistola metrica Ad se ipsum,* written during the raging of the Black Death, and appear now and then in later writings. It was in the hope of improving his prospects for eternity that he made his pilgrimage to Rome in the Year of Jubilee. Toward the end of his life diminution of fear and increase in hope are reflected in his last letters to Philippe de Cabassoles. But even the final *canzone* to the Virgin closes with an entreaty that she commend him to the mercy of her Son.

Petrarch exalts God the Father as creator, and as the source of life, truth, grace, and blessedness. Most of his appeals for help from Heaven are addressed to Christ, whether the help asked be for Petrarch himself, or for the Church, or for the world. In the two latter cases the appeals sometimes take on a quality of despairing remonstrance, as in these outbursts:

> But Thou, oh Christ, Sun of Justice, all-seeing, and all-illuminating, how is it that Thou hast allowed this cloud of shame to rest upon this earth of ours?
>
> Oh Thou good Jesus! What kind of a world is this? Hast thou averted thine eyes from us because of our sins?

Similar phrases pervade a letter that begins with the exclamation "Woe to thy people, Christ Jesus," and continues so long in the same exclamatory vein that it becomes in effect a letter addressed to Christ: only in the very last sentence is there a reference to a mortal addressee. Petrarch's references to the third Person of the Trinity are very few indeed.

His references to the Virgin are few in number and for the most part of slight significance; but his intention to build a chapel in her honor in Arquà and his writing of the final poem of the *Canzoniere* indicate a real devotion. In his Will he implores the aid of the Virgin and of the Archangel Michael "and of the other saints whom I have been wont to invoke hopefully as intercessors for me with Christ." To St. Augustine he refers more than a thousand times, but rather as an inexhaustible source of wisdom than as an object of worship or petition.

He regarded the Church as the most sacred of institutions; and he deplored bitterly the all-too-human indulgences with which its Babylonish court was stained. He thought of the ecclesiastical profession, in which he was himself enrolled, as an honorable one, and he received readily the perquisites to which, in the practice of the time, it entitled him; but he never thought of his profession as a ministry, and he consistently refused to accept any office that would have involved the cure of souls.

Both in the second Book of the *Secretum*, written probably in 1343, and in the self-portrait prefixed, some thirty years later, to the Letter to Posterity, Petrarch analyzes his own moral status, using the familiar categories of the Seven Deadly Sins. In the *Secretum* his culpability is debated, sometimes at length, between his more critical self, represented by "Augustinus," and his more usual self, represented by "Franciscus." In the Letter to Posterity there is no debate: the several statements are direct, simple, and brief.

In the case of pride, Augustinus charges Franciscus with pride in his intelligence, in his learning, in his eloquence (that is, his literary skill), and his good looks. Franciscus denies the validity of these charges, saying that his only sign of intelligence is his recognition of the slightness of his intelligence, that his learning has brought him a mass of cares rather than satisfaction, that he is tormented constantly by his inability to express his concepts rightly, and that intelligence, learning, and eloquence have alike proved powerless to quiet the storms that rage in his soul. He admits that in his youth he had been vain of his good looks, but asserts that all such vanity is past. In the Letter to Posterity he says:

> I have seen pride in others, but not in myself; and though
> I have been a man of slight value, in my own judgment my
> value has been still more slight.

Petrarch was too intelligent not to have realized the exceptional quality of his own gifts; but he was also constantly aware of his limitations. He met with such extraordinary evidences of esteem from many other men that it must have been hard for him to resist entirely the influence of their opinions. But such pride as he had was tempered both by a harassing sense of his insufficiencies and by recognition of the abilities that he possessed as being gifts bestowed upon him rather than achievements of his own. Many of his references to himself and to his writings are so depreciative as to seem expressions of false modesty; but their modesty, even if exaggerated, is not necessarily false. Such pride as he had seems never to have given offense to his friends. He had causes for pride, but he had also corrective causes for self-dissatisfaction. He cultivated humility; he felt, eventually, the chastening effects of old age; and at the end of his life he could say, without conscious error, and thinking perhaps of the more obvious manifestations of pride, "Sensi superbiam in aliis non in me."

Even Augustinus finds Franciscus guiltless of envy; and in the Letter to Posterity envy is not even mentioned.

Augustinus next charges Franciscus with avarice; Franciscus repudiates the charge as being utterly absurd; but Augustinus renews it, linking with it the charge of ambition. Franciscus says that he does indeed want enough to provide him with his daily food, and that he does want to lay something by against the insidiousness of old age; and when Augustinus bids him define the limits of his desires he replies: "To be neither in need nor in abundance; to be neither inferior nor superior to other men." In the continuing argument Augustinus stresses the sinfulness of clinging to earthly concerns and of failing to meditate on death; but he admits that Franciscus has never debased himself to the use of the despicable methods commonly employed in the attempt to win honors; and he does not succeed in convicting Franciscus of setting undue store either on means of support or on honors. In the Letter to Posterity Petrarch writes: "I have always greatly despised riches—not in themselves, but because of my hatred for the toils and cares that are their inseparable companions." He says repeatedly in other letters that he desires nothing more than a mean between poverty and wealth; he refused offers of ecclesiastical positions that would have been both lucrative and honorable; and when possible papal benefactions were in view he made it clear that while he would welcome a relatively small benefaction, he would not want a large one—and that it would not trouble him in the least if no benefaction at all should be forthcoming. He accepted gifts or substantial favors from the Correggi, from the Visconti, and from Jacopo and Francesco da Carrara; and he was in fact comfortably off. To Boccaccio, in his real poverty, Petrarch seemed to be rich; other friends, now and then, questioned him on this point; and it was generally believed that he was at least well-to-do. But he was certainly not avaricious. The last sentence in his Will reads thus: "I, Francesco Petrarca, have written this: I would have written a very different Will if I had been rich, as the foolish commonalty supposes."

No charge of gluttony is brought against Petrarch in the *Secretum;* and in the Letter to Posterity he states that he has been content in his frugality.

Nor does Augustinus charge Franciscus with wrath as a besetting sin: he merely says that although Franciscus is often moved unduly to indignation he is quick to recover his usual good nature. In the Letter to Posterity Petrarch writes: "My wrath has often been harmful to myself, but never to others." These assertions, however, are open to question: it is hard to think of the *Invectives* as being matters of merely momentary excitement; and it is hard to believe that anyone who had been attacked in one of them could ever have forgiven or forgotten.

With regard to the two remaining sins, incontinence and *acedia*, the case is very different. Franciscus pleads guilty at once to the charge of incontinence: even his prayers have not availed to bring him relief. Augustinus bids him to renew his prayers, with more complete contrition and resolution, and to remember that incontinence, even more than any other sin, prevents attainment of the vision of God. In the Letter to Posterity Petrarch again admits his sinfulness in this respect, but asserts that after his fortieth year he had, by the grace of God, overcome this temptation.

As a seventh sin, *acedia* (which usually means "sloth"), Petrarch reports his liability to occasional fits of extreme depression. These fits, he says (speaking through the person of Franciscus), seize him so tenaciously that they bind and rack him for whole days and nights, which are for him times not of light and life, but of infernal darkness and bitter death. They are marked by "humane conditionis odium atque contemptus"—that is, by "hatred and contempt for the human state." His depression is due, at least in part, to certain purely personal causes: he has not attained what he regards as the necessary mean between poverty and wealth; he is not his own master (he was still in the service of Cardinal Colonna); he has no family home (his father having been exiled from Florence); and he is compelled to be much in Avignon, of which he draws a most repellent picture. Augustinus, speaking in this instance as an exponent of classic wisdom rather than of Christian precept, points out flaws in Franciscus' thinking, but devotes himself to possible cures rather than to condemnation. Fortunately for Petrarch, the intensity and the frequency of these fits diminished within a few years, and finally disappeared. There is no trace of them in the Letter to Posterity.

Of his mentality Petrarch has this to say in the self-portrait that he prefixed to his Letter to Posterity: "My mind was well-balanced rather than acute, capable of undertaking good and beneficial study of any kind, but attracted chiefly to moral philosophy and to poetry." He adds that in the course of time he came to prefer sacred to poetic literature; and that his special interest was in antiquity, most of all in ancient history. His mind was amazingly inclusive. His awareness of the whole human experience covered not only the present and the past but was projected into the future; and it ranged widely in space as well as in time: a notably wide spatial survey is referred to in Chapter XVIII. It was inclusive also in subject matter: he wrote on princely government, on the qualities desirable in a military commander, on the decay of military discipline since ancient times, on the medical profession, on the legal profession, on education, on the spread of Christianity, on the location of "Ultima Thule," on the worthlessness of astrology, on the requisites for a successful dinner party, on illustrious women, on the choice of a wife, on allegory, on diet, and on Fortune. He was well acquainted with the ancient philosophers; but he was not himself a profound thinker, and he never wrote anything of his own in the field of pure philosophy. His thinking was notably acute, however, in the areas of historical and textual scholarship. He wrote frequently and extensively in the field of practical moral advice, treating many special topics in letters and in some of his other writings, especially the *De remediis utriusque fortune*. His memory was not less than extraordinary. It was supported, to some extent, by signs that he had made on the margins of his books; but he was not by any means dependent on such signs. He seems to have been able to hold in mind the substance of the whole vast range of his reading, and to quote numerous apposite passages at will. He was, for his time, uniquely introspective: it is to this characteristic that we owe the *Secretum*, the Letter to Posterity, and many of his poems.

Petrarch was an ardent Italian patriot. He loved Italy as being the land of his fathers and his own native land; he loved it for its matchless beauty; and all Italy was suffused for him with the glory of ancient Rome. His love of Italy shines in many of his letters—most notably perhaps, in a passage, summarized in Chapter XXVIII, that occurs in his first letter to Urban V—and receives eloquent voicing in two of his greatest poems, the *canzone Italia mia*, summarized and quoted in part in Chapter X, and his Latin salutation to Italy from the pass of Mont Genèvre, quoted in full in Chapter XIX. His love of Italy was reinforced by his conviction that Rome was the one and only proper seat both for the papacy and for the Empire. He deplored the fragmentation of Italy, and hoped for its unification through Cola di Rienzo. Warfare between Italian states seemed to him to be a terrible thing: he did his utmost to avert war between Venice and Genoa. He repeatedly attacked Italian use of mercenary troops as being stupid, disastrous, and altogether shameful.

Petrarch was also a public-spirited citizen of Christendom. It was not only for the good of Italy, but for the good of all Christendom, that he endeavored over and over again to persuade popes to return to the city that had been divinely ordained as the seat of the papacy, and to persuade Charles IV to return to the city of Augustan authority and of Augustan peace. It is quite possible that Petrarch's first letter to Urban V had some influence in bringing Urban to his decision to return to Rome: that return, to be sure, proved to be temporary, but it served as prelude and precedent for the definitive return of Urban's successor. Petrarch's letters to Charles IV and his interviews with him did not serve to dislodge him from his Bohemian kingdom.

The profession from which Petrarch derived his livelihood was ecclesiastical; but his real vocation was that of study and writing. For this double activity he required a high degree of personal freedom; and he succeeded in finding such freedom almost always and almost everywhere—except in Avignon. His freedom was not incompatible with acceptance of enlightened patronage by worthy patrons; and it was under the conditions of such patronage that much of his work was done. His clearest statement on this matter is quoted at the beginning of Chapter XXIX.

Thanks to such freedom he was able to write abundantly: he wrote less, however, than he might have written if extensive study had not been for him a necessary concomitant of his writing and if he had not been a perfectionist. His intellectual restlessness led him to the writing of works of various kinds; and the combination of his restlessness and his perfectionism resulted in his leaving several of his works slightly or more than slightly incomplete. But his total production is very substantial in quantity, and very high in quality.

In addition to the writings that are about to be listed, he left a good many uncollected Italian lyrics, some discarded portions of the *Triumphs*, a few bits of Latin verse, a few prayers, his Will, and about seventy-five uncollected letters, most of which have been published in a modern collection known as the *Epistolae variae*.

The collections and individual works that he finished, at least in considerable part, are these:

> The *Canzoniere*
> The *Triumphs*
> *Africa*
> *Bucolicum carmen*
> *Epistolae metricae*
> *De otio religioso*
> *De remediis utriusque fortune*
> *De viris illustribus*
> *De vita solitaria*
> *Epistolae familiares*
> *Epistolae seniles*
> *Epistolae sine nomine*
> The (four) *Invectives*
> *Itinerarium syriacum*
> The (six) *Orations*
> *Psalmi penitentiales*
> *Rerum memorandarum libri*
> *Secretum*

All of these collections and individual works are valuable in themselves, some of them extremely valuable; but they all have a very special additional value. For Petrarch the works of the ancients that he read so constantly and so carefully were not merely books: they were emanations of personality. His writings are, for us, emanations of one of the most remarkable and one of the friendliest personalities of our own past.

Note on Sources

Our knowledge of the life of Petrarch is derived mainly from his own letters, of which nearly six hundred are extant, and from his other writings. Additional information is derived from letters written to him, of which about eighty are extant, from documents, and from certain other sources. The enormous task of evaluating the evidence thus made available, of solving the many problems that present themselves, and of dating hundreds of elements as exactly as possible has been shared, especially in the present century, by many scholars, among them Antonio Avena, Giuseppe Billanovich, Umberto Bosco, Carlo Calcaterra, Enrico Carrara, Henry Cochin, Arnaldo Foresti, Lino Lazzarini, Ugo Mariani, Guido Martellotti, T. E. Mommsen, Pierre de Nolhac, Francesco Novati, Paul Piur, Pier Giorgio Ricci, Fortunato Rizzi, Vittorio Rossi, Giuseppe Rotondi, B. L. Ullman, Marco Vattasso, and Roberto Weiss. References to their studies may be found in earlier Petrarchan books and in forthcoming studies of my own.

Three of the bits of verse translation that are contained in the present book are taken from my *Petrarch at Vaucluse*, which is published, also, by the University of Chicago Press; and much of the material in Chapters XX–XXXVI is taken, with the permission of the Mediaeval Academy of America, from Petrarchan books of mine that have been published by that Academy.

Index of Works of Petrarch

Identifying List of Letters

This list is designed to enable the reader to identify the letters from which quotations are excerpted, and certain other letters that are especially notable.

The abbreviations *F*, *S*, *Sn*, and *Met* stand, respectively, for the four collections—the *Familiares*, the *Seniles*, the *Sine nomine*, and the *Metricae*—that were made by Petrarch himself. There are extant 77 prose letters that he did not include in any one of his collections. Of these, 59 were collected, under the title *Epistolae variae*, in the nineteenth century; the other 18, known as the Miscellaneous Letters, are to be collected in a forthcoming publication. The abbreviations *Var* and *Misc* stand, respectively, for these two collections.

Pages	Letters	Pages	Letters
3, 4, 7	S X 2	72–73	F VII 7
5	Met I 7	75	{ F VII 15
8	F X 3		Met III 6
11	Met I 2	76	F VII 10
13	F IV 1	78	F XXIV 5
14	F VIII 1	78–79	F VIII 1
14–15	S V 2	79–80	Met I 14
20–21	Met I 6	81–82	F VIII 2–5
30–31	F V 7	84	F VIII 10
31	S XVI 7	84–85	F X 3
32–33	F VI 3	85	Met III 25
33	Met II 3	86	F X 4
35	Met II 5	87	F I 1
40–41	F V 3	88–89	F IX 13
44–45	Met II 18	89	S VII 1
46	Met II 10 and 17	89–90	F XXIV 8
50	F V 10	90–91	F XXIV 11
51–52	F XXIV 3	92	F IX 10
53	F XXIV 4	92–93	Met I 1
55	{ Met I 10	95	F XI 1
	F III 19	96	F XXIV 7
57–58	F III 18	97–98	F X 1
60	Met III 5	98	F XI 8
64–65	Var 48	98–99	F VII 17
66	Var 38	102	F XI 5
69	Var 40	103	F XVI 2
70	Sn 2 and 3	105	F XI 6
72	F VII 5	107	F XIII 8

General Index

In entries in which a dozen or more references are given, the more important ones are marked with asterisks.
Place names are entered only in certain special cases.

Joan, Queen, 36, 41–42, 53–54, 60, 110–11
John II, 154, 158, 169, 172–75, 181
John XXII, 10
Joseph, 48
Joshua, 87
Judas Maccabaeus, 87
Judith, 48
Jupiter, 23, 69
Justina, St., 90, 102

"Laelius," 9*, 31, 56, 58, 72, 92, 115, 120*, 125, 128, 145*, 147, 158–59, 161*, 163, 168–69, 190–91*, 252
Lancelot, 23
Laura (Laureta), 8*, 12, 15, 17–18, 20–23*, 37*, 48*, 57, 76–78*, 80–81*, 83, 85, 86*, 87, 108*, 128, 160, 215, 244, 245*, 251–53*, 254
Lauria, Ruggiero di, 119
La Verna; see Alvernia
Law, 1, 4–9, 11–12, 34, 171–72, 214
Lawrence, St., 203
Liége, 10
Linus, 172
Lionel, Duke of Clarence, 211
Livy, 16, 26, 52, 89–90, 102, 136
Lombez, 9, 11, 13, 30, 248
London, 158
Longo, Matteo, 106, 229
Louis of Hungary, 74, 111
Louis of Taranto, 60–61, 110–11
Luca, Don, 30, 84, 111, 119
Lucretia, 48
Luzzara, 92

Mago, 42, 184, 189
Malatesta, Pandolfo, 151–58* passim, 180, 183–84, 187, 191, 203, 211–12, 231, 236
Malatesta, Paolo, 23
Malaucène, 12
Malpaghini, Giovanni, 196, 205–6, 208–11, 215, 217, 243
Manasseh, 174
Mandello, Giovannolo da, 159
Maria (of Pozzuoli), 41

Mark, St., 135, 185–86
Marsili, Luigi, 241, 249
Martini, Simone, 12, 23, 77, 254
Martinus Theutonus, 152
Mary, 223, 231, 243–44, 265
Mary Magdalene, St., 18–20
Masinissa, 23, 87
Matilda, 160
Medicine, 113–14, 123–24, 165, 169–70, 172, 198–99, 224–28, 230
Mercury, 46
Mézières, Philippe de, 193
Michael, 255
Mileto, Roberto da, 40–41
Modena, 50, 119
Moggi, Moggio dei, 45, 74, 188
Monet, Jean, 107, 127
Monet, Pierre, 107, 127
Monet, Raymond, 18, 107, 122, 144, 224
Monselice, 186, 197
Montpellier, 4–5, 248
Montrieux, 36, 58–60, 117, 121, 125–26, 137–38
Monza, 134, 144
Morando, Neri, 137, 144
Muglio, Bernardo da, 193
Muglio, Pietro da, 171, 188, 193, 212–13, 250
Mussato, Albertino, 24

Nelli, Francesco, 94–95*, 101–2, 109–20 passim, 126, 129–31, 133, 150–58 passim, 160*, 167, 170, 177* 180–83, 190–91*, 252
Nero, 176
Nice, 39, 122
Novara, 154, 161

Očko, 152
Orpheus, 172
Orvieto, Raimondo di, 63, 66

Pagazzano, 158, 165–66, 212
Palestrina, 40
Palladius (Bishop), 141
Palladius (Rutilius Taurus Aemilianus), 79, 91, 141

Pancaldo, 224
Papazurri, Bartolommeo Carbone dei, 195
Pardubic, Arnost z, 117, 152–53
Parenzo, Ser, 1
Paris (city), 10, 25, 173–74
Paris (person), 23
Parma, Giovanni da, 148–50
Pastrengo, Guglielmo da, 12, 44, 51–52, 93, 117, 133
Paul, St., 171, 203
Penna, Luca da, 250
Pepoli, Giovanni de', 212
Perugia, 40, 232–33
Peter, St., 201, 203, 226–27
Peter Damian, St., 181–82
Peter I (of Cyprus), 193, 212
Petracco, Gherardo, 2*, 3, 6–7, 8*, 9, 12*, 21, 36*, 57, 58–60*, 84–86, 101, 102–3*, 117, 121, 125–26*, 134*, 137, 224, 232*, 254
Petracco, Ser, 1–5, 8–9, 16, 192
Petrarca, Francesca, 37, 177–78, 193, 200, 211–12, 232, 252
Petrarca, Francesco, *passim*
   Accidents, 2, 50, 94–95, 131, 165, 249
   Archdeaconate, 56–57, 78
   Art, 12, 23, 27, 130–31, 160, 223, 254
   Astrology; *see* the general topic above
   Books as persons, 20–21, 52, 114, 208
   Books owned, 1*, 5–7*, 10*, 11–13, 15–17*, 23–24*, 51*, 94–96, 134, 136*, 145*, 150, 164, 207, 215–16
   Canonries, 10–11, 32, 56–57, 76, 82, 119, 186, 188–89, 197
   Chaplaincies, 9–10, 27, 42
   Consolatorie, 31–32, 76, 78–79, 188, 226
   Copying and copyists, 10, 51, 150, 153, 159, 198, 200, 238, 246; *see also* Malpaghini
   Criticism and hostility, 45–46, 81, 111, 119, 215, 220–21, 233–36
   Death rumored, 45, 189, 224, 229

Discoveries, 10, 51
Dogs, 20, 60, 106–7, 229
Drawing, 92
Dreams, 22, 30–31, 69
Educational opinions, 98–99
Eyeglasses, 197
Fame, 15, 17–18, 37, 45, 47, 146, 186, 197, 245, 253
Fishing, 54, 124, 253
Florentine citizenship, 11
Florentine offers, 99–100, 197
Florentine patrimony, 99–100, 126–27, 170, 192
Fortune, 33, 174–76; *see also* the references for the *De remediis* in the Index of Works of Petrarch
Gardens and planting, 30*, 75–76, 79*, 81, 84, 91, 101, 106*, 131, 133*, 155, 163*, 179*, 212, 221*, 223, 227, 253
Godfatherhood, 135, 212, 232
Government, letters on, 111, 241–43
"Grand climacteric," 204, 212
Horses, 2, 4, 40*, 50*, 94–95*, 107*, 131*, 143–44, 216, 222*, 231*, 233*
Houses, 17*, 30*, 44–45*, 78, 82*, 83, 96–97, 130*, 145, 167*, 179*, 185–87*, 195, 198, 200, 207, 219, 221–23*, 227*, 229, 230, 232
Illnesses, 45*, 47, 177*, 196*, 216, 218–19, 221–22*, 224–25*, 229–30*, 251*
Italy loved and praised, 85, 88–89, 127, 147, 153, 202, 214, 236, 259–60
Joint habitation proposed, 59, 61, 82–83, 90, 252
Journeys (main), 3, 6*, 10*, 13–14*, 26, 39–40*, 52–53*, 62, 74, 93–95, 104–6*, 127*, 129, 152–53*, 173–76*
Languages: French, 174; Greek, 33–34, 74–75, 136; Provençal, 3
Law; *see* the general topic above
Manner of life, 8, 20–22, 33, 44–

PHOENIX BOOKS

PHOENIX BOOKS

PHOENIX BOOKS

 PHOENIX SCIENCE SERIES

PHOENIX BOOKS